IGNITE YOUR LIFE

THE WORLD'S LEADING ENTREPRENEURS & PROFESSIONALS
REVEAL THEIR SECRETS TO IGNITE YOUR HEALTH, WEALTH & SUCCESS.

IGNITE YOUR LIFE

CELEBRITYPRESS®
Winter Park, Florida

CONTENTS

CHAPTER 1

THE POWER OF PERSUASION

BY BRIAN TRACY

Persuasion power can help you get more of the things you want faster than anything else you do. It can mean the difference between success and failure. It can guarantee your progress and enable you to use all of your other skills and abilities at the very highest level. Your persuasion power will earn you the support and respect of your customers, bosses, coworkers, colleagues and friends. The ability to persuade others to do what you want them to do can make you one of the most important people in your community.

Fortunately, persuasion is a skill, like riding a bicycle that you can learn through study and practice. Your job is to become absolutely excellent at influencing and motivating others to support and assist you in the achievement of your goals and the accomplishment of your business objectives.

You can either persuade others to help you or be persuaded to help them. It is one or the other. Most people are not aware that every human interaction involves a complex process of persuasion and influence. And being unaware, they are usually the ones being persuaded to help others rather than the ones who are doing the persuading.

THE POWER OF MOTIVATION

The key to persuasion is motivation. Every human action is motivated by something. Your job is to find out what motivates other people and then to provide that motivation. People have two major motivations: the desire for gain and the fear of loss. The desire for gain motivates people to want more of the things they value in life. They want more money, more success, more health, more influence, more respect, more love and more happiness. Individual wants are limited only by individual imagination. No matter how much a person has, he or she still wants more and more. When you can show a person how he or she can get more of the things he or she wants by helping you achieve your goals, you can motivate them to act on your behalf.

President Eisenhower once said that, "Persuasion is the art of getting people to do what you want them to do, and to like it." You need always to be thinking about how you can get people to want to do the things that you need them to do to attain your objectives.

THE POWER OF FEAR

People are also motivated to act by the fear of loss. This fear, in all its various forms, is often stronger than the desire for gain. People fear financial loss, loss of health, anger or disapproval of others, loss of the love of someone and the loss of anything they have worked hard to accomplish. They fear change, risk and uncertainty because these threaten them with potential losses.

Whenever you can show a person that, by doing what you want them to do, they can avoid a loss of some kind, you can influence them to take a particular action. The very best appeals are those where you offer an opportunity to gain and an opportunity to avoid loss at the same time.

There are two ways to get the things you want in life. First, you can work by yourself and for yourself in your own best interest. You can be a "Robinson Crusoe" of modern life, relying on yourself for the satisfaction of your needs. By doing this, you can accomplish a little, but not a lot. The person who looks to himself or herself completely is limited in his or her capacities. He or she will never be rich or successful.

THE POWER OF LEVERAGE

The second way to get the things you want is by gaining and using leverage. Leverage allows you to multiply yourself and get far more out of the hours you put in rather than doing everything yourself.

There are three forms of leverage you must develop to fulfill your full potential in our society: other people's efforts, other people's knowledge, and other people's money.

OTHER PEOPLE'S EFFORTS

You leverage yourself through other people's efforts by getting other people to work with you and for you in the accomplishment of your objectives. Sometimes you can ask them to help you voluntarily, although people won't work for very long without some personal reward. At other times you can hire them to help you, thereby freeing you up to do higher-value work.

One of the most important laws of economics is called "Ricardo's Law." It is also called the Law of Comparative Advantage. This law states that when someone can accomplish a part of your task at a lower hourly rate than you would earn for accomplishing more valuable parts of your task, you should delegate or outsource that part of the task.

For example, if you want to earn $100,000 a year, in a 250-day year, you need to make $50.00 per hour. That means you must be doing work that is worth $50.00 per hour, eight hours per day, 250 days per year. Therefore, if there is any part of your work like making photocopies, filing information, typing letters, or filling out expense forms that is not valued at $50.00 per hour, you should stop doing it. You should persuade someone else who works at a lower hourly rate to do it for you. The more lower-level tasks you can persuade others to do, the more time you will have to do tasks that pay you higher amounts of money. This is one of the essential keys to getting the leverage you need to become one of the higher paid people in your profession.

Management can be defined as "getting things done through others." To be a manager you must be an expert at persuading and influencing others to work in a common direction. This is why all excellent managers are also excellent low-pressure salespeople. They do not order people to do things; instead, they persuade them to accept certain responsibilities, with specific deadlines and agreed-upon standards of performance. When a person has been persuaded that he or she has a vested interest in doing a job well, he or she accepts ownership of the job and the result. Once a person accepts ownership and responsibility, the manager can step aside confidently, knowing the job will be done on schedule.

In every part of your life, you have a choice of either doing it yourself or delegating it to others. Your ability to get someone else to take on the job with the same enthusiasm that you would have is an exercise in personal persuasion. It may seem to take a little longer at the beginning, but it saves you an enormous amount of time in the completion of the task.

OTHER PEOPLE'S KNOWLEDGE

The second form of leverage that you must develop for success in America is other people's knowledge. You must be able to tap into the brain power of many other people if you want to accomplish worthwhile goals. Successful people are not those who know everything needed to accomplish a particular task, but more often than not, they are people who know how to find the knowledge they need.

What is the knowledge that you need to achieve your most important goals? Of the knowledge required, what knowledge must you have personally in order to control your situation, and what knowledge can you borrow, buy, or rent from others?

It has been said that, in our information-based society, you are never more than one book or two phone calls away from any piece of knowledge in the country. With on-line computer services that access huge data bases all over the country, you can usually get the precise information you require in a few minutes by using a personal computer. Whenever you need information and expertise from another person in order to achieve your goals, the very best way to persuade them to help you is to ask them for their assistance.

Almost everyone who is knowledgeable in a particular area is proud of their accomplishments. By asking a person for their expert advice, you compliment them and motivate them to want to help you. So don't be afraid to ask, even if you don't know the individual personally.

OTHER PEOPLE'S MONEY

The third key to leverage, which is very much based on your persuasive abilities, is other people's money. Your ability to use other people's money and resources to leverage your talents is the key to financial success. Your ability to buy and defer payment, to sell and collect payment in advance, to borrow, rent or lease furniture, fixtures and machinery, and to borrow money from people to help you multiply your opportunities is one of the most important of all skills that you can develop. And these all depend on your ability to persuade others to cooperate with you financially so that you can develop the leverage you need to move onward and upward in your field.

THE FOUR P'S OF PERSUASION

There are four "Ps" that will enhance your ability to persuade others in both your work and personal life. They are power, positioning, performance, and politeness. And they are all based on perception.

1. **Power:** The more power and influence that a person perceives that you have, whether real or not, the more likely it is that that person will be persuaded by you to do the things you want them to do. For example, if you appear to be a senior executive, or a wealthy person, people will be much more likely to help you and serve you than they would be if you were perceived to be a lower level employee.

2. **Positioning:** This refers to the way that other people think about you and talk about you when you are not there, your reputation. Your positioning in the minds and hearts of other people largely determines how open they are to being influenced by you.

   In everything you do involving other people, you are shaping and influencing their perceptions of you and your positioning in their minds. Think about how you could change the things you say and do so that people think about you in such a way that they are more open to your requests and to helping you achieve your goals.

3. **Performance:** This refers to your level of competence and expertise in your area. A person who is highly respected for his or her ability to get results is far more persuasive and influential than a person who only does an average job.

   The perception that people have of your performance capabilities exerts an inordinate influence on how they think and feel about you. You should commit yourself to being the very best in your field. Sometimes, a reputation for being excellent at what you do can be so powerful that it alone can make you an extremely persuasive individual in all of your interactions with the people around you. They will accept your advice, be open to your influence and agree with your requests.

4. **Politeness:** People do things for two reasons, because they want to and because they have to. When you treat people with kindness, courtesy and respect, you make them want to do things for you. They are motivated to go out of their way to help you solve your problems and accomplish your goals. Being nice to other people satisfies one of the deepest of all subconscious needs, the need to feel important and respected. Whenever you convey this to another person in your conversation, your attitude and your treatment of that person, he or she will be wide open to being persuaded and influenced by you in almost anything you need.

THE POWER OF PERCEPTION

Remember, perception is everything. The perception of an individual is his or her reality. People act on the basis of their perceptions of you. If you change their perceptions, you change the way they think and feel about you, and you change the things that they will do for you.

You can become an expert at personal persuasion. You can develop your personal power by always remembering that there are only two ways to get the things you want in life, you can do it all yourself, or you can get most of it done by others. Your ability to communicate, persuade, negotiate, influence, delegate and interact effectively with other people will enable you to develop leverage using other people's efforts, other people's knowledge and other people's money. The development of your persuasion power will enable you to become one of the most powerful and influential people in your organization. It will open up doors for you in every area of your life.

About Brian

Brian Tracy is Chairman and CEO of Brian Tracy International, a company specializing in the training and development of individuals and organizations. Brian's goal is to help people achieve their personal and business goals faster and easier than they ever imagined.

Brian Tracy has consulted for more than 1,000 companies and addressed more than 5,000,000 people in 5,000 talks and seminars throughout the US, Canada and 69 other countries worldwide. As a Keynote speaker and seminar leader, he addresses more than 250,000 people each year.

For more information on Brian Tracy programs, go to: www.briantracy.com

CHAPTER 2

EMBRACING A GREAT LIFE FROM YESTERDAY'S EXPERIENCES

BY DR. AMARA ANNE ONUJIOGU

There is much knowledge in the past that makes us more aware in the future.

So many people think and feel that you must just forget about the past and move on. For me, it's my entire past that has given me the information, awareness, and valuable experiences that I needed in order to be where I am today. And it is a good place, despite the fact that it does not always feel so. However, I realized over time, and through age and wisdom, one important thing:

We make our good places in life; life just doesn't hand them over, but it provides the ingredients.

I grew up in Nigeria and lost my mother at a very young age. She died giving birth to her tenth child. In fact, because I was only five, I don't remember what she looked like nor do I have even a photograph of her. All I know is what people tell me—that we looked alike. As a result, the woman she was has had little impact on my life, but her absence created a lasting void in mine.

With the help of my older siblings and a new wife who was also my mother's cousin, my father raised me. No woman could fill the gap that my mother's absence created. In spite of a tough situation, my father did the best he could from his upbringing and mindset, making his every action align with one goal: <u>raise a daughter that would be a suitable wife when the time came</u>. **Every decision that was made in my life for me was focused on making me that "one type of person" that my father envisioned.** I remember his usual warning: *"Sit well, cover your legs so that you can get a husband."* He was just thinking and acting like everyone else in his culture. And for a great while, I thought I was doing the right thing by trying to be that woman, regardless of which culture I found myself in.

Then political unrest came to Nigeria, and I found myself in a refugee camp for three years, lingering between a new beginning and the turmoil I was in. It came with a price! Although I had this feeling that there was more, I still had no idea how to go about getting to "more." Would I be accepted? Was I smart enough? Was I even good enough? I'd never thought I'd really get the chance to go somewhere else. **I'd settled for my fate:** <u>to be immersed in a Nigerian culture and do what I hoped would be thought of as good and respectable</u>. All these fear-driven thoughts were there, yet I did long to experience freedom in my life. I could not avoid the feeling, although it would have been easier to smother it out at times.

Eventually, I did get to the United States at the age of 23 to join my fiancé, who had left a few months earlier. He was a young gentleman with a golden heart and I thought I was set for life. I was excited and scared and nervous. Then at the age of 32 he died from heart failure. My world collapsed! I was cracked, scared, and suddenly a single mother, plus in a strange environment without any family around. It took me years of adjusting and a few years later, I finally found another Nigerian man that I thought would be the one. We did get married, but I quickly found out he was the wrong type of "one." I was the wife to a very traditional Nigerian man. I was in a new place and surrounded by expectations from my old culture.

The Nigerian culture that I had left followed me right into my home, and it consumed me.

Doing what I was trained to do, I tried to be the best wife possible. I followed my husband's wishes, tried to make him proud, and put everything that I'd learned my entire life into action. <u>Then it hit me— like a ton of bricks—no matter what I did, it was not good enough</u>. I wasn't as good of a wife as he felt he deserved and he revealed that polygamy was in his blood line and that was okay—he had options. I wasn't the mother I should be to my children in his eyes, and I couldn't have the dozen children he wanted. *Really, according to him, I wasn't anything of significance in spite of my education and loyalty to him.* And sadly, like many women from all areas of the world who are in these situations, I believed him.

When someone is beaten down in some way, he or she eventually believes what is being said by that "person of significance" who is the head of the family. It doesn't even matter what others say. I was lucky to have a brother-in-law, a profoundly calm man who also believed in the way a Nigerian man should treat his wife according to custom, but he felt bad for me because he saw a quality in me and affectionately named me "Mother Love." This was a name that inspired me, even though I didn't know how to run with the inspiration for a great many years. It's a name that I'm still known by to this very day, only with a "Doctor" added in front of it after I earned my doctorate degree.

So life went on, and I kept trying to learn and grow and be better. I went to school and received many degrees, including: Doctor of Education in Health and Family Life Education, a Master of Science in Public Health Administration, and dual Bachelor of Science degrees in Nursing and Chemistry. This type of commitment to education and growth took a lot of work, but learning brought me such great joy, even when it was so trying. After all, it had to be done in addition to striving to be the ideal Nigerian wife and mother. And before I knew it…forty years passed me by.

Then, it happened. **I realized that my great potential in this world wasn't going to be fulfilled if I kept my situation as it was.** I kept praying for change to finally come. Luckily, his family situation back home in Nigeria provided me with an exit plan. It was divine intervention! I left my husband and Boston, where I'd lived since moving to the United States. It was so scary, yet exciting. It was fresh and new and I forced myself to be committed to finding a place where I could celebrate me and my freedom. My self-esteem wasn't there, but I knew it was time to stop spinning my wheels for others and pursue what was mine to offer others—mine to offer the world!

better family, we are teaching the examples that our children, spouses, and others we meet need to learn in order to truly create global change. This change is based on principles and values that not only make families stronger, but also individuals' wiser. One thing that I often hear from men I coach is this: <u>If I had this insight years ago, I would have made better choices, been a better husband, and father</u>. For me, these bitter regrets blow my mind and encourage me to reach out even more to younger men.

Poverty is a condition that most in third world countries experience their entire life. Part of it is due to poor choices that a culture can force us to make. They never know of anything else, experiencing hunger more regularly than hope. This can change with a stronger sense of family and purpose. And when people are not worried about their basic needs, such as food and shelter, they can then focus on their internal needs much easier. The pressing questions that all humans have, regardless of where fate chooses to have them born, exist in us all. Who am I? What is my potential? How can I fit in? What will make me happy and fulfilled? These are challenging questions and not easy to answer alone. That's where a strong family structure can help, heal, and offer hope.

A culture that does not respect human dignity or protect women and children must be trashed.

We are all in this crazy, mad, and glorious world together—for the good and the bad. In a very conscious manner and deliberate way, I take every opportunity I can to make sure that I'm part of the solution—the one who delivers good.

Since I've begun my journey through coaching and my non-profit, I have noticed incredible differences. There is still a long way to go, but I gain more energy for the momentum every day. I have seen differences already. The people I connect with walk away with the ability to spread that message. It's like pollen being spread on the wings of bees to all the flowers, only its caring, kindness, and compassion are being spread from person to person. A little bit can go a long way. We have a long way to go, but if we commit, we'll get there—one person at a time. This message of hope and positive front never fails. Embrace it and you will be amazed!

About Amara

Dr. Amara Anne Onujiogu has an amazing passion for family life and values. Her compassion and love for all people—wanting them to have a better life—is a driving force behind this chapter. It's the beginning of the journey she has put into play.

Empowering people is the main goal for Amara today. She is naturally compelled to give people hope, especially from those who live stagnant in a world of unfulfilled dreams—regardless of the reason. Her journey has been as compelling as it has been inspirational. She has been widowed at an early age, being left a single mother, endured four decades of a turbulent marriage, emerging from it not only as a survivor, but also a role model with a powerful message. According to Amara, "It is never too late to begin again with a renewed determination, more clarity, serenity, and wisdom."

In 1971, at the age of 23 and after three years very tough years in a refugee camp, Amara moved to the United States from Nigeria. It was the end of the civil war there and she settled in Boston, where she wasted no time taking advantage of her new opportunity. She went to college, earning degrees including: Doctor of Education from Boston University; a Master's in Public Health Administration from University of Massachusetts, Amherst; a Bachelor's in Nursing from Boston University; and a Bachelor's in Chemistry from Emmanuel College in Boston, MA. During this time, she also raised her family, and worked hard as the co-owner and Executive Director of her family business, which focused on the pharmacy and real estate industries.

With over thirty years of professional experience in health care administration, including directing health care centers, nursing homes, home health agencies, and health and nursing educational programs, Amara has the knowledge and expertise to make all her goals for helping others and for helping others dreams come true. She is also an advocate for public health issues, international health, and family life education. Amara engages in finding solutions for problems facing families, especially those with roots in the developing world. She is very active with her Relationship Training and Motivational Speaking engagements.

Amara recently founded a non-profit organization, AmaraCares.org. Its mission is to harness the unnecessary wastes of the western world and reuse them for the benefit of starving human beings worldwide, which she calls "Turning waste into grace." She also offers coaching and consultancy services for those who wish to promote better family lives and further awareness about the major triggers of family dysfunction.

Dr. Amara Onujiogu's passions hover around family, marriage, relationships, and empowering future parents and families. She knows that everyone can lead better and fulfilled lives through creating a suitable family environment. This type of safe, secure environment is vital for success and the avoidance of triggers of dysfunction, which are debilitating for many families. For more information on Amara's mission, contact her at: DoctorMotherLove@yahoo.com, or visit AmaraCares.com.

CHAPTER 3

IT'S A GOOD THING YOU DON'T KNOW WHAT YOU DON'T KNOW

BY GLENN WARNER

Valentine's Day, a few years ago, I got a present from my wife, Shelley. The box was big and heavy. As I opened the box, I felt like a kid at Christmas. I love getting presents from my wife. It was a 3D printer! My wife got me a 3D printer. WOW! What a great wife. Unlike me, we started out slow. We watched all the videos and read the manual on how to use it. Now it was time to print. We started with our names, then worked up to harder prints. Next was a bracket we needed for a client. It was amazing; if we could think it, we could print it.

After two days, I was 3D printing anything and everything I could think or dream of. The 3D printer allowed us to make any dream come true. We found many online sites for models and CAD programs to help us along the way. Our website (www.gorillamaker.com) has a list of sites where you can freely download models and our favorite programs. A few more days went by and the unimaginable happened. The 3D printer broke. My world of 3D printing came to a very abrupt end. We boxed the printer up and sent it back. After purchasing another, more expensive 3D printer, we were printing again. All is right in the world. Or so I thought. The new printer didn't last much longer than the first one. Are you kidding me? My 3D printer was broke, again. As I talked to other enthusiasts, checked out the forums and asked more questions, I was surprised to find out I was not alone. To everyone else, this was acceptable. "Print out the broken parts," they would say. It's all a part of being a 3D printer owner. How is this right? Why do people believe this is "just another day" in the 3D printing world? It seems crazy that it's OK to fix your own printer.

What bull! We work hard to save for the fun toys. I should not be expected to "fix" what I buy before I can use it. Yet every day I would go to my workshop and do exactly that. My mind screaming; "Why is this broken? How much longer will it take to repair?" A couple of weeks go by. No real solution foreseeable. The voices in my head still yelling and getting louder with every passing day. How could 3D printer owners not be going insane with all the repairs? All that time and money wasted. As the days passed, the conversations in my head got stronger, louder, screaming with such convictions. My frustration finally exploding, I said to myself, I could crap out a better 3D printer than this. I would call it GorillaMaker. It would be made out of aluminum, all-metal parts, and professional controls. Then I'd powder coat it so it looks like those twenty-five thousand dollar printers but sell it for five thousand. I'll show them. Big value, giant build area, professionally built and all with an affordable price tag.

Back straight, shoulders high, I trekked up the stairs to share my news with my wife. "Shelley," I hollered, "guess what!" BAM! That's when her hands went up. Is that a timeout signal she's giving me? Oh no, what have I done now, I thought. To my surprise, she already knew. She says to me, "I know, I know... we are going to make 3D printers. And we are going to call it GorillaMaker.com. I have already secured the domain name and started on the website." What? How could she have read my mind? She knew what I wanted to make, what I wanted to call it. How could she have known? So I asked. Her response, "you've been screaming it from your workshop for weeks." And here I thought I was talking to myself.

So I knew what I did not like about 3D printing. Blue tape, glue, hair spray, harsh chemicals, hot end issues, even bed leveling topped the list. Yet do-it-yourselfers saw this as normal. I knew I needed to do it better, make it bigger. It is amazing how easily we accept what others tell us. This is not right. My personal mission is to guide others to reach their greatness by fixing their broken stuff. OK, so this isn't a person, but the same holds true. The 3D printer industry is broken and needed to be fixed.

As a serial entrepreneur, my mission has grown. It's not just about people anymore. It's bigger than one person. There's an entire industry that needs fixing. Staring me straight in the face, mocking me, begging me to take them on. Challenge accepted! Back in my workshop, I spent months designing. Drawing up the case; all aluminum, no wood or plastic parts on this bad boy. Even went as far as making sure the hot ends were all metal. Now what to do about the heating bed. It needs to be polymer coated. No more blue tape or toxic chemicals. Over the next three months, I discovered so many ways on how not to build a 3D printer. Our core group stuck with it and worked many long nights to make things right. We dared to do what others could not or would not do.

You might be asking yourself, "Who's this core group he's talking about? Where did they come from?" Our core group is a business support group I've nurtured through the years looking to make the world a little more 3D. We are engineers, assemblers, marketers, web developers, graphic designers, videographers, salesmen and so much more. We lead, we follow, we help each other out and I make sure we stay on track. I help them see further, pushing them along. We are always improving, moving forward with new ideas, new technology. We are always asking, "How do we make 3D printers better?" Well, we started with all aluminum cases and parts. Added a two-year warranty. Unheard of, you say? Yes, it is. We make sure each part in our printers aren't just the best it can be; it's ALL that it can be. There is no fear of changes. We embrace change. We are continuously striving to make our 3D printers better every day. We offer free upgrades to all our customers, all the time. People say to think outside the box. We left the box behind, there are no limits here. We are not the norm. We are not your average company with average views. We pride ourselves on being a cut above the rest. Our 3D printers have very high standards.

It is our belief that the 3D printer industry will skyrocket. They will not just be for the big companies. Home owners will have their own professional 3D printers to create and print from. From last minute gift ideas to cookie cutters. Let's not forget the cool toys you can dream up. We empower schools and libraries to grow with our 3D printers. Our children are the future and we provide so they can succeed.

The secret to our success is we are willing to do what others won't do.

We didn't just fix it and slap a pretty red bow on top. We provide training, support. We go beyond what is expected and provide the unexpected. Our first 3D printer, the GM3D500, has over a cubic foot of build area. We built a professional series printer for manufacturing and prototyping shops. We quickly realized that was short-sighted. Teachers, educators, even librarians were in awe over our craftsmanship. They wanted a great printer, at an affordable price with an outstanding warranty. Throw in training and they were over the moon. What a wonderful feeling to know you are changing lives around the world. Dreams become a reality with a 3D printer.

You don't know what you don't know. Take a moment and let that sink in. It is unbelievably true. We decided to go to New York for the "World's Largest Maker Faire." Talk about not knowing anything. It took over four hours just to setup on Friday night. To get ready for what they were predicting would be over 55 thousand visitors in two days. Then it happened. It was early on Saturday and they started coming in droves. Picking up flyers, business cards, asking, "where did you come from?" We were a hit. A drop in the ocean that people were swimming towards. It wasn't until Intel stopped by that I really knew we were in for the ride of our lives. One of the world's largest chip makers wanted to interview me, a hillbilly from Kentucky, who's making waves in New York. Intel was doing video segments on Makers from the show and were intrigued and amazed with our printers. What an honor. There was more excitement that weekend. Representatives from Colleges and Universities, including MIT, Cornell and Stanford stopped by. Even NASA wanted to see who was causing all the excitement in the 3D printer world.

Days later, back in Kentucky, the phones were ringing off the hook. Emails pouring in from schools wanting to order our GM3D500 3D printer. Never underestimate the value of going to trade shows, talking to the masses or even doing 'spur of the moment' interviews. This changed how others viewed us. We keep raising the bar for 3D printers and other manufacturers are looking to us for ideas. One step at a time. Or should I say one broken item at a time. As we began prototyping our printer, problems would arise. How many more would there be? That may be overwhelming, but not if you take them on; one at a time. This process has served me well, in all aspects of my life.

Why 3D printers? They expand your mind. Help to build on your dreams and ideas. Part of our mission is to help our children to grow. They will be our next leaders after all and they should be smarter than us. That's why we offer such a large discount to schools and libraries. Our children are the dreamers and inventors of the future. What better way to empower them to dream than to show them how they can bring their dreams to life?

When I was a kid, I loved to watch Star Trek. Scotty could make anything with their replicator machine. Need a screwdriver? Push a few buttons on the replicator and viola, there it is. Science fiction at its finest. Who could have imagined that becoming a reality in my lifetime? NASA recently experimented with that concept and their 3D printer that was located on the Space Station. An engineer on Earth emailed a file for a wrench to the Space Station and then printed it. They 3D printed a working wrench in space. It doesn't get more Sci-Fi than that.

Let's cut to the chase now. I love to help people and companies become great. I love working with our core group every day and watching them grow. I love 3D printing, the bigger, the better. I take it as a personal challenge when something is broke. I will fix it. Coaching individuals, even companies gets me excited. Working with people who want to do better; who want to grow themselves and their business. Our company has grown at a rate of 10% per month over the past year. This is not by accident. We make unrealistic goals and take action every day to shape them into reality. Goal setting is where most people struggle. Think Bigger! I tell them. Shoot for the stars, you won't be disappointed. What are your goals? What are you willing to do differently in your life or business that will impact others? Never stop learning or growing. For me, it started with a book. One book turned into five then fifty. Now I'm up to reading a 150 books a year, one page at a time. Now we have the greatest 3D printer in the world. What's holding you back?

About Glenn

From a very early age, Glenn Warner had the drive to understand what made things tick. He needed to know how to make things tick better. Growing up, he saw the dawn of the tech revolution and that only added to his passion for understanding creativity.

Having worked up through the ranks of a Fortune 500 company for over a decade, Glenn ultimately found "big business" slow to change. As a firmly-established Information Technologies expert, he struck out on his own and founded American Computer Solutions. With a standard for providing the very best solutions for his clients' needs, ACS took root.

Always seeking the next challenge, Glenn knew there was more to do. Seeing the unlimited potential and endless capabilities in a barely-tapped industry, Glenn dove headlong into 3D printing and thus GorillaMaker was born.

With many successful businesses flourishing at the same time, many people asked, how does he do it all and can he help me succeed too? Glenn has worked with many companies that have started out very small and watched as they doubled and tripled their income. Glenn loves working with broken companies to help them succeed as large as they can dream. Over the past five years, Glenn has helped many companies grow. One company had over a million in sales "pre-Glenn". Two years later that turned into five million. Glenn spent countless hours working with owners and their staff giving them the tools they needed to be successful. It's all about changing the culture so they can prosper for years to come.

Glenn is a big believer in the BNI concept of 'Givers Gain'. With that, Glenn will give any company thirty minutes of his coaching for free. All they need to do is ask. How can you know what you don't know? That's why we need coaching. To have the tools to become more successful. Glenn has had many people help him over the years. Michael E. Gerber, the author of the E-Myth, changed his life. He took time out of his day to lead Glenn on the right path and gave him the tools to become successful. He not only guided but inspired Glenn. Even going so far as to saying he has many books in him yet to be written.

Glenn loves to visit his clients so he can see the progress for himself. Inevitably they all tell him how their sales have increased, as well as productivity. Those types of results are what drive Glenn to take them to the next level.

When you first meet Glenn, you will undoubtedly find his energy infectious. In just a few hours, he will have numerous avenues to getting your company on the right track. Even if you think your company isn't broken, you will find that there are many things you can do differently to make your business more successful.

"I fix broken stuff."

Call Glenn Warner at 859-918-9900 or visit: GorillaMaker.com. You have an obligation to make abundant amounts of money so people who rely on you can live a prosperous life too.

CHAPTER 4

UNIVERSAL PATH TO HEALTH AND HAPPINESS
—15 Practices Used by People all Over the World

BY DR. GARY EPLER

Good health and the feeling of happiness propel us through life with strength, energy, and vitality. Imagine the feeling of being healthy and happy throughout the day. My research has taken me throughout the Western and Eastern world, and after years of observing successful and extraordinary people, I discovered 15 practices they use to bring them health and happiness.

Follow these practices, and you will begin to look forward to the day filled with excitement, adventure, creativity, and pure enjoyment. Filled with confidence, you love who you are. People want to be with you. You're grateful. You're helpful. And you improve the lives of people everywhere you go.

Life is about feeling good. About being creative. About enjoying the day. Follow these 15 practices from people all over the world, and you're bound to see results.

The first practice: Love life. Have the attitude that it's going to be a great day filled with new experiences, meeting new people, and seeing friends. Start the day with gratitude for the opportunity to have an exciting day. Start the morning with anticipation and the simple expectation: "This is going to be a great day!"

Let me tell you about my friend and workout partner John. In 2002, he lost a kidney to cancer and in 2008, he had a pancreas cancer removed that sent him to the ICU for 40 days after surgery. From that near-death experience, he exercised his way back to life. Then he was told spots in his lungs were growing. These spots were slowly growing metastatic tumors from the kidney cancer that had seeded the blood 13 years previously. He had to decide whether to continue observation until his lungs filled with tumors or to choose surgery instead. He chose life despite the one-in-five chance of dying from the operation. He wasn't interested in waiting two to three years for death. The highly skilled surgeons removed 22 tumors from his lungs, and the technological advances helped him through the first day. But, he developed a pneumonia complication that gave him a 1-in-a-100 chance of surviving. Then his remaining kidney failed, forcing him to dialysis and a 1-in-1000 chance.

A few days later, a massive heart attack left him on the extracorporeal mechanical oxygenation (ECMO) machine with a 1-in-10,000 chance of surviving, then he had a stroke, moving his odds to 1-in-100,000. At day 30 in the intensive care unit, he developed blood clots that gave him a one-in-a-million chance of survival. He had phenomenal surgeons, medical doctors, and support equipment plus hundreds and thousands of prayers, and theta healing. All of these helped, but he survived for one reason. He did his part, he wanted to live. He loves life! He can't wait for the day to start. He can't wait to see his wife, his daughter, his three sons, to see his friends at workout, and he can't wait to go to work. He enjoys every minute of the day and shares his love of life with everyone near him.

This extraordinary person exemplifies the first universal practice: love life.

The second, third, and fourth practices are as old as life itself: Eat, sleep, and exercise.

Practice 2: Eat the right foods in the right amount. There have been tremendous strides in knowledge about nutrition during the past decade. For example, the powerful anti-inflammation properties of omega-3 fatty acids and the dangers of the inflammatory properties of omega-6 fatty acids. Eat lean proteins. Limit omega-6 fatty acids found in processed foods, farm-raised fish, and force-fed cattle. Choose slow-burn carbohydrates such as spinach and broccoli, sources of fiber that don't cause insulin and blood sugar spikes. Limit or eliminate added sugar, fried foods, and sodium.

Practice 3: Sleep eight hours every day. Science has told us the energy chemical in the brain called adenosine is gradually depleted during the day's activities. Eight hours of sleep is needed to restore the balance of adenosine; five is not enough and ten is too much. Chose a time to go to bed, add eight hours, and get up, not before and not after. You can take a daytime nap but only for 15 minutes – anything longer will reset your natural sleep pattern and you won't sleep at night. Finally, do not fall asleep watching television.

Practice 4: One hour of vigorous exercise every day will give you the energy needed to get through the day. This produces the feel-good neurotransmitters and hormones such as endorphins, dopamine, and serotonin. Exercise together in a group such as spinning, body pump, or dance class; this produces oxytocin, the bonding hormone. Numerous studies have proven that exercise both reduces stress and improves concentration.

Practice 5: Learn something new every day. Read books, listen to CDs, take a class, or find a coach to help you grow and improve. This will give you energy, make you more interesting, make life more enjoyable, and make you more alert. The more obscure the topic and the further away from your work, the better. Consider studying a foreign language and its culture or taking a dance class, distant viewing, an economics course, or a philosophy course.

Practice 6: Create alpha-brainwave time every day. What's alpha-brainwave time? Day dreaming. Meditating. We have five different brainwaves during 24 hours. Beta-brainwave activity occurs during our typical waking day. Alpha-, theta-, and 15 minutes of deep-sleep delta-brainwaves occur during sleep. Newly discovered gamma waves are fast and may occur during peak performance. Learn to experience the alpha-brainwave and theta brainwave state while awake. How? The traditional way is with meditation, and a new way is eyes-open meditation during yoga or a walk. The Norwegians have a term, "Friluftsliv," which describes the alpha-brainwave feeling a person develops when outside in free air. Alpha-brainwave time decreases stress by lowering you adrenalin levels. You go from the flight-or-fight state to the stay-and-play state. Meditation (just like, exercise discussed above) results in release of the feel-good neurotransmitters and hormones including endorphin, dopamine, and serotonin; it also balances the left and right sides of your brain. We need the left brain to function in society – it helps with discernment and doing the right thing, but it is rigid and dominant.

Meditation shifts some of that activity to the right brain – the social and creative brain, making the day more enjoyable. An interesting benefit of meditation is that people may depend on external activities for pleasure and enjoyment, but this is an internal job – meditation brings that pleasure inside. Science-based benefits include increasing mirror-neuron function, which improves social interaction and increasing the life of telomeres at the end of your chromosomes for increased lifespan.

Practice 7: Engage in positive social interaction every day. Positive daily interaction with clerks, shop owners, restaurant staff, and coworkers produces energy and the bonding hormone oxytocin. One important aspect of positive social interaction is not judging people. Walk into a room filled with people, look around, and have no judgment: no one has faults; they are who they are without your feelings about who they should be. This makes you feel good. Judging people means you are comparing yourself to others for validation of who you are. Being nonjudgmental frees the need for comparison resulting in increased personal energy and sense of well-being.

Practice 8: Have compassion. Have compassion for yourself and others. This is a wonderful word. Tibetan monks meditate by repeating this word over and over for hours, months, and years. You can feel their warmth and kindness. This compassion can combat negative emotions from others. The nature of our lives is to seek happiness; and compassion and kindness contributes to other people's happiness.

Practice 9: Grant forgiveness. Practicing forgiveness is done regularly by people who enjoy life. We know that not forgiving has no effect on the other person or bad event, and only hurts you. Dwelling on the person or event causes chronic stress, taking hours, weeks, and even years away from an enjoyable, creative life. After going through denial, anger, and depression after a toxic situation, forgive as fast as possible to free yourself from blame and excuses.

Practice 10: Manage stress. People have always learned how to manage acute stress. The flight-or-fight response caused by a surge in adrenaline results in increased heart rate and blood pressure, and shutting down the stomach. Examples include an argument, a parking ticket, a dripping faucet – all part of day-to-day living. For healthy people, the stress response is triggered, lasts for a few minutes, then dissipates. The body is well-equipped to handle this without harmful effects. Helpful techniques to dissipate stress include a few belly breaths, yoga breathing with equal in and out breathing, and repeating a mantra such as "love and peace" from 45 to 60 seconds.

Chronic stress is a killer. This usually results from a work setting with a tyrannical, controlling boss, supervisor or coworker; loss of income; an uncontrolled situation such as an alcoholic or drug-using family member; or caring for a spouse with Alzheimer's or other disabling condition. Chronic stress resets the adrenalin level resulting in rapid heart rate, increased blood pressure, shutting down of digestion, and inflamed arteries. A healthy response is to manage chronic stress by first eliminating or reducing the cause. Explore fear as a basis for stress. Use the neuropathway bypass technique by replacing the face of the person or the distressing event with 90 seconds of repeating "love and peace" for 14 days. As previously mentioned, it pays to also develop and maintain a daily exercise program to reduce stress. Positive social interaction with compassion and forgiveness also keeps chronic stress in control. And alpha-brainwave time is excellent management for chronic stress.

Practice 11: Be grateful. Being grateful is such a wonderful feeling; it instantly makes you feel good. Stressed out, on the verge of panic? Take a couple of belly breaths and think of ten things in your life to be grateful for. Grateful for being alive. Grateful for your family, your spouse, your friends. Grateful for your house or apartment, your car, your pets. Being grateful makes you a good person and attracts other grateful people into your life.

Practice 12: See the good in all things. This one is easy for some people – for others, it must be learned through practice. When you're faced with a new situation, rather than seeing its problems and negative aspects, pause instead and search for the good. This will allow you to fully enjoy the situation if it's a positive event – or to move toward a solution if it's a problem.

Practice 13: Help someone. When you see people who need a little help with something minor, give them a hand. You feel good, and you bless that person with a boost of energy. The more you help people, the more people will help you. Be nice to people.

Practice 14: Self-healing. Machines are built to repair themselves, and so can you. Healing is the process of restoring physical health from injury or disease and restoring mental, emotional, and spiritual health. You can use your mind to enhance this process. Learn everything possible about the anatomy of the injury or mechanism of the disease process through your doctor and the Internet. Use your best treatment option available, such as antibiotics, medications, and surgery.

Now, use your mind. You need to have a positive approach to the injury or illness. This will let you avoid the neurolinguistic trap, which is repeatedly thinking of and verbalizing negative feelings (complaining) about the illness – this counterproductive activity establishes a new neuropathway sending you down the road of perpetual aggravation and worsening the process. Have compassion for the diseased organ system. Use controlled breathing, equal breaths in and out. Breathe in healing energy and send it where needed. Visualization is fundamental. Use this technique while in the alpha- or theta-brainwave state. Mentally send energy to the specific body part that needs healing such as the knee or organ system such as the heart. The more specific, the better.

Next, replace dysfunctional cells beginning with one healthy cell to replace the injured cell. Visualize replacing two cells, then four, and eventually replace one million cells. With your mind, renew damaged DNA of your cells. Persist; over time these methods can contribute to healing.

Practice 15: Be yourself. Learn how to be your true self – and experience total freedom. I discovered a parasite while in medical school, a lung disease soon after, and I discovered how to treat diseases all over the world. Finally, I discovered myself, which was the best discovery of all. You do not want to be who your parents wanted you to be, who your teachers and professors wanted you to be, who society wants you to be. You do not want to be that someone you have created in your mind that you will never be. You want to discover and be the real you. Keep in mind that the person you discover is not static and fixed but alive in a state of flux with invigorating change. Be yourself. This gives you freedom from unnecessary decisions and stress, and the freedom to live life the way you want.

Follow these 15 practices for an extraordinary life filled with energy, creativity, health, and happiness. You are in charge. You control your life. You can do this better than anyone else. Your chance of success is unlimited.

About Gary

Dr. Gary Epler is a world-renowned health leader and a Harvard Medical School professor. He is an authority on health, nutrition, fitness, and executive health excellence. He has impacted the lives of people throughout the world through his speaking engagements, books, and teaching.

Recognized yearly since 1994 in "The Best Doctors in America," Dr. Epler believes personalized health empowers people. He has written more than 110 scientific publications and four health books in the critically-acclaimed "You're the Boss" series including: *Manage Your Disease, BOOP, Asthma,* and *Food.* Dr. Epler's latest book, Fuel for Life: Level-10 Energy is about living a high-energy life filled with enjoyment and creativity. He is currently writing *The Universal Path to Health and Happiness: 15 Practices Used by People all over the World.*

Dr. Epler discovered the treatable lung disorder *bronchiolitis obliterans organizing pneumonia* (BOOP), and he is regularly called upon to help individuals from around the world with this rare lung disease. He found a new parasite in South America, chronicled the nutritional needs of North Afri¬can children, and managed the tuberculosis refugee program in Southeast Asia. In addition to conducting clinical and research work, Dr. Epler strives to educate. He became editor-in-chief of an educational program in critical care and pulmonary medicine offered by the American College of Chest Physicians.

Dr. Epler was one of the Boston Celtics team doctors. He was Chief of Medicine at a Boston Hospital for 15 years and is currently at the Brigham and Women's Hospital in Boston. *Business Week* acclaimed him for his development of e-health educational programs that enable patients to manage their health and disease. Dr. Epler was recognized as one of *Boston Magazine's* "Top Doctors in Town."

Dr. Epler ran seven marathons including Boston, New York, and proposed to his wife, Joan at the start of the Paris Marathon; and for their first anniversary, they ran the original Greek marathon together. He delivered the 20th baby from a mother who named the baby after him. He has taught medicine throughout the world and was fortunate enough to save a dying infant in South America from an overwhelming parasitic infection by using the sap from a fig tree. He saved a baby who choked on a donut during a little league baseball game that he was coaching. He is a radio and television personality.

Dr. Epler has written a Hollywood medical thriller movie script about a doctor who puts his hospital in lockdown mode when he realizes that a group of terrorists plan to use one of his patients infected with an Ebola-like virus as a biological weapon. He is active in the community. He coached soccer, basketball, hockey, baseball, and club baseball at Boston College. He lives in the Boston area with his wife, Joan.

Gary R. Epler, M.D.
Epler Health, Inc.
1-800-279-1455
Website: www.eplerhealth.com
Facebook: https://www.facebook.com/eplerhealth?fref=ts
Twitter: https://twitter.com/EplerHealth
LinkedIn: https://www.linkedin.com/home?trk=nav_responsive_tab_home

CHAPTER 5

YOUTH LEADERSHIP: IT'S OUR RESPONSIBILITY

BY JEAN MORRIS

Do you worry about your children? If you're anything like me, you worry about them all the time. Whether they're an infant, a toddler, a teenager, or an adult, you still worry.

Ever since my daughter, Taylor, was a little girl, I wondered who she would grow up to become. Would she be respectful of herself and others? Would she feed the right emotions? Would she develop good habits? Would she be responsible? Would she be able to handle stress and loss? Would she ever fail a test, lose a friend, or get left out of a group? These are the type of questions I ask myself every day. The reflection helps me to learn and grow so I can provide the best possible conditions for the healthy development of my child. It is my responsibility to be the positive role model in my daughter's life, especially since her eyes are always watching me.

I was fortunate to learn, at a very young age, that there are both wins and losses in life. My parents would allow my five siblings and I to settle our disputes amongst ourselves. Since I was the youngest, I often lost. Perhaps I didn't get the extra dessert, the best seat at the movies, or to ride "shotgun" on the way home, but I did receive my parents' approval for being kind-hearted and good. I learned that a small loss in life could turn out to be a great win in the end. You see, all losses trigger a response that's either positive or negative; one that moves you forward in growth or leaves you feeling stuck. I had a choice to accept my losses and learn from them, or feel sorry for myself and blame others. Over time, these negative responses can lead to more serious self-destructive behaviors like drug and alcohol abuse and self-harm.

When Taylor was in her teens, she struggled to find her own identity. She was bullied at school for being different and directed her anger inward. She began to cut herself "to take away the pain," she said. She would bottle up her anger to the point where she "didn't know what else to do." I tried to help her but she wouldn't talk to me. I arranged for counseling so she could talk to someone, and all I could do was continue to love her and support her. I still worried about her and the more I worried, the more she withdrew. It felt like I was losing her.

Throughout the next year, Taylor had broken into a house with "friends"; she started to lie and steal; she ran away from home, more than once; she dropped out of school; and she attempted suicide by overdosing on prescription medications. I was scared, overwhelmed and exhausted. I had to figure out a way to help my daughter develop a positive self-image and lead herself through life in a confident and responsible manner. I needed to play a more active role in helping Taylor develop her leadership abilities so she could live into her potential and become all that she could be.

At first, I drew upon my own abilities as a leader. My first exposure to a formal leadership course was in nurses training over 20 years ago. Nurses have to be competent in making quick decisions based on good clinical judgment to ensure the best possible outcome for the patient. Although I was competent, it wasn't enough.

When I was in my early 20's, I enrolled in the Canadian Armed Forces (CAF) as a Nursing Officer and spent my first 12 weeks in a Leadership Development Program in Borden, Ontario. In this program, I learned a lot about discipline, tolerance and teamwork. Every morning we had to be outside at 5 a.m. for a 5-10 Km run. Afterwards, we'd have "the next 40 minutes" to shower, get dressed, eat and prepare for room inspection. If your room wasn't spotless and you weren't standing at attention at your bedside when the Directing Staff arrived, you failed inspection and would have to perform extra duty training that evening while others were resting. You quickly learned how to work in teams to support each other in completing all tasks and objectives. Teamwork and camaraderie are paramount in the CAF. If you cannot hold your own and be an active part of the team, then you fail. This form of leadership was not going to work with my daughter. I couldn't just tell Taylor what to do because she would simply find a way to disagree and argue with me. Taylor needed to be an active participant in her own learning. I realized that I was not going to be able to help Taylor grow and develop as a leader with my current knowledge and style of leadership. I, therefore, enrolled in a Masters Program in Organization Development and Leadership at Saint Joseph's University in Philadelphia, PA. This 20-month program focused primarily on corporate leadership, executive coaching and teamwork; yet, it did help me to better understand the importance of self-development and continuous learning in life. I incorporated many new leadership principles into my relationship with Taylor. I asked more open-ended questions that helped her think into herself and her actions. I learned to listen at a different level, listening for clues into what Taylor was really saying. Our relationship evolved nicely. Taylor returned to school, made new friends, and started believing in herself again. She was happier; and so was I.

What I realized through my experiences is that leadership is more than just a skill to develop; it's a way of life. When you get up each day and choose your attitude, just like you'd choose your clothes for the day, you feed the right emotions and you lead yourself in life. When you choose to think differently and approach each day with a learning attitude, you become open to opportunities and you lead yourself in life. When you accept your wins and learn from losses, you move forward in change, building your unique, yet human, character and you lead yourself in life. When you begin to think about your goals and dreams and make intentional choices to get you there, you create a sense of hope for the future and you lead yourself in life. My own learning and self-development throughout my Masters program has helped me become a better leader in my life, while helping Taylor become the leader of her own.

Taylor is now 22 years old. She works as a photographer for a local studio and she's confidently leading her own life. She continues to receive coaching services to help her stay focused on her goals and dreams.

The next step for me was to learn how to help other parents, and their children, live a lifestyle of leadership. I want to be able to help thousands of teens and young adults, across the globe, take control of their lives and become our great leaders of the future. I explored a variety of learning opportunities until I finally found the John Maxwell Leadership Team. John Maxwell is the world's number one leadership expert who has written over 70 books on leadership. John has built a team of certified coaches, worldwide, who've learned how to help others live a life of significance. His leadership principles shape the lives of everyone who comes in contact with him. He helps people become the heroes of their own life stories. I joined John's team and became one of his certified coaches, speakers, teachers and trainers in August 2015. Since that time, I've been coaching teenagers and young adults, both in private and group sessions, to reflect on who they are and decide on who they want to become. I help equip the young person with the skills necessary to meet the challenges of adolescence and adulthood and achieve his or her full potential.

Youth leadership programs support the young person in developing their ability to:

1. Learn from loss

2. Feed the right emotions

3. Think differently

4. Become a better communicator

5. Build a sense of hope

6. Be intentional in their choices

1. LEARN FROM LOSS

Failure and loss are inevitable in life. When we develop an understanding that we're all imperfect beings who make mistakes, then we are better able to learn from them and move forward in growth. We become open and honest with ourselves, realizing that failure is not the end of the road, but simply a small detour on the road to success.

2. FEED THE RIGHT EMOTIONS

Negativity is everywhere. We hear about crime and violence every day on the television, on the radio, in the newspaper, and even on social media like Facebook and Twitter. It's hard not to get sucked into the negativity. It changes the way you perceive yourself and the world around you. In the words of Hendrie Weisinger in *The Power of Positive Criticism*, "People who project negativity typically have lower self-esteem. They feel badly about themselves and their negativity is simply a reflection of those feelings." Conversely then, a positive person who has positive self-esteem has respect for themselves and others. They have a healthy self-image with positive thoughts and opinions about themselves. Positive people are happy. They are comfortable with who they are. They feed the right emotions and kick negativity to the curb.

3. THINK DIFFERENTLY

When we face challenges in life, it's difficult to maintain our perspective. Sometimes, we blow things out of proportion. We argue and fight until we can't even remember what we were arguing about. We must learn to use critical thinking in our experiences to determine their importance. We can use our learning from previous experiences to guide us in our future ones. All experiences can therefore help us see new perspectives that will open doors to new opportunities. The way we think about our experiences and ourselves is the most important factor in determining our success in life. As such, we need to encourage our youth to think positively and to learn how to cope with emotional stress by helping them build a positive self-image.

4. BECOME A BETTER COMMUNICATOR

Most youth are comfortable with communicating through email, text and social media, but when it comes to face-to-face communication, they struggle. Speaking to large or small groups, or even one-to-one conversations can be intimidating and frightening for many adults, let alone our youth. Communication training helps us learn how to formulate and express our ideas, as well as to listen at a different level without interrupting. Corporate leaders and business owners are looking for people who express themselves clearly and confidently, and are comfortable in their communication. I think Jim Rohn said it best when he suggested we "take advantage of every opportunity to practice your communication skills so that when important occasions arise, you will have the gift, the style, the sharpness, the clarity, and the emotions to affect other people." Helping our youth develop good communication skills will help them experience greater self-confidence and personal growth. Let's start communicating better with our children so they, too, can learn the power of effective communication.

5. BUILD A SENSE OF HOPE

By definition, hope is "a feeling of expectation and desire for a certain thing to happen" (Wikipedia.com). Building a sense of hope in our youth helps them look forward to the future. However, if the young person has experienced any type of loss, or a persistent situation that they could not change, or a terrifying event where they've been out of control, they lose hope in their ability to change their life or their situation. They develop a sense of helplessness and believe that any efforts to change their life are futile. When we lose hope, we are certain that we'll be rejected and that our actions won't make a difference. If we lose hope, change is next to impossible. When we help our youth see how specific actions lead to specific outcomes, we help them make better choices and build hope for the future. Over time, they will see that their actions are having a positive affect on their life. They'll be able to start exploring their goals and dreams and living for tomorrow. They will learn to take risks to achieve success. When our younger generations start to believe in themselves, they are capable of creating significant change in their own lives, and in the lives of those around them.

6. BE INTENTIONAL IN YOUR CHOICES

If our life isn't moving in the direction that we want it to be, it helps to write down what we really want to accomplish in life to help make the world a better place. When we identify what we're passionate about, it makes it easier for us to take the required actions to get us there. The only person responsible for our actions is our self. So, we must act to create real change in our lives. One way to help our youth take action and create forward momentum in life is to help them develop good daily habits. A habit is formed when you perform an action over and over again until it becomes unconscious and you perform it without thinking. Some daily habits that help our children become successful in life include, but are not limited to:

- Setting priorities and completing important tasks first
- Reflecting on your day to determine how you can do things better
- Reading more books on leadership and self-development

When we make intentional choices that are aligned with our goals and dreams, success and significance are more likely to occur. If we allow our youth to passively accept life as it occurs, they will always struggle. But, if we coach our teens and young adults into making good, intentional choices, we help them move forward in growth and success.

With the many challenges facing our youth today, we have a responsibility for providing them with the best possible chance for success. Youth leadership programs equip our youth with the necessary skills to navigate through life. Let's provide them with the map, the compass, and the direction so they can find their way.

Thank you for reading this chapter. ~ Jean Morris

About Jean

Jean Morris is helping her clients develop the necessary skills to become great leaders in life. She helps them to build on their strengths and explore their weaknesses in order to reach their full potential. Her passion is for helping teenagers and young adults transition into their own lives and lead their way to success. Jean opened her own coaching and speaking business in 2014, providing value to others in her community. Her vision is to help thousands of youths, and their parents, worldwide, to lead lives of significance and live out their dreams.

Jean began adding value to others by providing competent, kind and professional nursing care to Canadian soldiers. She has a natural leadership style that encourages others to do more and be more. In the early 1990's, Jean transitioned into Occupational Health Nursing and began coaching health care practitioners and affiliates on how to manage their own health and wellness needs.

Through this work, Jean became interested in the health of organizations. She returned to school and graduated with her Masters Degree in Organization Development and Leadership from Saint Joseph's University in Philadelphia, PA.

Jean has become an expert in providing leadership development programs to individuals, groups and organizations. She coaches teenagers and adults, as well as CEO's, Executive Teams, and Business Owners, helping them to create momentum and move forward in their leadership and success.

Jean is on a new journey of becoming a best-selling author. She has partnered with Brian Tracy in co-authoring the book entitled, *Ignite Your Life*.

Please feel free to contact Jean for additional information:

Jean Morris, BSc-N, MSc, CPC
www.taketheleadconsulting.ca
www.johnmaxwellgroup.com/jeanmorris
Email: jeanmorris.takethelead@gmail.com

CHAPTER 6

EMBRACING DYSLEXIA BY LIVING AN UN-STOPPABLE LIFE!

BY LUCIE CURTISS

For the longest time, basically my entire adult life, I lived with the notion that I was never quite good enough to be a real expert, a top leader, a speaker on a stage or a role model because I felt I concealed a secret. The truth is that I am imperfect. Yes, that is true. I'm imperfect. I'm dyslexic, definitely dysgraphic and probably dyspraxic. Fortunately, after years of personal development courses with supportive and like-minded people, I was able to break free from the idea that perfection was needed in order to succeed at the top of my field and to make a difference in the world. One step at a time, my beliefs and my views about my imperfection changed because of the power of words. . . words spoken by people who care about me and who want the best for me. Words are very powerful tools that can empower or disempower the recipient. Words can change a person's life in a fraction of a second. Words influence us so much yet often people neglect to think twice about their effect, especially the effect they can have on vulnerable and impressionable children.

Too often, words are used blindly without thinking and realizing their power on others. The words you use can even change the trajectory of someone's life without you ever knowing about it. In his book, *The Four Agreements*, Don Miguel Ruiz talks about four agreements – the first of which is, "Be Impeccable with Your Word." In his book he goes on to say: "All the magic you possess is based on your word, and you cast spells all the time with your opinions. You can either put a spell on someone with your word, or you can release someone from a spell." This book profoundly changed my life in many ways by making me realize how my words influence others. Today, I use my words to empower dyslexic children to succeed in life. My mission is to preserve their self-esteem and to help them enjoy an UN-Stoppable life.

When I was in school, I struggled with reading, writing and math. I reversed numbers (203 became 302). I interchanged 's' and 'c'. I confused left and right. However, my biggest challenge was with reading long and complex paragraphs. Fortunately, I instinctively found ways to adapt and cope. Today, I still live with those same challenges, I just approach them differently and with a new perspective.

Growing up, determination and perseverance were my best friends. Back then, I was unaware of my dyslexia. I had never even heard of dyslexia. I did, nonetheless, have a gut feeling that something was up; yet I chose to ignore it. Understanding and mastering skills taught in the classroom when the teacher was explaining them orally was easy for me. My difficulty showed up when I was physically reading a book, especially a very large text book. I would disconnect right then and there. This was a pattern I followed for the longest time even throughout my college years. I kept this affliction to myself in silence for way too long. I would read and reread the same paragraph over and over and still the information would not "stick in my mind". So, without even realizing it, I relied heavily on paying close attention in class and visualizing the information by developing a photographic memory. And, on multiple choice tests, I used the process of elimination to find the correct answers. In the end, I made it through and began a new chapter for myself outside the doors of formal education.

After college, while working in pediatrics, through a chain of events, I finally figured out I was dyslexic. At the age of twenty-five, I moved to the United States to work as a registered nurse. (I was born in Canada and my first language is French.) Moving to a new country, living very far away from home for the first time and communicating in my second language (English), brought up many issues that I had buried years ago. Issues like difficulties with word and name pronunciation, letter reversals and speech issues were greatly disturbing my life. That's when I decided to look into what was the underlying cause of my struggles.

The dots started to connect. I was finally matching my symptoms to what dyslexia looked like. It has a name, d-y-s-l-e-x-i-a. Finding that out was a turning point for me, and that's when I realized that my life was about to change.

A few years and a couple of major surgeries later, my son was born. His name is Felix-Alexander. His nicknames are FeZander and Baba. I remember when he was very young, about five months old, he was energetic, full of life and crawling all over the place. He crawled everywhere while his friends were barely able to move. As he got older, around four years old, he sat for hours designing engineering books and creating models of machines. He wanted his creations to be useful in making the world a better place. During that time period, he started reading, and boy was he struggling. In first grade, the mechanics of writing were laborious for him and decoding words while reading was painfully difficult. He also had a lisp. Even though we were, at that point, still in major denial, we slowly started linking my learning issues with his and we realized we needed outside help and fast. My husband's knowledge as a pediatrician came in handy and reinforced our desire to get services in place as soon as possible. And, by then, our daughter Chloe, who was twenty-one months younger was catching up fast. Even FeZander was feeling the pressure and saying how his sister was reading better than he was.

In our household, we were experiencing one extreme to another. One child was struggling with reading while the other was excelling It was shocking to us to see the contrast. Chloe was reading chapter books at four while FeZander was barely getting through a simple book like Dr. Seuss/P. D. Eastman's *Go, Dog. Go!* Thus, this is when our journey with dyslexia really took form. We spent the next four years helping our son overcome dyslexia by finding the right tutors, the right tools and the right strategies to remediate his learning difficulties and assist him in achieving his greatest potential. We all knew he was very smart and just needed assistance and guidance in learning. It was imperative for him to learn with a different approach and we found it just around the corner.

We also changed the family's diet and lifestyle and saw major improvements in his focus and concentration abilities. We were finally on the right path. FeZander turned his life around with hard work and sheer determination. He went from a struggling reader to an avid reader of complex and intricate subject matters. And, today, he's a creative and eager writer. He even writes "movie scripts" for his own enjoyment.

While on this journey of guiding and supporting our son to overcome dyslexia, my husband and I started taking personal development courses to enrich our lives. I enjoyed these experiential courses tremendously as they built my self-confidence and gave me more clarity about my life purpose. Along the way, we met numerous successful and brilliant people who inspired us to live meaningful lives filled with joy. However, because of my lingering altered beliefs about my imperfection, I still found it improbable for me to achieve the same level of success as those people whom I admired. As much of a go-getter I felt I was, at the same time I felt I did not belong in this elite group at the top. You know, those people we admire, those who consistently succeed in life and attain their goals with gusto? I'm always up for a challenge. Nevertheless, the top achievers were somewhat mystical people in my view, almost superhuman. I imagined these perfect beings with glamorous and prestigious lives who would not be able to relate to someone like me. How could they identify with me? They are too perfect. They own the perfect house, perfect body, perfect car, perfect ideas, perfect business.

It was only a few years ago, while at a personal-development course, no less, that my husband pointed out to me that my imperfection was my gift. For a moment I paused, then tears of joy filled my eyes for the next twenty hours. I was sobbing like a baby and could not stop myself. The next day, we were back in class and I remember telling the person next to me, "I'm OK, don't worry." I just experienced a monumental self-discovery and my emotions were running on high speed. These wet salty tears flushed away years of self-doubt, self-neglect and self-judgment. I finally got it! My journey through imperfection is my message and my gift to share with the world. Looking back at my life, I realized that I had gone from struggling in school to an entrepreneur, and from a dyslexic to an author in one lifetime. Think about it, if I was the picture of perfection as perceived by our society, how could I inspire others to overcoming dyslexia and live a passionate life? I wouldn't have a clue about dyslexia or how to help anyone who struggles with this challenge if I didn't have my own obstacles to overcome.

Living with the duality of dyslexia is how one gets to understand the ups and downs of daily life with dyslexia. Turning this difficulty around by embracing the gifts it brings along the way helped me show by example, to the kids we want to inspire, that anything is possible. Dealing with the challenges, the obstacles, the failures and experiencing the creativity, vision and success are what opened my eyes to the beauty of dyslexia. One has to live through it before one can fully understand and appreciate the complexity of this gift. The secret magical gifts that accompany this complex condition are worth discovering.

Dyslexia is such a broad and complex field of expertise. So many people need to come together to share their knowledge, experience and research to bring awareness to this great cause. Everyone has a specific role to play and each one is needed to debunk all the myths associated with dyslexia. Some people are scientists who do brain research and testing to find out what parts of the brain are affected and why. Some people are educators and teachers who approach learning in a more holistic and visual way. Some people are doctors, like my husband, who help their patients get the services they need in school. Some people are psychologists who help guide and counsel the students. Some people are speech therapists who help dyslexics communicate clearly with the world. And, some people are dyslexics like me who empower and motivate the kids to find their inner strengths and gifts, so they can live fulfilled and exciting lives regardless of their adversities. We all come together, in our own and special way, to show dyslexics how wonderful and valuable they truly are. We remind dyslexics that they are loved and are valuable members of our society.

I feel very lucky and blessed in my life. I'm married to a supportive and understanding husband who loves me for who I am and I have two wonderfully energetic and lively kids who make me laugh. Life is good and there's lots of laughter in our home. Yet what brings me the biggest joy is seeing my son so happy and fulfilled in his life. It's one of my biggest accomplishments. Having contributed to helping my son overcome dyslexia by finding the right tools and strategies to help him achieve his goals and potential makes my day. Empowering him by encouraging him along the way made him UN-Stoppable. Today, nothing stops him and he's an impressive young man with a love of learning that is so infectious. One can't see in others what one doesn't see in oneself. By living with dyslexia I had to work very hard, and now I can appreciate it in my son and others, this determination to succeed.

After about four years of remedial classes, hard work and lots of perseverance, my son finally attained a level of independence and success in reading and writing that enabled him to join a private school where his intellectual potential and great thinking abilities were being recognized and appreciated. Now, he's enjoying the ride and spreading his wings.

After seeing first hand what love, compassion, understanding, healthy living and the right tools and strategies can do to help a struggling child, we decided to share this information with other parents and with my husband's patients. After many years of researching ways to help our son overcome dyslexia and seeing him grow and succeed beyond our wildest dreams, this is when *Dyslexic AND UN-Stoppable*, the company, the book with tools and strategies, the cookbook, the tutorials, the videos and the documentary (still in progress) were born. Our main goals are to empower dyslexics and help them find their inner power. Everyone on this earth is born with a gift. Sometimes we just need a little help to rediscover what it is.

One of my mentors strongly reminded me on the last day at an intensive boot camp that I feared success more than I feared failure. His insisting I had the fear of success was definitely somewhat confrontational for me and my ego. (Today, I'm still challenged by it to some degree.) It was a fact. I was, deep down, more afraid to succeed fully than to fail miserably. Succeeding by putting myself out there for the world to see and exposing all my flaws was one crazy proposition. In spite of my fears, after much contemplation and because of the nagging thoughts of spending the rest of my life relinquishing my dreams, I chose to share our success with the world. Choosing to just live a comfortable life and not sharing what we learned on this journey through dyslexia, would have been more of a disappointment than failing while trying. So after all these trials and errors, we are here sharing our story with you.

Success is not about finally being perfect. Success is about perseverance and following your passion. Success is about never giving up on your dreams. Are you still willing to let dyslexia or any other excuse stop you from becoming healthy, wealthy and successful?

About Lucie

Lucie M. Curtiss, R.N., is an entrepreneur, mother, pediatric nurse, business manager of a successful pediatric practice, and author of the *Dyslexic AND UN-Stoppable* series. She, along with her husband, Dr. Douglas C. Curtiss, a Yale-trained pediatrician and Amazon #1 best-selling author, are the co-founders of Dyslexic AND UN-Stoppable, LLC.

Together they researched and found the most effective methods to help their son overcome dyslexia by using the right tools, healthy lifestyles, positive reinforcement and a more holistic approach to learning. After seeing the results firsthand of their son's success, Lucie teamed up with Doug to help parents of kids with dyslexia find the tools and strategies and make educated choices, to help their children rise to their fullest potential. Their mission is to empower dyslexic children to become UN-Stoppable and overcome dyslexia by rediscovering their inner power. They are here to remind dyslexics that they are SMART!

CHAPTER 7

FOUR SIMPLE ELEMENTS TO CONTROL DIABETES FOR LIFE

BY REGGIE CHANDRA, PhD

DIABETES: THE PROBLEM

Diabetes is a chronic metabolic disease that is spreading rampantly. The Centers for Disease Control and Prevention estimates that 9.3% of the population has diabetes—up 300% in the last 30 years. Today, nearly 21 million American adults have been diagnosed with or suffer from diabetes and more than 33% of our population lives with pre-diabetes. Some diabetic diagnoses are genetically based; however, Americans' sedentary lifestyles, combined with terrible diets, cause most of this epidemic. For example, the average American consumes 100 to 160 pounds of toxic, inflammatory, chlorine-bleached, chemically-refined sugars every year—which lead directly to the rise in diabetes, heart disease, and cancer.

There are two main types of diabetes: **Type 1** and **Type 2.** Both involve the body's inability to regulate blood glucose levels. Type 1 diabetes occurs when the body does not produce enough insulin on its own. Many experts have considered Type 1 a childhood problem, but it manifests in adults as well. It is also considered an autoimmune disease and can be caused by destruction of the pancreas for any reason. Ignored or improperly managed, Type 1 diabetes can lead directly to loss of extremities, coma, and death. Many doctors assert that the patients with

Type 1 must have insulin injections daily to survive and that there is no known cure.

Type 2 diabetes accounts for 90-95% of all diagnosed diabetes cases and occurs when the body becomes resistant to insulin's effects. Doctors acknowledge that Type 2 can often be managed with regular exercise and proper diet but should never be ignored. However, reports show that the side effects of the medications for managing both types of diabetes can cause more problems than they remedy. Hence, many holistic doctors are now searching for and finding evidence of natural cures for Type 2 diabetes and alternative treatments for Type 1.

THE KEY ROLE OF MINERALS: CHROMIUM

Diabetics, mostly due to medications, must deal with depleted vitamin and mineral levels. These depletions can place patients at increased risk for disease and ailments. Physicians fail to mention this aspect of diet during evaluation and check-ups. Moreover, many diabetics overlook the role of the diet, especially mineral and element supplementation, in improving outcomes and potentially reversing the disease. However, data shows that getting the proper vitamins and minerals is crucial in helping with recovery. Vitamin and mineral supplements help the body recover to normal levels, which can then assist the body with self-healing. Important players include: Vitamin E, Cinnamon, B vitamins (especially B-6 and B-12), Biotin, Chromium, Magnesium, Calcium, Potassium, Zinc, L-taurine and Vitamin C. Of these, the two that appear most relevant are Chromium and Magnesium. In concert with another key nutrient, Calcium, these minerals are essential for the proper regulation of metabolic activities within our bodies.

Chromium, a very abundant element in our environment, exists in several oxidation states: metallic, trivalent and hexavalent Chromium. The latter is primarily produced by industrial processes and is highly toxic. However, metallic and trivalent chromium are quite beneficial and, in fact, are essential for human health. In addition, the body has the ability to detoxify toxic forms of Chromium to safer forms. High levels of Chromium are found in foods such as broccoli, raw cheese, green beans and grass-fed beef.

Chromium is known to enhance the action of insulin, a hormone critical to the metabolism and storage of carbohydrate, fat and protein in the body. It was initially identified when patients on total parenteral nutrition developed severe signs of diabetes. These symptoms were reversed after supplemental chromium was provided.

Chromium also appears to be directly involved in carbohydrate, fat and protein metabolism, but more research is needed to determine the full range of its roles in the body. We know that Chromium deficiency impairs the body's ability to use glucose to meet its energy needs and raises insulin requirements. In fact Americans have been shown to only ingest 50-60% of the minimum suggested intake, suggesting normal dietary intake may be suboptimal.

Another compounding factor is that chromium absorption is very low but can be enhanced by Chromium Picolinate, which has been shown to increase absorption to near 2.8%. In addition, consumption of refined foods, including simple sugars, exacerbates the problem of insufficient dietary chromium as these foods contain little chromium and in fact, increase its excretion from the body. Chromium loss also increases during pregnancy and as a result of strenuous exercise, infection, physical trauma or stress. It also decreases as we age. As a result, it has been suggested that chromium supplements may benefit those of us who may be deficient.

In addition, studies suggest that chromium supplements might help to control Type 2 diabetes or the glucose and insulin responses in persons at high risk of developing the disease. Diabetic patients seem to have reduced chromium levels, and it appears they also have altered chromium metabolism (both absorption and excretion appear higher).

While inconclusive, several small studies have provided key insight to the effects of chromium supplementation on blood lipid levels in humans. In some studies, 150 to 1,000 mcg/day had decreased total and low-density-lipoprotein (LDL) cholesterol and triglyceride levels and increased concentrations of apolipoprotein A (a component of high-density-lipoprotein cholesterol known as HDL) in subjects with atherosclerosis or elevated cholesterol or among those taking a beta-blocker drug. These findings are consistent with the results of earlier studies.

More recent studies conducted as part of the male health care professionals follow-up study demonstrated that lower total chromium levels (measured from toenails – a good measure of long-term intake of trace elements) were correlated with an increased risk for myocardial infarctions, but only in subjects with BMI (Body Mass Index) measurements over 25 (kg/m^2). A second study conducted with the same group showed that diabetic men with prevalent cardiovascular disease (CVD) had lower chromium levels than those diabetics with no CVD and much lower than healthy control subjects. This demonstrates a clear correlation between adequate chromium levels, diabetes and CVD prevention.

These results were also confirmed in a European study (EURAMIC) where researchers demonstrated that toenail chromium levels had a clear inverse relationship with the risk of myocardial infarction in men. In addition, an evaluation of 15 studies using chemically-defined compounds and the proper 'controls' demonstrated that chromium supplementation showed positive effects in 12 of these 15 studies. This data indicates that impaired glucose tolerance can be improved or normalized, even in spite of a reduced insulin output, with chromium supplementation.

THE KEY ROLE OF MINERALS: MAGNESIUM

In addition to chromium, magnesium studies have revealed its significant role in diabetes care and reversal. Magnesium is thought to play a role in glucose homeostasis, insulin action and pancreatic insulin secretion, but the exact mechanisms have not been determined. Magnesium functions as a cofactor for several enzymes critical for glucose metabolism and decreased levels were shown to decrease tyrosine kinase activity at insulin receptors (essential for activation of insulin binding) and to increase intracellular calcium levels, both leading to impaired insulin signaling.

There is also a correlation between magnesium levels and insulin sensitivity. A number of studies demonstrate an inverse association between plasma or erythrocyte magnesium levels and fasting insulin levels and/or insulin sensitivity in both diabetic and healthy individuals. In addition, there is an association between dietary magnesium and homeostasis, which is further supported by data showing magnesium supplementation improves insulin sensitivity in non-diabetic individuals. Further data from clinical case studies and cross-sectional studies provides evidence that there is indeed a correlation between blood magnesium levels and Type 2 diabetes.

Another factor important to the proper uptake of magnesium is the level of calcium in the diet. Both minerals have similar chemical properties and share the same regulating system, including gut absorption and kidney reabsorption, as both are monitored by the same receptor. Therefore, in clinics, hypomagnesaemia (low magnesium) is commonly linked to hypocalcemia (low calcium). In fact, studies demonstrate that changes in dietary calcium/magnesium balance affect systemic inflammation responses in animal models. They also may antagonize each other in other physiological activities, including oxidative stress and insulin resistance, which may be involved in the development of Type 2 diabetes and many other diseases. In fact, in some recent small studies, calcium and magnesium supplementation has been shown to reduce insulin resistance in obese patients.

Holistic studies also show that increased magnesium intake can reverse diabetes as it regulates normal blood sugar levels and provides correct immune response and function. These studies suggest that magnesium is best taken into the body through skin absorption and can be sprayed on the body by using a magnesium chloride solution in a spray bottle. Holistic doctors recommend that patients rub coconut oil on their skin an hour after spraying magnesium to avoid their skin drying out. If patients do not wish to use the spray, there are vitamin supplements or magnesium oil. Magnesium can also be found in foods such as dark leafy greens, nuts and seeds, and fish (salmon, tuna).

The bottom line: research suggests that these two minerals, and more, play a significant role in Type 2 diabetes regulation, treatment, prevention and potential reversal.

THE KEY ROLE OF EXERCISE IN DIABETES

In addition to supplements, diabetics should include exercise in their daily activities. Patients should be careful to consult a physician to the level of exercise that would be best for their specific situation. The diabetic patients can then tailor their exercise regimen to their specific condition.

Data supports the role of physical exercise in helping prevent or control

Type 2 diabetes and may also benefit those with Type 1 disease. One study demonstrated that those who do not exercise routinely might have up to a 1.9 fold increase in developing impaired fasting glucose levels. Importantly, as little as 30 minutes of moderate physical activity daily may offer protection. To lower A1C levels (glycosylated hemoglobin, a measure of average blood glucose levels over 3 months), a greater benefit was seen with increased levels of exercise and activity, especially in women. This change in A1C levels occurs after 8 weeks of structured physical activity, independent of changes in body weight.

A number of other studies demonstrated similar results. In a randomized controlled trial, 16 weeks of progressive resistance training resulted in reduced A1C levels, increased muscle glycogen stores (a measure of glucose uptake by muscle), and reduced prescribed 'diabetic' medicine doses in 72% of exercisers. A second publication reviewed 25 individual studies and determined that both aerobic and resistance exercises had a positive effect on both Type 1 and Type 2 diabetes patients. However, this effect was enhanced in Type 2 diabetics, believed to be due to increased glucose uptake into skeletal muscle, reducing the amount of blood glucose (and reducing A1C). Aerobic and resistance exercises also significantly improved insulin sensitivity. Two additional studies showed that even moderate activity was associated with reduced mortality risk in individuals with diabetes. In addition, the first demonstrated that physical activity combined with modest weight loss lowered the risk of Type 2 diabetes by up to 58% in high-risk populations; the second showed that exercise alone (expenditure of 2000 calories per week through exercise) resulted in a 24% reduction in the risk of developing Type 2 diabetes (again, in high-risk patients).

Two systemic reviews of current literature reinforced the role of physical activity combined with diet in reducing Type 2 diabetes incidence. In one review, the data showed a significant decrease in incidence, body weight, and fasting blood glucose levels in those who participated in routine activity. In addition, these studies showed improved blood pressure, significant improvement in total cholesterol, reduction in LDL and triglyceride levels, and improved HDL levels.

In the second review, nine randomized controlled trials for at-risk patients and 11 trials for diabetic patients were analyzed. Seven studies demonstrated that lifestyle interventions decreased the risk for diabetes for up to 10 years post-study. All these results indicate that exercise can reduce the severity or prevent Type 2 diabetes and provide the added bonus of reduced heart disease, potential for weight loss, and improved overall general well being.

THE KEY ROLE OF DIET IN DIABETES

Finally, a diabetic's diet can assist mineral supplementation to help reverse diabetes. Diabetic patients can make wiser dietary choices to maximize their diabetes management.

Avoiding processed foods of any kind and switching to naturally occurring foods can make a drastic difference in the diabetic's lifestyle. For example, diabetics should avoid processed sugars and processed oils and replace them with natural cane sugar and natural oils such as olive, coconut and red palm. They should also increase the amount of high fiber foods (fresh vegetables, fruits, nuts and seeds) to slow glucose absorption (low glycemic index). Substituting green tea for sodas adds an extra benefit, as the ECGC (Epigallocatechin gallate) antioxidants increase insulin sensitivity and reduces blood glucose levels. In addition, green tea helps with insulin uptake into the cells and liver glucose production. Most doctors recommend 4-6 cups of green tea a day. Lemon water can also help by balancing pH levels. These are just a few examples.

Note that doctors also recommend patients adjust how they are eating and drinking. Smaller meals more often are better than three big meals. Eating more slowly while chewing carefully and thoroughly allows the body to process the food slowly and avoid as many spikes. Also, rather than gulp drinks, patients should sip or drink slowly. Pace does make a difference.

The point here: mineral supplements and wiser dietary and lifestyle choices allow doctors to treat their patients from a holistic standpoint. This works to correct and prevent the disease, empowers the patient to create conditions for optimal health and helps move the patient to a point of healing where medicines and insulin injections are no longer necessary. Traditional medicine treats the disease; alternative medicine treats the person. Alternative nutrition follows a structured plan that adjusts with the person, rather than following a "one-size-fits-all" diet. The evidence supports this: controlling blood glucose through modification of diet and lifestyle should be a pillar of diabetes therapy.

CONCLUSION

With the increased dangers and side effects of mainstream drug treatments for diabetes, doctors and patients are hunting for better treatments and methods for managing and reversing diabetes. Research has identified new methods to treat diabetes, showing the importance of minerals and diet in overcoming the diabetic epidemic. Chromium and magnesium are two key minerals in assisting patients with diabetes management and reversal. Proper diet provides a strong foundation to a life without insulin injections and damaging drugs. People deserve to live without side effects and fears; natural, holistic cures can change the lives of diabetics across the world. For more information on this topic, the reference list can be obtained at hello@unmarketing.agency.

About Dr. Reggie Chandra

Dr. Reggie Chandra is an entrepreneur, husband, dad, and friend whose purpose in life is to love, to be loved and to create. He lives his purpose. He expresses his love for his family by creating magic moments for them. His love for the community is expressed through his inventions, time, and resources that he spends supporting charitable organizations and mentoring younger entrepreneurs.

In 2007, Reggie invented InSync, a device that synchronizes traffic signals and reduces automobile crashes by 30%. His company, Rhythm Engineering, owns 95% of the US market in this technology and has been listed in the Inc. 5000 for three years. *Inc. Magazine* listed it as the 64th fastest-growing company in the US and Deloitte Fast 500 listed Rhythm Engineering as the 43rd fastest-growing company. Rhythm Engineering holds four patents and continues to invent new and disruptive products that revolutionize the industry. Rhythm Engineering solutions operate in over 2,000 intersections in 31 states and positively impact over 4,000,000 motorists daily.

Dr. Chandra has invented other products/solutions and has founded six other companies besides Rhythm Engineering. He has also developed a solution to run those companies without physically spending time "in" them. He is always working "on" his businesses rather than "in" them. A self-proclaimed dreamer, Reggie leads by communicating a vision, developing a plan, and stepping back to allow his team to go to work on making the dream a reality.

Reggie's other products/solutions also include Dream Cultures, (www.dreamcultures.com) where he offers a system for employees to create and live their Dream Life. Dr. Chandra is a true visionary and believes in a team environment where each employee, as a unique, remarkable and indispensible person, has the ability to contribute brilliant ideas, passion, and feedback. In everything he does, Dr. Chandra seeks to challenge the norm, think outside the proverbial box, and identify new solutions that create value and success.

As a result of his talents, Reggie was recognized as one of the United States most inspirational CEOs by *Esquire Magazine* in 2012. Sir Richard Branson, after meeting with Reggie declared that: "You should be awarded a Nobel Prize." Governors, entrepreneurial groups, and engineering organizations have also recognized Reggie for his contribution to society.

Reggie lives in Loch Lloyd, Missouri, with his wife of over 27 years, Jenny, a board-certified physician, and their two daughters, Joan and Jubilee. Joan is a final-year medical student and Jubilee is a high school student. He continues to support the community and the advancement of new technologies to make life simpler, easier and safer.

CHAPTER 8

SKYROCKET YOUR BUSINESS AND LIFE!
—Unearth your personal brand and stand out from the crowd

BY DR. SHAHAB ANARI

Does any of these sound like you?

1. **I'm a student, wondering what career is right for me.**

2. **I'm a college graduate, looking for a fulfilling job.**

3. **I'm not happy with my current job. I want to make a change.**

4. **I'm an employee. I think I've learned enough in my present position. I want to get promoted.**

5. **I'm an entrepreneur, looking for a way to earn more money and, at the same time, be able to spend more time with my family.**

6. **I want to win more clients, customers, or patients and increase my business.**

7. **I'm in transition to a new field or market. I want to build credibility and new relationships.**

8. **I'm a C-level executive, willing to position myself as a thought-leader and a sought-after expert in my field.**

9. I'm a busy, accomplished professional, and I want to make sure I will maintain my popularity in the long run.

Can you see the common theme in all these seemingly different situations? After fifteen years of experience in lifestyle and business coaching, I believe what all these people share is 'the need to stand out' and the single remedy I'd propose is 'personal branding.' Personal branding is the process of creating a recognizable unique promise of value that will establish you as the obvious choice for your target audience. Just as any company needs to differentiate itself from the competitors, any aspiring individual has to stand out from the competitors and have a tall presence in the marketplace. Here are my three steps for you to do that:

STEP1: DISCOVER YOUR PERSONAL BRAND

1. Know yourself:

According to a recent Gallup study, more than 85% of adults hate going to work. I believe this is mainly because most people have no idea what they really want in life. I firmly believe if you don't truly know your life purpose, you'll just spend most of your life reacting to anything that will come your way, without pursuing a genuine vision. I've come up with a set of absolutely foundational questions for you to realize how much you truly know YOU (You need to be focused and in a calm place to do this exercise, and you might want to talk to your friends and family to come up with the best answers.)

• *What are your core values in life?* To find your values, think of people you admire very much. These could be world leaders, scientists, artists, your teachers, friends and family, dead or alive. What makes you think highly of them? This indirectly demonstrates to you what your higher values are.

• *What are your main talents and passions?* Think of the times in your life when you demonstrated peak performance, some moments you experienced utmost pleasure because of something you had done, or things you loved doing in your free time when you were a child. Also ask yourself what you're known for doing well among family, friends and colleagues.

• *What are your top skills?* Suppose you're applying for a job and writing a resume. What gifts will you want to show off most?

- *What are your vision and mission in life?* If you were endowed with eternal life and a never-ending amount of money and you didn't have to do one day of work for money ever again, what would you spend your money on? Think of both yourself and the other people in the world you might want to impact. What would you start doing right now if you knew you wouldn't fail?

- *What are your strongest beliefs?* First think of your empowering beliefs: Those convictions that keep you going during tough times. Then think of the limiting ones: The beliefs that have held you back from doing what you've always wanted. Then, think about the life references that have led you to believe in that way. For example, *I believe I can never be a good singer. That's because whenever I sing karaoke, people start laughing at me.*

- *What would you call your main attribute if you were to limit yourself to one?* For example, do you represent the archetype of a Caregiver most of the time? Do you consider yourself a Ruler who puts everything to order? Are you an Outlaw? Or a Magician?[1]

You have probably had a hard time writing down answers to these questions. Honestly, this is an ongoing process of self-discovery as you flex your mental muscles and reflect upon who you really are. However, by thinking about these questions regularly, you get to know yourself better each and every day.

2. Define your target audience:

I remember one day a young lady came up to me and told me about her idea about building a language academy where all the instruction was done by phone. When I asked her who the service was intended for, she replied just like lots of entrepreneurs mistakenly assume: 'Everyone!' You see everyone is no one. You have to define your specific audience. If you try to be everything to everyone, you'll be nothing to no one. Your target audience could be the companies you'd like to be hired by or people to whom you'd like to sell your products or services. Be as specific as you can. A great way to define your

---

1. For a comprehensive definition and analysis of each archetype, refer to Brand You, by John Purkiss and David Royston-Lee, chapter 7.

target audience is to create an audience persona. When creating your audience persona(s), consider including demographics, behavior patterns, motivations, and goals.

3. Devise your value proposition:

Everyone who's worked with me has heard me say over and over, "Don't be just another same boring member of the herd." Your value proposition, in essence, is the unique value you provide for your audience that sets you apart from the others. What makes you different from your competitors? A good value proposition answers three essential questions:

- *What are your audience's pressing problems?*

- *What is your problem-solving promise?*

- *How are you different from the others?*

STEP 2: CREATE YOUR PERSONAL BRAND

1. Build your brand:
Now that you have unearthed your identity, described your target audience and defined your distinctive value, it's time for you to learn how to build your personal brand.

- *Act in tune with your identity.* The way you behave must be in accordance with the image you'd like to portray. I had a client who was struggling with establishing his role as a project manager. When I attended one of his meetings with his team members, the reason became obvious. He was cracking jokes all the time. Obviously, his behavior wasn't in line with his desired identity as a ruler.

- *Dress consistent with your identity.* I sometimes notice young college teachers having a hard time establishing themselves because their attire is more appropriate for a teenage audience than for a college.

- *Try to be a thought-leader.* At meetings and seminars, be the first person to make thoughtful comments or ask insightful questions. Stay informed, write great content on your weblog, and write for prestigious magazines.

• *Associate yourself with powerful brands.* You may have noticed that great speakers and writers refer to strong brands in their speech or writing, and this makes people see them in a more reliable light. Also, choose wisely who you keep company with. Jim Rohn said, "You're the average of the five people you spend time with."

• *Never stop networking.* Use these tips in networking:

   - Volunteer for jobs/internships/responsibilities where you can make important connections.

   - Be a genuine listener. React to what people are saying instead of focusing on what is in it for you. Be positive and honest in the emotions you express. Promote yourself only when they ask you to talk about yourself.

   - Give and you will receive. Always try to do something of value for people first before asking them for help or referrals.

   - Try to connect to key players and influencers. If you don't think you can approach them easily, find out about their new endeavors, and send them an email offering to help in some way.

   - Establish a relationship with people you meet. Don't just get their business cards and forget about them until you need them. Refer business to them, or at least remember them on Holidays.

• *Be visible.* When I first came to Canada, I attended any seminar and meeting relevant to my field that I could. The more often I attended, the more visible I became to the influencers' vigilant eyes.

• *Ask your happiest clients/customers for testimonials.* Among the best tools I've always used to build my credibility are testimonials, which I constantly use in my offline and online branding.

• *Ask your existing network for referrals and recommendations.* Some won't but there's definitely no harm in asking.

- *Prepare your marketing toolkit,* including your business card, personal brochure, and direct marketing package (and your book, if you have one). All these items should carry your logo, full name and slogan, and be congruent and convey the same image and message. Use this kit both to keep in touch with previous clients regularly and to shock-and-awe your new prospects.

- *Write your one-year personal branding plan and act upon it.*

2. Create your brand online:

At the time of writing this book, 3.2 billion people (around 40% of the world population) have an Internet connection. In 1995, it was less than 1%. Considering the huge effect of the Net on our lives, here is how you can make yourself, in William Arruda's words, Digitally Distinct.

- *Google yourself.* Find out how much information there is on the Web about you and how positive and relevant it is. If there is very little information or it is either negative or irrelevant to who you are, you have got some homework to do!

- *Harness the power of social media.* In September 2015, Facebook reported that it had more than 1.44 billion active monthly users. When you add LinkedIn, YouTube, Twitter, Instagram and others, you realize why social media have gained such an undeniably huge impact. A survey by Bullhorn in 2012 showed that almost 97.3 recruiters used LinkedIn as a recruiting tool.[2]

Make sure you use social media correctly. Here are some tips:

- Build profiles. Choose the social network(s) that is(are) most relevant to you and your target audience. For example, LinkedIn is a professional social network and is probably not ideal for teenagers wishing to socialize.

- Be authentic. Personal branding is not about projecting a fake image which is meant to deceive people into working with you. Act professionally and present your genuine

---

2. http://www.forbes.com/sites/susanadams/2013/02/05/new-survey-linked-in-more-dominant-than-ever-among-job-seekers-and-recruiters-but-facebook-poised-to-gain/ Accessed in September, 2015.

personality without exposing too much of your personal life.

- Be congruent. Check that your title, bio, experience, education and even the headshot for your profiles are almost the same across different social networking platforms. Besides, if you mean to use social media professionally, use your full name and not some fancy meaningless invented ID. ElephantOnFire would not be the best Facebook profile name if you're desperately trying to reach out to recruiters.

- Be careful about perceptions. Dan Schawbel writes in *Me 2.0*, "Perception is reality…. The point is, in personal branding little things matter. Each move you make is a chance for you to enhance how people perceive you." You must have heard stories about employees being fired because of some tweet they made, or a college student getting toasted because of some ill-judged pictures he posted on Facebook.

- Be networking all the time. Try to connect with people, reply to their comments, engage your followers and fans and build a relationship based on humility and respect. The time and energy you put in pays off big time in the long run.

• *Claim your own land online.* One of my 'musts' for personal branding is setting up a website. If you are determined to stand out, it's inevitable that you have a personal website, under your own domain name. Make sure your website has

- user-friendly navigation

- a clean attractive design

- a blog where you post great content to keep engaging the visitors to your website

- an 'about me' page where you showcase your unique value proposition

- a 'contact me' page where your people can find you

- testimonials and multimedia to boost your credibility

- social media links to encourage visitors to spread the word

- free stuff as lead magnets to collect data from prospects

- a marketing system in place to regularly get in touch with your audience

Remember your website is not a static 'window' to show stuff to passers-by, but a dynamic environment where you engage with your audience.

STEP 3: MAINTAIN AND EXPAND YOUR PERSONAL BRAND

1. Focus on quality:
Over time, it's been proven to me that competency is THE most important factor in career success, much more than marketing, sales pitches, and connections. To ensure the best quality:

• *Always (over-)deliver what you promise.* Go the extra mile for your audience.

• *Continuously plan your moves, measure your progress, and correct any problems.*

• *Listen to your audience and act accordingly.* After all, they are the people who put food on your table.

• *Don't sell yourself cheap just in the pursuit of being more visible.*

• *Focus single-mindedly on one goal at a time.* Dividing your attention in so many directions will only cause frustration.

2. Update yourself:
Each night, ask yourself "What have I learned today?"

• *Read.* I always start and finish my days with 30 min of reading. Never cease to learn and apply your new knowledge to your job.

• *Be creative* to stay ahead of copycats.

• *Attend seminars and join special-interest groups and associations in your field.*

3. Deal with people prudently:

- *Follow the golden rule.* Treat others as you would like to be treated.

- *Always respect your supporters and fans and those who stood beside you at difficult times.*

- *Respect everyone in your network.* I think a major reason why most of my competitors speak well behind my back is because I always show the utmost respect for them, no matter how experienced they are.

- *Ignore jealous people.* Their jealousy is a vivid indicator that they believe you are better than them.

- *Don't take negative comments personally.* Haters mostly hate themselves for not achieving the great things that you did.

- *Remember you are a role model.* It doesn't matter if only a hundred people know you or you have tens of millions of fans throughout the world. If you're aspiring to improve your personal brand, try to act as if everyone's watching you all the time. Serve people, give to charities, be humble, and your personality will shine through the crowd.

There are so many subtle aspects to personal branding which I obviously can't cover in such a short chapter. However, I've provided you with the indispensable fundamentals. Don't forget your Personal Brand is a work in progress, and it definitely takes time and effort to turn your dreams into reality. However, if you commit yourself to this 3-step process, your efforts will undoubtedly be paving the way to your amazing personal brand!

About Dr. Shahab Anari

Dr. Shahab Anari is a speaker and coach who helps his clients build a memorable authentic personal brand. He teaches how you can stand out from your competitors and become recognized as the trusted expert among your audience. Having fifteen years of experience as a coach and speaker, Shahab has the natural gift of making complex procedures very easy to follow and implement. Through his books, workshops, seminars and speaking engagements, he has reached out to more than 1.5 million individuals and helped them on their path to success.

"My greatest joys in life have always been learning and teaching. I used to be a very inquisitive child who was in the habit of taking things apart and failing to put them back all together! The interesting thing was that my Mom rarely told me off for this behavior and actually attributed what I did to the fact that I was intelligent and I always wanted to know more. For this reason, I developed a keen interest in learning and growing.

At school, I was a really good student, almost always being in the top three in my class. I used to study hard and actually enjoyed it. In 1997, I entered the best medical school in the country. This achievement led to people coming up to me and asking me to help their kids with their studies. And so I did! While being a medical student during the day, I started teaching and coaching students in the afternoons, and after a while, I started making a name at it.

Encouraged as I was, I began reading books on the topic of personal development and started trying to figure out what I used to do unconsciously that brought about my good results. Besides, I gradually realized I didn't like to be a medical doctor and I decided that was definitely not something that fired me up to go to work every morning. So I devoted all my time to coaching and speaking, and after 5 years, I was fully booked for the next whole year! I was invited to hold workshops and speak at events and seminars, which ultimately ended in me writing several best-sellers, appearing as a guest expert on TV programs, and, finally, starting my own business."

Shahab's message for those who seek to build their personal brands is:

"First, discover your life purpose."

His goal is to help his clients unearth their unique values, talents, skills and experiences and use that one-of-a-kind combination to portray their authentic self to their specific audience in a systematized marketing procedure. Shahab's clientele ranges from college grads looking for a fulfilling career path to well-established professionals who want to maintain and enhance their brands and businesses. Shahab was selected as one of America's Premier Experts™ in 2015.

You can connect with Shahab at:
www.shahabanari.ca
info@shahabanari.com

https://www.linkedin.com/in/shahabanari
https://instagram.com/shahab_anari
https://www.facebook.com/shahab.anari

CHAPTER 9

FROM 11¢ IN FIVE BANK ACCOUNTS TO A MULTI-MILLION DOLLAR REAL ESTATE BROKERAGE

BY MARNIE BENNETT

Pursue your dream and if you believe you can achieve it, you will. From the time I knew that I wanted to be a millionaire through real estate, I was driven by this thought: "Winners do what losers don't." It may seem harsh to say "loser", but what I consider a loser is a person who does not work hard, never reaches their full potential, and never finds their passion in life. It's never easy being successful, but how you move forward after a failure or a knock down and strive for success is truly the definition of a winner.

You may be thinking "successful people are workaholics, they are always working." That's a misconception that most people have— they don't understand the mindset of an entrepreneur. Entrepreneurs love what they are doing and are so passionate and so driven that time becomes irrelevant because failure is not an option. A true leader must "give up to go up"so they can provide for their family and loved ones.

A humble start…

Doing the best we can with what we have as a starting point is the foundation for everyone who wants to succeed. For me, I gained awe and inspiration from a woman who worked so hard and had so little—my mother. *I was raised my entire life by a single mom when this was not fashionable and was in fact, almost universally stigmatized.*

Being the only child in my school class who had only one parent was not easy—for my mom or me. I was only seven years of age when my parents separated and it was tough. But not as tough as watching my mom go through something she had to deal with her entire life—breast cancer. At this time, breast cancer treatment didn't have the resources it does now. Mom had some harsh realities to deal with, which meant I had those same harsh realities by default, including:

- Watching her go to the hospital time and again, left lingering with a hope that she'd be coming back home soon and praying every night that God would let her live.

- Seeing her stress about having no money or support, for either herself or for raising my younger sister and me. I remember vividly how tough that was.

This was my reality. I tried to be a mother and raise my younger sister when Mom was sick. And when she wasn't sick, she did the best she could with her very limited skill-set and energy. She had a clerical job in government, but it was often sporadic. After all, she was in and out of the hospital almost every year for sixteen years, for surgeries for her cancer. Sadly, more of her life was spent recovering than it was actually spent getting to live it to the fullest. Yet she never complained.

One thing about Mom was that she was determined, setbacks and all, to leave something behind for her daughters. She wanted us to have a chance to do something more and not have to go through those same challenges. This is when real estate first had an impact on my life.

The power of property…

After my parents first got divorced, we lived in a horrible apartment. It wasn't a good place—for anyone—but it was the only option we had. My mom had the vision to know that there must be a way to get to someplace better—a way to make it work regardless of her financial and health situation.

After much diligence, in the divorce settlement my mother got our family house back. It was there that she saw the potential in owning a home for all our futures. *It was nothing we could ever afford on her income alone, so she got innovative, knowing that having this home was a way for her to give us something more than what we currently had.* She rented rooms out to college students, teachers, and other boarders. The three of us lived in one bedroom.

It wasn't the most comfortable, but there was a vision there and we made it work!

I was ten by that time and had a lot of responsibility. I needed to take care of the home, which meant that I had a lot of manual labor chores. I cut the lawn and did all the shoveling, changed the winter storm windows to screens when spring came, cooked, cleaned, shopped for groceries, and did whatever Mom needed help with. Yes, I complained sometimes, but I was so inspired by my mom's actions and determination that what I learned far outweighed those moments.

There I was living a hard life, but one with lots of love. Everything was centered around money, everything was costed out, which meant that money was quite often on my young mind. I decided that in addition to school and my chores at home, I also wanted to get a part time job so I could make my own money. When I was 14, I lied about my age and said I was 16 just so I could work. *This inner drive was building and I was learning so much.* **If you want it, you can achieve it**—that was my mantra—even before I knew what a mantra was.

And life goes on…

Life blessed me with allowing me to marry my high school sweetheart and I had three wonderful children by the time I was 28 years old. Although we were happy, we were far from wealthy. One day while doing our monthly bank reconciliations, my husband and I laughed when we totalled up those five accounts' balances and realized that we had all of 11 cents in the bank. At that time, I was a stay-at-home mom and worked part-time at a major retailer and I worked in insurance; and I had a girlfriend who was in real estate. Just like today, it was not easy to try to have a career while juggling a young family. It takes work, and it takes planning! For me, insurance wasn't exciting or remunerative, but what I saw my girlfriend doing seemed like it was. I was interested and we started talking. An idea was born which was new at that time, but is common today:

We would become a real estate "team", helping each other to be good in our careers and better for our families.

Then we got to work in the resale business! We'd take turns watching each other's kids while our husbands were at work so each of us could do what was necessary to drive our success. The irregular hours were difficult, but we found the support from each other that helped us out. And we grew and I loved the industry and was ready for my next step— new home sales.

I went to work for a builder and developer and experienced great success quickly, selling 75 homes in eight weeks. These new homes were not built—the sales came from viewing blueprints—and I gained recognition for my sales expertise and my love of the real estate industry deepened with each sale. *Within 5 years, I was the Executive VP of a large custom home builder.* No other woman had a position like that. From there, it kept going, because I kept growing, both in knowledge and passion for the career I had chosen. Before I knew it, I was ranked #1 for sales in Canada.

Having found my passion in the new home industry, I felt the sky wasn't even the limit. And then… the owner of the company I worked for died of a sudden heart attack and the family took over the company and booted me to the curb at the age of 40. Poof! Gone in an instant! And along with it, my job, my future, and my passion and my livelihood – but not my drive or support!

In those defining moments…

Anyone who reaches a certain stage of success will have a defining moment. *It's what you do with that moment that matters.* How do you get back up? How do you talk yourself up and regain focus and reposition yourself? This is what I've learned:

> **Every 10 years I have to reposition myself, making sure that I am taking my skills onward to a higher and higher level. If I am going to go bankrupt or lose my job it is because of one thing—me! Don't be fearful of change - embrace it!**

You don't have to actually get fired to understand that it is devastating. I never wanted to experience that lack of control over my life again like I did that day, making that single incident pivotal—a life changing moment for me—but it did lead me to incredible heights of success. The feeling of being so disrespected led me to have the strength, fortitude, and confidence to launch a new home sales and marketing company, which became an industry leader and remains so today.

My boutique company sells millions of dollars of real estate in hours representing international developers. Each day I have the privilege of working alongside some of the most brilliant, innovative self-made billionaires in the world. Daily, I get to work and meet with the most incredible leaders of business, plus I have the privilege to learn and grow from these people. In addition, we have created a one-of-a-kind team that strives to be the best and in my wildest, most optimistic dreams I would never have envisioned this. *I certainly would not have considered it as such at the time, but when I look back I was blessed to have been fired, because I would never have pursued this dream.* If I had not been pushed to take a different and self-responsible path in life then I would never have…

- Built up a credible, innovative, and unique new home sales and marketing business

- Begun selling millions of dollars of new home sales in hours

- Used my "out-of-the-box" thinking for inventive marketing and strategizing

- And most shockingly, become a marketing consultant for my former competition!

In addition, what made everything take on an even more rewarding "shine" and lead me to another, higher level of business achievement was that by that time, my three children were adults - one even was married - and they wanted to become a part of this extraordinary business that I'd created. It forced me to "up my game" again and make sure that I was offering them the tools they needed to run wild with their passion, creativity, and dreams for their own lives and their own futures. It cemented that we are a "strong family," which excites me more than even real estate. I love my family so much; knowing that we can all be a part of this amazing opportunity is so inspiring—each and every day. It is the heart of the legacy I want to leave behind.

Building the legacy…

The relationships I built with developers and builders in my career were a highly personal thing. They were doing business with ME—because they knew ME and what I could do. There was no assuming that they'd give my children that same benefit of the doubt. Something had to change, and here's what I did:

I added a "resale pillar" to my organization chart and went to work for an existing international brokerage, knowing full well I would never stay because I wanted my own brokerage someday. I put a plan into place that included growth, training, mentoring, education, and the most incredible sales systems that would help me create the team that was geared to be the best in the world.

The results proved that I'd been successful in my approach. I became #1 Worldwide for sales for this international brokerage – selling more homes than 113,000 other realtors – I was on the top of the mountain. This was no small feat, as I was the first female ever to reach #1!

As an entrepreneur, I found ways to recognize business opportunities when the US economy was failing and the recession was causing so many foreclosures, and short sales. I went to the US with a group of Canadian investors; we were buying up homes for our clients in Arizona. I made alliances with many American realtors. True entrepreneurs recognize business opportunities and they don't wait—they find a way to make it happen. Today, we have an international referral network that works for our clients. We have built up incredible business relationships in China, United States, the Emirates, and Latin America, to name a few. We have sold over 10,000 properties, and we sell hundreds of properties a year with a very small, elite, professional team.

How is that possible? *With the most innovative systems that get our sellers top dollar in the least amount of time!*

What we offer is very unique, and our consumer programs are unsurpassed. We guarantee that we will sell your home in 29 days at a price acceptable to you or we'll buy it! For all our buyers if you don't love your house anytime in 2 years we will buy it back or sell it for free. We also offer:

- Free staging of up to $10,000 in free furniture for your vacant home

- Home Warranties so you can sell or buy with peace of mind

- Never get stuck owing 2 homes—we will buy your home, guaranteed

- Offering off-market properties, or distressed sales for real estate worldwide

Because of all these systems—even in a slow economy—we are able to grow annually by 35% to 50%, which is phenomenal growth in any industry, and particularly in real estate.

Our glass is never half empty, it is always overflowing because there is always an opportunity for success somewhere else!

Today, I have a boutique real estate brokerage, "The Bennett Property Shop" in Canada's Capital, Ottawa. Our office is a 1878 landmark heritage house which is just steps away from the Peace Tower, where the Prime Minister is our neighbor. I vividly remember the day I purchased our heritage office and it really hit home to me that, *"Yes, you can achieve your dreams, and the only person holding yourself back is you. If you believe it, you can achieve it."* For over 5 years I had envisioned owning a landmark heritage home in the downtown core. I had no idea which one I just knew someday it would happen. Then suddenly I heard about the possibility of a heritage office coming onto the market – it wasn't yet for sale – I called the owner —and made a cash offer of over $1 million with no conditions within 30 minutes of viewing. To this day I still can't believe it is ours. It just shows you how hard work, determination and careful planning can lead to great success. **It's hard to imagine that all of our wealth building and our family real estate legacy started with us having just 11¢ in 5 bank accounts.**

About Marnie

Marnie Bennett is an educator, mentor, and wealth coach to clients who seek to master the art of the wise real estate transaction. Known for her kind heart and generous spirit, she is highly committed to showing individuals how to maximize their potential in real estate.

As broker, founder, and shining-star of The Bennett Property Shop Realty, Marnie has built a one-of-a-kind boutique real estate brokerage in Ottawa, Canada, with a business philosophy based on exceptional personal service, leadership, innovative policies, and practices. With a team of 25 elite sales representatives, the sales volume speaks for itself—over 10,000 homes sold for top dollar since 1994 and over $3.6 billion in residential sales. Today, she is also recognized on an international level for both her sales records and mentoring success.

Passionate and committed about her calling, Marnie says, "Some people feel boxed-in by their professions, with no room to breathe. I've never felt that way. I've shaped my career in a way that allows me to explore my strengths; one of which is connecting with people. If there's a chance for me to share what I know with others, I'll jump at it."

An ardent educator, Marnie works with aspiring and established real estate investors by engaging them with her in intense, one-on-one mentoring sessions. As a wealth coach, she helps clients to design and execute custom-made plans of action. And for those dipping their toes in the waters for the first time, Marnie continually creates educational opportunities that are fun, practical, and easily understood.

Marnie has a substantial media presence, frequently making appearances on CTV and CBS news channels. She has written a nationally-syndicated column, Property Talk, for CanWest Global newspapers, while her Home Smarts column appears regularly in New Home and Condo Guide magazine. She appears on a weekly real estate show, Experts on Call: The Real Estate Hour. Marnie has also co-authored two books:

- *Death of the Traditional Real Estate Agent; Rise of the Super Profitable Real Estate Sales Team* with Craig Proctor and Todd Walters
- *Ignite Your Life* with Brian Tracy

Her awards include:

- *Daniel Passante Entrepreneurship Award*

- *Ottawa Business Woman of the Year*

- *Top Dog Award* from Craig Proctor Real Estate Systems in recognition for being the best, most productive agent in North America

Growing up with a single mother who struggled financially, Marnie is particularly passionate about helping other women discover their aptitudes for business, investment, and entrepreneurship. To this end, she's developed the "WOW [Women on Wealth] Workshops," and also participates in the "Invest and Dress for Success" fashion shows.

Marnie also has a love of athletics and her national pride has inspired her to sponsor Olympic hopefuls. She and her family are long-time supporters of young Canadian soccer and hockey players, billeting members of the Ottawa 67, and working for a renewal of soccer fields throughout Ottawa.

You may reach Marnie at: marnie@bennettpros.com
Or visit her website: www.bennettpros.com.

CHAPTER 10

PUTTING YOUR MISSION TO WORK: PRINCIPLE-BASED PROSPERITY

BY J.W. DICKS & NICK NANTON

While in college, he wrote a term paper on the need for a special overnight delivery service, since he believed society was entering a computerized information age. He detailed how the idea could be made to work. His professor wasn't convinced – and gave him a "C" on the paper.

It was another setback for a boy who had already experienced many. He was born with a congenital birth defect, as well as a hip disorder that forced him to wear braces and walk with crutches for most of his boyhood. He was to face a conflict of a much different sort after college, when, as a Marine, he was sent to serve in the Vietnam War and became a platoon leader. There he learned some important leadership lessons as he was put in charge of a group of soldiers with very different backgrounds and personalities. Vietnam also sparked a passion to build, after he saw so much useless destruction.

His first job, after leaving the service, was working for his stepfather, a retired Air Force general who had a company that overhauled older aircraft and modified their engines. That didn't last long, so he thought again about his overnight delivery idea. He went back to the plans he laid out in his term paper, a "hub and spokes" proposal in which packages from all over America would come to a central location, and then be flown out at night when airports were fairly empty. When he inherited

$4 million when his father passed away, he put it all into starting his "unfeasible" business. In 1971, his company was finally airborne - and became a huge overnight success. That's when Fred Smith decided to do something really radical with his already-revolutionary business, Federal Express.

Smith knew that in order to guarantee the best delivery service, he had to create a unique relationship with the employees the company relied on to make it excel. In his mind, if his people were made a part of the decision-making processes and treated as well as possible, they would perform at a higher level and, as a result, increase business revenues. He called it the PSP philosophy (People-Service-Profit) and, in 1973, its implementation caused FedEx to become one of the first companies in the world to formally view employees as a means for achieving long-term growth.

The next step was to manifest that philosophy to both the employees as well as the outside world. To accomplish that, FedEx went ahead and created "The Purple Promise," which played off the color of the company's logo and consisted of only seven words: "I will make every FedEx experience outstanding."

Smith's term paper may have gotten a "C," but no rational business analyst would give the company he built that low a grade. The company has become the number one overnight delivery service in the world, handling more than 3 million packages in over 200 nations every single business day. Not only that, but in 2013, Fortune magazine named FedEx one of the top companies to work for.[1]

FedEx truly succeeding in making PSP its company-wide mission. In the words of its website, "The Purple Promise is more than what we say — it's what we do. It unites us. Every one of us at FedEx is committed to making every experience outstanding."[2]

An Organizational Mission (or as we call it, an "OM") can give a business integrity, a sense of purpose and a powerful profile that attracts hordes of customers and clients, when chosen wisely and properly put into practice. And that's just what Fred Smith did with FedEx.

---

1. http://archive.fortune.com/magazines/fortune/best-companies/2013/list
2. http://www.fedex.com/purplepromise/docs//en/fedex_pp_booklet.pdf

It all begins with finding whatever your Life Mission (LM) happens to be, a topic that will be covered in detail in our forthcoming book on Mission-Driven Businesses. Once you tap into whatever drives your passion, as Smith did, the next challenge is to find a practical way to translate your LM into a practical real-world application. To do that, you have to understand what kind of OM will most effectively do that.

For example, Fred Smith's LM was not to build a company that would be a shining example of customer service. No, his passion was to create the first international delivery company that could follow through on shipments quickly and efficiently; creating the PSP model was his way of bringing that innovative business model to life. Similarly, the Zappos company, the online shoe retailer, was created to bring Tony Hsieh's LM of customer service to life; selling shoes was almost an afterthought, as he actually had little interest in that field prior to the company's birth.

In other words, when it comes to OMs, there is more than one way to skin a cat, as politically incorrect that phrase might be these days.

THE THREE TYPES OF OMS

An OM should be a huge "moon shot" type of goal, one that is doable if extremely difficult; it's an objective that should keep you busy for a number of years, if not your entire life.

Our research has shown us that the bulk of OMs fall into three main categories, which we're about to reveal. As you read through these, consider which type might work best for your specific LM.

OM Category #1: Social Benefit
Social Benefit OMs are aimed at improving life at a local, national or even international level – and the specific mission may not even have anything to do with the actual product involved. Both Ben & Jerry's as well as Newman's Own, pursue charitable OMs that, for the most part, have very little to do with the actual food products these brands sell.

OM Category #2: Buyer Benefit
When you embark on a Buyer Benefit OM, you must grant your customers and clients a clear and distinct advantage over buying from a competitor. As we've already noted, Fed Ex and Zappos both employ this OM; other similar OMs include Walmart's low price guarantee,

Ebay's auction process and Amazon's extensive selection of products. In each of these cases, the business is committed to a huge Buyer Benefit similar companies can't or won't offer – and that in turn gives its brands a huge defining positive that creates ongoing success.

OM Category #3: Disruptive Innovation
The final type of OM is the Disruptive Innovation OM, which such huge fast-growing tech companies such as Uber, PayPal and Amazon have embraced. The Disruptive Innovation OM shares some crossover with the Buyer Benefit OM – because it does involve finding a way to serve the customer at a higher level. The difference, however, is the benefit a disruptive company delivers is far more wide-ranging; it's actually a radically new way of operating a traditional business, such as the way Uber turned the traditional taxi business on its head.

CREATING YOUR ORGANIZATIONAL MISSION

Keep these three categories in mind as we now get into the nuts and bolts of composing your OM through the following four-step process.

1. Restate Your Life Mission.
Your LM will guide you to the right OM if you allow it. Think about the main objectives contained in your LM and what kind of impact in the real world you would like to make with them.

2. Determine What "Moon Shot" Goal You Want to Pursue
Remember the OM represents how you're going to translate your LM to a concrete objective. John F. Kennedy's original Moon Shot goal of putting a man on the moon within a decade was a response to a more abstract mission of catching up to the Russians, who badly outpaced the U.S.A. in the early days of the space race. He saw the OM of putting a man on the moon as a way to galvanize NASA and the scientific community at large into winning that race.

You may want to help with the fresh water crisis in undeveloped countries. Or advance the cause of cancer research because you lost your parents to that disease. Or you may have a gift for music that you want to somehow serve the world with. In each of these cases, unless you set your mind to a specific "Moon Shot" goal, your efforts will be scattershot and unfocused.

Your "Moon Shot" goal could involve:

- Raising a certain amount of money for a cause

- Creating a certain level of valuation for your company

- Raising your profile to a certain level in your industry that would allow you to do more, achieve more and have more resources (for example, an actor wanting to win an Oscar so he can have his pick of projects)

- Breaking a specific barrier or reaching a certain threshold in your field (for example, curing cancer, creating an entirely green business, etc.)

This part has to be your call – but it's best to be ambitious. This is a long-term goal, not a short-term one – and it should be one that *does* make you a little nervous. That will motivate you to work hard and achieve more than you ordinarily would. So…shoot for the moon!

3. Determine the Best Organizational Solution.

By "organizational solution," we mean what kind of structure do you need to have in place to carry through with your Moon Shot goal? Is it a matter of retooling your current business to connect it to your goal? Should you set up a nonprofit (or team up with an existing one)? Or do you need to create an entirely new business to really complete your Moon Shot? This may be something you'll change up down the line, but, for now, it's best to have a rough idea of how you can realistically take the first steps to your OM.

4. Finalize Your OM.

Your OM should be a statement of your Moon Shot goal together with your organizational solution. JFK's would be, "We're going to put a man on the moon, and we're going to give NASA all the funding and resources it needs to accomplish that goal."

What's yours? And what structure will you use to achieve it? The answer is *your* OM.

PUTTING YOUR OM TO THE TEST

Once you've decided on a potential OM, it's a good idea to give it a further theoretical road test. With that in mind, we've prepared a set of six questions you can ask yourself to determine whether this mission is really going to perform as you'd like.

• Is it simple?

To fulfill your OM, you're going to have to get people on board to help you out. That means it should be easy to understand and explain. Like a great "elevator pitch," you should be able to convey the basic thrust of the mission in less than thirty seconds – or, even better, in a breathtaking sentence that will impress the listener. So practice your OM out on a few people you trust (both in terms of judgment and discretion – you don't want it repeated to others before you get a chance at making it work!). Make sure it garners a positive reaction from your preview audience and be open to any reasonable feedback.

• Is it sustainable?

As discussed, an OM can sometimes generate extra expenses or a drain on profits, as well as a strain on resources and personnel. So think carefully about whether it's a OM you can realistically work towards while supporting yourself and growing your business. If the initial outlook is problematic, consider the kinds of adjustments you can make that might enable it to be a doable long-term commitment.

• Is it memorable and unique?

An effective OM should be something people find compelling and out of the ordinary – a goal that people have been *wanting* a business or individual to do. While it's hard to reinvent the wheel, your OM should at the very least be an attention-getting proposition that will make potential customers, clients or supporters seriously consider working with you.

• Is it delivering a big enough benefit?

Another important aspect of your OM should be the benefit it actually delivers to your buyers or your cause. If it's a business benefit, then it should make a big impact in terms of money, convenience, access, price or quality of product or service. If it's a cause benefit, it should also deliver a big awareness or fundraising component (ideally both). It can also be a big *intangible* benefit – such as Chick-fil-A's public display of what it considers to be Christian values, which is attractive to those who share those values and makes them feel good about eating there. Call it a *spiritual* benefit if you will, but it's still a powerful one.

• Does it play into your strengths?

If you're a technophobe who is considering an OM based on a mobile app or website, are you able to compensate for your lack of ability with a gifted programmer? If your OM is charity-based and you have absolutely no experience with nonprofit endeavors, are you motivated to learn enough to do it correctly? It's best if your OM substantially ties into your abilities and experience, so you can carry it out at the highest level. If the OM is beyond your skill set, then, at the very least, you will need to commit to hiring the right talent to help you follow through on it.

• Is it part of your belief system?

Imagine if it was suddenly revealed in the media that Chick-fil-A was secretly run by Muslims pretending to be Christian in order to boost profits? Imagine if Ben & Jerry's was secretly funded by the Koch Brothers in order to trick liberals into giving them money? Both these scenarios are, of course, patently ridiculous, but what isn't ridiculous is *committing to an OM you don't really believe in.* If you don't and the public finds out, you could at some point experience a severe backlash that could harm your business (a danger we'll discuss at more length in a later chapter).

Having a sincere motive behind your OM is essential. Uber's disruptive mission came from a genuine desire to provide a better cab experience, Google's famous mantra, "Don't be evil," came from the founders' desire to be better than certain old-school corporations that worshipped money over morality, and Tony Hsieh's conception of Zappos employee culture came about because of his disillusionment over how it felt to work at other companies that didn't seem to care. In each of the above cases, the company's success came from a founder's genuine desire to change things in a substantial way – to make some aspect of their business *better*. This kind of powerful emotional component that inspires an OM is often described as "fire in the belly."

OMs can be difficult to work towards – and it takes a certain kind of passion to see it through. But the effort pays off in both attracting lots of new customers and keeping them loyal once they arrive. There's no question that a business with a mission enjoys more benefits than one without – so there's also no question that you should consider putting one into action at your organization!

About Nick

An Emmy Award-Winning Director and Producer, Nick Nanton, Esq., is known as the Top Agent to Celebrity Experts around the world for his role in developing and marketing business and professional experts, through personal branding, media, marketing and PR. Nick is recognized as the nation's leading expert on personal branding as Fast Company Magazine's Expert Blogger on the subject and lectures regularly on the topic at major universities around the world. His book *Celebrity Branding You®*, while an easy and informative read, has also been used as a text book at the University level.

The CEO and Chief StoryTeller at The Dicks + Nanton Celebrity Branding Agency, an international agency with more than 1800 clients in 33 countries, Nick is an award-winning director, producer and songwriter who has worked on everything from large scale events to television shows with the likes of Steve Forbes, Brian Tracy, Jack Canfield (*The Secret*, Creator of the *Chicken Soup for the Soul* Series), Michael E. Gerber, Tom Hopkins, Dan Kennedy and many more.

Nick is recognized as one of the top thought-leaders in the business world and has co-authored 30 best-selling books alongside Brian Tracy, Jack Canfield, Dan Kennedy, Dr. Ivan Misner (Founder of BNI), Jay Conrad Levinson (Author of the Guerilla Marketing Series), Super Agent Leigh Steinberg and many others, including the breakthrough hit *Celebrity Branding You!®*.

Nick has led the marketing and PR campaigns that have driven more than 1000 authors to Best-Seller status. Nick has been seen in *USA Today, The Wall Street Journal, Newsweek, BusinessWeek, Inc. Magazine, The New York Times, Entrepreneur® Magazine, Forbes,* FastCompany.com and has appeared on ABC, NBC, CBS, and FOX television affiliates around the country, as well as CNN, FOX News, CNBC, and MSNBC from coast to coast.

Nick is a member of the Florida Bar, holds a JD from the University Of Florida Levin College Of Law, as well as a BSBA in Finance from the University of Florida's Warrington College of Business. Nick is a voting member of The National Academy of Recording Arts & Sciences (NARAS, Home to The GRAMMYs), a member of The National Academy of Television Arts & Sciences (Home to the Emmy Awards), co-founder of the National Academy of Best-Selling Authors, a 16-time Telly Award winner, and spends his spare time working with Young Life, Downtown Credo Orlando, Entrepreneurs International and rooting for the Florida Gators with his wife Kristina and their three children, Brock, Bowen and Addison.

Learn more at www.NickNanton.com and:
www.CelebrityBrandingAgency.com

About JW

JW Dicks Esq., is a *Wall Street Journal* Best-Selling Author®, Emmy Award-Winning Producer, publisher, board member, and advisor to organizations such as the XPRIZE, The National Academy of Best-Selling Authors®, and The National Association of Experts, Writers and Speakers®.

JW is the CEO of DNAgency and is a strategic business development consultant to both domestic and international clients. He has been quoted on business and financial topics in national media such as the *USA Today, The Wall Street Journal, Newsweek, Forbes*, CNBC.com, and *Fortune Magazine Small Business.*

Considered a thought leader and curator of information, JW has more than forty-three published business and legal books to his credit and has co-authored with legends like Brian Tracy, Jack Canfield, Tom Hopkins, Dr. Nido Quebin, Dr. Ivan Misner, Dan Kennedy, and Mari Smith. He is the resident branding expert for Fast Company's internationally syndicated blog and is the editor and publisher of the *Celebrity Expert Insider,* a monthly newsletter sent to experts worldwide.

JW is called the "Expert to the Experts" and has appeared on business television shows airing on ABC, NBC, CBS, and FOX affiliates around the country. His co-produced television series, *Profiles of Success,* appears on the Bio Channel - along with other branded films he has produced. JW also co-produces and syndicates a line of franchised business television shows and received an Emmy Award as Executive Producer of the film, *Mi Casa Hogar.*

JW and his wife of forty-two years, Linda, have two daughters, two granddaughters, and two yorkies. He is a sixth generation Floridian and splits his time between his home in Orlando and his beach house on Florida's west coast.

CHAPTER 11

ATTRACTION MARKETING MAY BE IN YOUR FUTURE

BY JILL KLUNK

Some people know what they want when they are young, but I didn't. Some people graduate from college at 22, ready to blaze a career, but I didn't. Some people take off focused. . . full speed ahead, but I didn't.

Yet I am here to tell you that I have succeeded despite the roundabout, stop-and-start route I've taken through life. With the example of my hardworking parents, and my own dogged persistence and openness to change, I've done well in management and in real estate, and now in Attraction Marketing. I'm a boomer enjoying life and work. And now, finally, both are on my own terms.

But they weren't always. Unloading trucks, unpacking merchandise and stocking shelves for J.C. Penney was my first job. Next, I did the same thing at a men's clothing store. A customer, noticing my strong work ethic, offered me a job at his company, writing technical manuals for a defense contractor. "I know nothing about that," I told him. "We'll teach you," he said. I learned every day.

At Allis Chalmers, I put together procedure manuals about nuclear reactors, again, this was something I knew nothing about until I began. Then I moved on to a graphic arts company where I assembled text books for colleges. At my next job for a company which was building tanks and trucks, I wrote technical manuals. My boss asked me if I'd try supervising workers, and I said, "Well, I've never done that, but sure, for three months, I'll do it. After that, if you think I've done a good job, I'll expect a raise and a title. Within a few months, I was manager of the department, and eventually, Manager of Logistical Support. I was making more money and handling more responsibility. But after 16 years, a change of executives led to my parting ways.

Meanwhile, I had gone to college, a course here and there, for many years. At first I thought I wanted to teach PE, but then I wasn't sure. I was basically spinning my wheels like a hamster in a cage, not getting anywhere. I found myself torn between the hopes of higher education and the need to pay my bills. If I could just get certified in this or that, I could get a job that would allow me not to struggle so hard to merely survive. But then one day, I discovered my employer had an education assistant program. I joined in a heartbeat and began taking three courses a semester. It was do or die. I did, and graduated with a B.S. in Business Administration.

Life led me south to Myrtle Beach. After taking inventory of my peripatetic career, I realized I had developed strong managerial skills, an ability to write, and recent experience in lease management. To work in lease management in South Carolina required a license, but if I secured a real estate license, I could do both leasing and selling. No brainer! I began doing both, focusing on the baby boomer generation retiring to the South.

Nudged by a friend, I tried marketing on the Internet. My first YouTube video, on finding retirement homes in Myrtle Beach, went "viral" in my market. Since then I've made more. I put myself online with a website and not one, but four blogs. Before my online marketing, I was kind of flopping out there, but after, traffic picked up big time.

Now I sell one to two homes a month at an average price of $127,000. My niche is 55 and older. I'm a boomer so I can relate to my clients. I know their issues—getting older, needing good medical care, having nearby shopping, surviving after a spouse's death, even nursing homes.

Not long ago I sold a house to a couple, 83 and 84 years old respectively. They had lost everything to Hurricane Sandy. Their grandson, a neighbor, reached out to me. His father and he hoped the grandparents would move south, but they had lived in New Jersey all their lives. For three days I drove them around, showing them hospitals and doctors, places to shop, and how to get around. On the third day they asked, "Can we look at houses now?" While they ate lunch, I researched places they might like, and before the afternoon was over, they had found a home.

See, real estate is about more than knowing houses. It's about showing kindness and reaching out. It's about settling people down and making them comfortable. It's about exploring options. I always say real estate is a journey, and it is my responsibility to help people make sound decisions on that journey.

Recently I began my own business doing *Attraction Marketing*. Never heard of it? Neither had I, but you will. *Attraction Marketing* is attracting people to you—not to a product or to a company, but to you. You can do this by starting a website or a blog where people get to know you. If they leave their email address or phone number, you can establish a personal relationship with them, and keep in touch. Then, when they need a service you provide, they think of you. Or you can offer a service you suspect they might need.

When I started, I was looking for something not expensive to start up but with the potential to change people's lives. The service I provide is to help people create their own businesses. On my blog, I share my story, something I really enjoy doing. I teach people how to market themselves, how to set up websites, and how to blog. Some of my clients are stay-at-home moms and retirees wanting to try something different. Some are retirees wanting to take advantage of the Internet to share their travel photos or to write down family stories.

One reason I've succeeded, I think, is because people can relate to me. My father was the oldest of 13. He quit high school to help provide for his family. He worked in concrete, but when he came home, no matter how tired, he had a big smile for my four siblings and me. My mother believed in education and dragged us to the library every week. At night she heard us our flash cards and spelling words. They worked so hard.

I owe them so much. I've worked all my life, and I plan to keep going. I meet a lot of nice people through my work. Plus every day is a new learning experience.

When I look over my life, I see that another reason I've succeeded is because I've been open to change. Whether it was different jobs, or learning on the job, or moving from Michigan to Pennsylvania to Washington to South Carolina or adapting to technology, change has been a part of my life. Some boomers my age resist change, but where would I be without change? And who knows where I'll be a few years from now?

Retirement? Not now, maybe not ever. You know, I moved to Conway, right outside of Myrtle Beach, because I wanted to be near the beach. You know how many times I've been to the beach in the past ten years? Three maybe. When life is this exciting, who wants to go to the beach?

About Jill

Jill Klunk is a home-based business woman who specializes in blogging and attraction marketing. A baby boomer raised in Warren, MI, Jill has worked all over the US as a manager and realtor, achieving recent success and finding her niche while finding homes for retirees.

From humble beginnings as shelf stocker, Jill was either promoted or sought better jobs, eventually becoming a Logistics Manager. She started in retail stores but many years later was handling leases for the US Department of State. While working full-time, she earned a degree in Business Administration from Indiana Institute of Technology in 1995.

Then in 2005, Jill moved to coastal South Carolina and became a realtor in the competitive resort town of Myrtle Beach. She soon specialized in finding a new way of life for retiring boomers. With a new and secure career, she dreamed of becoming her own boss on her own terms. This led to researching network marketing, a field that allows her to work without the risk of business loans, employees or the overhead of a traditional small business. She continued her work as a realtor while building her home-based business on the side.

Along the way, Jill discovered that the Midwest values she grew up with could be a huge asset in her work. She sought out marketing education and at first reluctantly and later wholeheartedly employed technology to expand her businesses. What she discovered was that, though most network marketing companies are great, none provide the training she needed to become a pro. So she developed a brand of her own centered on her life and helpful personality. She said, "By attracting folks to me, to Jill Klunk, I could be of great service and develop a substantial business from home."

With the help of a new friend and now business partner, Tara Woodruff, Jill believes she has joined a community of the most amazing network marketing professionals on the planet. It has become her mission to combine her "never quit" attitude with the attraction marketing skills. "I want to help people push through the struggles in life and in business and create substantial incomes for real life change. I want to give more to the world, and network marketing Is how I am doing it."

You can connect with Jill at:
jillklunk@gmail.com
https://twitter.com/jillklunk
https://www.facebook.com/JillKlunkSellsConway
https://www.linkedin.com/in/jillklunk

CHAPTER 12

SUCCESS IS ACHIEVING YOUR DREAMS

BY CONRAD BRIAN LAW

My first defining experience with goals took place when I was in the fourth grade at Birney Elementary School. My teacher was retiring that year and they invited her class to the 6th Grade graduation because they wanted to give her an award. The highlight of the event for me was a ceremony where the brightest boy and girl graduates received awards and the honor of having their names placed on a plaque displayed in the school for all to see. Right at that moment, I decided that I would be one of the awardees.

For the next two years, I did everything I could to achieve my goal. I got the highest grades on all the tests and participated in instrumental music, glee club, safety patrol and other extra-curricular activities. I made sure that no one else had a chance to be considered. For the graduation I was selected as the master of ceremonies and wore a white jacket with a black bow tie. I remember thinking how special I was. Not only do I get my award for being the smartest boy, I also get to preside over the event. As I sat there waiting for my award, I thought how proud my family would be. When my moment of truth arrived I started getting out of my chair before I realized that my name was not the one that was called. The boy selected had the voice of an angel and had sung on the Ed Sullivan show in New York and on national TV with a group of students from Washington, DC.

All that I remember after that was going into the bathroom after the ceremony to cry. It was the worst feeling I had experienced in my life. I didn't understand how I could be so wrong about myself. This event had a significant impact on my life for the next six years. I promised myself that I would never feel that way again. After graduation I received a scholarship to attend a private school in Alexandria, Virginia as desegregation started taking place throughout the country. I didn't try to excel after that experience. I lowered my standards and realized that I wasn't as special as I had thought. I was satisfied with just being above average and stopped trying to be the best.

After the 9th grade at the private school in Virginia, I decided to return to public school in the District of Columbia. During my senior year of high school, I had an assignment to write an essay about my favorite teacher. Without hesitation I thought of Ms. Agnes Miller. She was never my classroom teacher but was always supportive and instrumental in helping me earn the scholarship to the private school. She took me into her home for a week and tutored me for the entrance exam. Then I thought about my 6th grade teacher, Mr. Alvin Parrish, during his first year as a teacher. I then realized that he was the reason that I didn't get the award that I had worked so hard to receive. He was trying to let me know that I had an arrogance about myself that wasn't healthy. Any arrogance that I felt, left with my self-esteem. I decided to write about him as my favorite teacher.

Later that year I decided to contact Mr. Parrish and found him in one of the local telephone books. Once he realized who I was, he asked me if I was the senior class president. I said no, I was the senior class vice president. He laughed at that revelation. He explained that I reminded him of how he was in college and discovered that he was not the smartest kid there. He was devastated and it almost destroyed him. He didn't want the same thing to happen to me. After that, I began feeling better about myself. I was special and no longer let the 6th grade incident define me.

I was still satisfied being an above average student but decided to pursue other goals. I had developed an interest in playing basketball even though I wasn't tall, coordinated or athletic. I tried out for my college team my freshman year when I could not dribble the ball with my left hand and was the last person cut from the team that year and my sophomore and junior years. I practiced all the time and read all of the books in libraries on how to play basketball. My senior year I tried out once again to the dismay and frustration of friends and family. They didn't want to see me disappointed once again. This goal had a deadline of my graduation from college. If I didn't make the team before I graduated, I never would. I could accept not being selected for the team. That was up to the coach and out of my control. The best I could do is try my best. I made the team my senior year and did fairly well.

I learned that not achieving your goal is not failure, but not trying your best is. I decided to try my best for everything I wanted to achieve and not worry about the outcome. I was able to turn my dreams into goals and performed the tasks to achieve them. This has been a constant theme in my life and I have been able to accomplish most of my dreams using that philosophy.

Throughout my personal and professional life, I have been able to achieve success by establishing goals to turn my dreams into reality. In 1990, I began conducting workshops for others showing how they can do the same. It surprised me that most people don't have an approach to achieving their dreams. After researching this topic for many years, I have found both an explanation for this condition and solutions to address it. The arrogance perceived by others is nothing more than self-confidence.

Remember when you were very young? Think about the first time you were alone with a flickering candle. When no one else was around, your curiosity led you to reach for the flame. If you got too close, it burned you. The next time you were alone with a flame, you left it alone. We live in a world that teaches us to avoid the things that bring us pain. It's human nature.

Another example is in high school. We might try out for a sports team or cheerleading squad and give it everything we have. If we don't make it, and most of us don't, it hurts. The more you care about a desired outcome, the more it hurts if you don't achieve it. Again, it is human nature to try to avoid those feelings of failure and disappointment. Eventually, many of us learn not to try too hard so that we won't be disappointed. Having worked with individuals from around the world, the feeling of disappointment is universal.

In many societies we are told when we are young that we can be anything that we want to be and do anything that we want to do when we grow up. Too bad they didn't tell us how to do it. The same people that were positive usually become negative as we get older and begin making mistakes or bad choices. Without positive feedback, it is difficult to maintain that optimism.

It's not the end of the world though. We continue our education and adopt a lifestyle that makes our life easy to manage. Instead of creating a world based on our internal dreams, we respond to the external world around us and live an ordinary life. But why settle for average when you can be extraordinary?

Up to this point we examined why most of us don't set goals, but it is even more important to determine how to achieve them and the wondrous things that happen when we do. Let's start by understanding what a dream is. A dream is a series of thoughts, images and sensations occurring in a person's mind. If we choose not to act upon this dream, it is nothing more than a fantasy. However, if it is a dream worth living, you must take action to turn that dream into a goal. A goal is a dream with a deadline that must be acted upon. Much has been written on how to achieve goals but not why most of us don't bother. It is a mistake that we can fix.

There is a well known story about a Goal Study that was conducted with students participating in the Harvard MBA program. In that year, the students were asked, "Have you set clear, written goals for your future and made plans to accomplish them?" Only three percent of the graduates had written goals and plans; 13 percent had goals, but they were not in writing; and a whopping 84 percent had no specific goals at all.

Ten years later, the members of the class were interviewed again, and the findings were astonishing. The 13 percent of the class who had goals were earning, on average, twice as much as the 84 percent who had no goals at all. And the three percent who had clear, written goals were earning, on average, ten times as much as the other 97 percent put together.

After exhaustive research it appears that this well-discussed study is nothing more than an urban legend or myth. However, evidence from actual studies indicate that real results are comparable. Most of us do not set goals because we are not guaranteed to achieve them and don't want to face the disappointment if we don't. Research conducted on seniors 70 years of age and older provide parallel results. Most individuals surveyed regret the goals they did not pursue because they were afraid of being disappointed. After a full life they realized that disappointment is a part of life and the only thing worse than being disappointed in not achieving a goal is realizing that you should have tried, and the reasons for not doing so are irrelevant.

The most important factor about one's ability to set and achieve goals is self-esteem. When you believe in yourself you are willing to try new things and don't need a guarantee of success. You realize that your success or failure in a particular activity does not define who you are. If you apply what you learn from your actions, you increase the possibility of being successful the next time.

The seven principles that will help you achieve your dreams by turning them into achievable goals are:

1. **Believe in yourself.** Understand that no one is responsible for believing in you, except you. You are also responsible for defining your value or self-worth. Often, we let those who are closest to us, define us. Sometimes the most negative people in our lives are our family and friends. We need to realize that the people in our lives that are always negative are not good for us and need to be ignored. If you don't find it within yourself, you won't find it anywhere.

2. **Acknowledge your most important dreams.** Identify those dreams that you care so much about that you are willing to work towards. These will become your goals. They are worth spending time and effort to accomplish.

3. **Visualize your goals.** Imagine how your life will be altered by achieving your goals. Cut out pictures that represent you enjoying the accomplishment of your goals.

4. **Write down your goals.** Be specific about what you want to accomplish, why you want to accomplish them and what steps need to be taken to accomplish them. Use action plans and task lists to track your goals. Documenting goals is the same for a business or organization as it is for an individual.

5. **Become a life-long learner.** There are always new things to learn and new ways of doing things. Learn how to define, develop and accomplish goals and utilize technology, philosophy and other tools to help you achieve your goals. Learning never ends and you should never stop learning.

6. **Share your goals.** Sharing your goals helps you to broaden your horizons. It allows you to determine where your support lies and who your advocates are. It is said that we become the average of the five people that we spend the most time with. Those should be individuals that are supportive of your goals and goal-oriented themselves.

7. **Prioritize your life.** Put the most important things in your life first. Goals can be personal, professional, family or business-oriented. Your goals should be reviewed often and you should be flexible in obtaining them but never lose sight of your goals. Your goals should be consistent with your core values.

The mystical Star Wars character Yoda said it best, "Do or do not; there is no try."

About Conrad

Conrad Brian Law is an international management consultant and the CEO of Applied Learning Solutions. Conrad has worn many hats and has constantly reinvented himself to achieve success in his personal and professional endeavors.

Entering the workforce as a clerk with a degree in Sociology and Archaeology, Conrad expanded his professional horizons to positions as a Research Economist, Quality Assurance Analyst, Computer Specialist, Business Analyst and Information Technology Project Manager working for the US Department of Labor. After an early retirement from the government, Conrad worked as a business consultant for the Maryland Small Business Development Center (SBDC) Network – providing technical assistance and training to the business community. Conrad also works with international organizations. He is an author, award-winning speaker and certified trainer of trainers.

Conrad's professional experience has given him an opportunity to develop and utilize a wide range of knowledge, skills and abilities. He has extensive training and conference presentation experience representing government agencies, the private sector and international non-profits. His training experience includes technical topics such as system administration, networking, software applications and database design. Additionally, Conrad conducts training in soft skills including entrepreneurship, career development, project management, leadership, supervision and professional development skills.

In 2010, Conrad established Applied Learning Solutions (ALS). Through ALS he designs, develops and implements instructor-facilitated online training in Equal Employment Opportunity, Early Care Education, Workforce Development and training for government and corporate employees. In 2015, he began working on projects with international organizations in Africa, most recently providing technical assistance and training in strategic business planning and goal-setting for a farmer's cooperative in Ghana.

Conrad co-owns and operates Freedom Manor, a meeting, training and event facility located in Fort Washington, Maryland with his wife and business partner, Amina Jones Law, and with the support of their children Alec, Toussaint and Taylour.

You can connect with Conrad at:
cblaw@ConradBrianLaw.com
866-599-4330
www.linkedin.com/in/conradbrianlaw
www.facebook.com/conrad.law.33

CHAPTER 13

BUILDING A GOLDEN CAREER FROM A BIG HEART

BY DEBORAH RENNA-HYNES

As you grow older you will discover that you have two hands, one for helping yourself, the other for helping others.
~ Audrey Hepburn

The way I have helped myself in life is the way I have helped my family. **My family is my big WHY.** They are constant reminders of the message that I carry with me every day, which is:

Think big. The bigger that your vision is, the bigger your goals are; and as a result, the bigger your success will be.

The intense desire and gratitude that I experience from helping others learn has always been a part of me. I love teaching, because as I teach I also learn and grow. Every day provides an opportunity for this type of nurturing to take place in my life, and the impact is profoundly rewarding.

If you want to teach, be a teacher.

For me, the decision to making teaching my career was highly logical. It was a worthy goal that I chose to pursue. I never regretted it—ever. For 25 years I was a teacher, starting out in a Catholic High School. Wow, the pay was low—even for the 70s! When I received that first job offer, I was so excited, but I was also startled. When I heard exactly what the pay was, I didn't know if my dream was something that could actually sustain me financially. When I heard what the offer was, I immediately made a call to my go-to source—my mother. I'll never forget it.

"Mom, they offered me $8,000 a year. Can I live on that?" I asked. *Please answer yes,* I thought.

Well, Mom didn't answer "yes." What she did say was, "You'll be creative, Debbie. You always have been."

What? That's it! But she was right; my creativity had always been an asset for me, allowing me to manage life when it seemed hard to manage. My childhood was different than many of the other kids in my school. My parents were divorced, which was taboo at the time, and when the parents' of the kids at school would get together for parties, someone would inevitably ask, "Is Debbie's family invited?" Only to be met with a whispered, "They're divorced." That was it—end of offer, followed by an awkward silence. I had to get used to it. And, of course there were many moves along the way, going from our family home to an apartment in another town. Then I had to start over at a new school and make new friends. It was difficult; especially for a very shy 13 year-old girl!

Despite having a "broken family," both my mom and my dad offered me insight through their personalities and skills that were beneficial to me, and the way I chose to explore and grow and navigate through life, regardless of what it brought me. My dad was in sales and always had multiple jobs; however, he was also always trying to get rich quick (we know how that often works out). My mom was in sales as well, and had the heart of an entrepreneur and a wonderful ability to visualize great things. Both of their methods had merit, but for me, I chose a custom blend of the two: I would be creative in sales, but not be fearful of taking risks. It was a sound philosophy for me.

If you want to be successful in this world, you cannot be accidental. You have to set your mind on a goal and the vision has to become even bigger.

The artist in me that knew I could design and create my own life sprung into action. I painted this picture in my mind that I knew could be achieved by only me—no one else could do it for me—and I latched onto it with all I had. *I felt how I could help others while helping my life to grow bigger and bolder and better with each passing day.*

If you want to invest in your future, invest in real estate.

I found my creative solution shortly after I began teaching. I decided that I would invest in real estate. The property I chose was a two family house and I began to put the numbers together, along with the help of my realtor at the time. *Something quite surprising to me was staring me in the face as I absorbed the financial analysis.* The numbers showed that I would be better off renting out both units of that two family home, instead of living in one myself. As a result, I stayed in my apartment, became the landlord to two, and started to earn income off of that property. I liked it and I envisioned more. That was the start. Afterward, year after year I found more creative ways to purchase multi-family homes… not a bad start for a 21 year old investor!

Eventually, my consuming passion for real estate demanded that I take the next step. After ending a 25 year career with no pension, I took another leap of faith and decided to go into real estate full time. I could do it—and better yet, I could do it the way I envisioned it should be for people who needed the use of a real estate agent.

- **I had one goal:** make sure every action I did was focused on helping people, whether it be teaching them or serving them with a genuine heart.

- **I had one need:** to learn to master real estate through observing and learning from those who really knew what they were doing.

Through educating myself and having discipline, I was able to take action and put systems into place. The results were quick success. I received my most cherished award, Realtor Associate of the Year in only four years. **This is how I do things!** At the time, most people received this award after being in the business 15-20 years. It never would have happened without the discipline I had to become better, both through learning and my skills as a teacher. This exciting approach to real estate that I'd found also offered me an opportunity to grow even further. I would find success, but I wanted to learn as much as I could so I could inspire others more. I sought out a real estate coach—a step that helped me further finesse my plans, goals, and vision—as well as helped me understand more about taking risks in the business that would lead toward creating a sustainable and profitable business. It's not just a job. It's a business!

With a very specific list of criteria, I began looking for the mentor and coach who could help me put together the type of business I envisioned myself running. They had to have experience in real estate, not just experiencing in talking about real estate. This individual must have a proven record of success and results, both as a realtor and as a coach. The person who would help me would also need to be someone that I felt worked from the heart, not just the love of financial gain. It took some looking, but I found that person; I found the greatest coach in North America. . . Craig Proctor!

The first time I spoke to my coach we talked about my specific hopes for real estate. I boldly said, "I am going to be very successful in this business and I am going to do it quickly." *Chances are that he had heard that before; however, I was not one to say things I did not mean. And I meant it!* What I created needed to:

- Have a structure that would support continued growth
- Embrace helping others, whether it be a client or a new team member
- Allow me to teach others, whether it be realtors or clients
- Follow a philosophy that my clients are my family—they are treated with all the compassion I have
- Have programs that appealed to my clients and showed them how their interests were my interests—their experience with me was of great value to me, as a person and as their professional realtor

This was the turning point that took me from just having tenacity for the business, to having a sustainable plan.

The merger of teaching and real estate—truly a way to use both hands.

When I think back to those days when I taught school I cannot help but reflect on all the wonderful lessons and experiences I received from the honor of teaching others. Without a doubt, it was educational for both the student and me. My greatest hope was that I was always offering my students even half of what they unknowingly offered me.

As I began my fully-committed real estate career, I was determined to keep the things I loved about teaching a part of my new experiences.

The opportunity to offer investors, home buyers, and home sellers an experience that was more innovative and geared toward making them more comfortable throughout their experience, was a huge motivator.

Today, I get to:

1. Have a wonderful, rewarding experience where I can watch others excel. Back when I taught art in school and my students produced their masterpieces it was so exciting to see their happiness with what they did. They gained confidence and when they gained acknowledgement through their work being accepted for a show, they felt achievement, which was so special to be a part of. Real estate offers those same types of emotions and opportunities.

2. Watch those who work in real estate have an explosion of growth in their income. I will do anything to help connect with those I mentor and coach on an individual level to help them rise up and achieve their goals. Seeing someone go from making $93K a year up to $500K in gross commissions income is a stellar experience.

3. Create opportunities to make amazing friends, while increasing the level of professionalism of the industry as a whole. People who conduct real estate business—really, all business—on a higher level are key factors in elevating the professionalism of those industries as a whole. It does not matter whether it is a family's well-being or on a consumer level, the growth is good. Since I am also an investor, I am doing what they are doing, which brings a connection and helps me to teach by example. My words have credibility. I am now the one who has applicable experience just like my two real estate coaches Craig Proctor and Todd Walters had for me.

The best in this business do not just tell people what to do. That is why I show them what I have already done, what worked, what did not, and how to optimize their individual situations. It is a custom blend—just like artwork!

An important part of being able to demonstrate success to others is to study it and apply it. This is a part of my daily routine, as it allows me to find the inspiration to keep the drive going steady for the career I love, shake it up whenever I need to, and keep offering a helping hand to anyone who needs it.

When people ask, I answer.

Everything I have learned is not meant to be kept locked away inside of me, protecting me and my income potential. It's meant to be shared. Everyone can have a win/win in the real estate industry if they put forth their best efforts and remember that a spirit of sharing information is much more fruitful than when we hoard it—it can only go rotten then!

There are many questions that come to mind when I go around talking with other Real Estate Celebrities and Entrepreneurs in other industries. Here are mine…

1. *What is your big why?* My family has always been my big why. To maintain a lifestyle that I never thought I would have as someone who grew up in a tough, single parent household where money was an issue, keeps me going. Knowing that my children are going to have incredible opportunities as a result brings me endless amounts of joy.

2. *What do you do daily before 9 AM?* Every day begins with reading from my devotional, where I draw great information that puts me in the right state of mind for a busy day. Then I go to check out my Social Media—which I have found to be quite refreshing despite what some think. The connections I make on there are very positive for me, and I delight in sending a positive message to others. I always take a half hour to read 'something Real Estate' so I can grow. And then, I am at the office and ready to serve between 8:00 and 8:30. I love getting my day started!

3. *What is most important to you?* Easily, it is faith and family.

4. *What is the one thing that separates you from other entrepreneurs?* My distinction is that I am an open book—not a secret keeper. I cannot imagine not sharing all the things that I have learned in life. I understand that being successful sometimes means being lonely, because others get jealous or just do not understand how you could make it. If I can help one other person avoid feeling that way, it is worth it to be an open book.

5. *How did you make money and what did you do to keep it?* Ah, the most challenging question! The main ingredient to making and keeping my money has been focus. I focus on how I approach my day, how I teach, and what I do to keep growing in the real estate business. **Everything**

I have done and continue to do is also driven by my core values and absolute commitment to helping others. This is not always easy, of course, because it costs money to make money and there have been times when that money was tight. I had faith, though, and knew that I would put a system in place that would work if I worked that system. So I did…and I still do. That's what risk takers do!

6. *Why do you do what you do every day?* My passion makes my life rewarding, which means that I do not have to think about my days as a "job." Working with those who want to become better through coaching, helping people with real estate needs, and being my authentic self make for some pretty amazing days. I always remember: **you cannot BS your way through life; you have to know the answers to the questions.**

I am an original by default, really. Simply being me and acknowledging what I can offer others has guided me to the ideal life.

About Deborah

Rochester Realtor Deborah Renna-Hynes wows real estate professionals when she travels to various offices in several states to hold office meetings on "How to be a Mega Agent." Originally from the New York City area, she holds a Bachelor's degree in Fine Arts from State University Geneseo and a Master's in Education from Nazareth College of Rochester. She was a high school teacher for over 25 years before entering into real estate in 2003. However, her career as a real estate investor began over 35 years ago in the Rochester, NY real estate market.

With a strong desire to combine education and real estate, turning her career over to her passion was a logical choice for Debbie. It was a merger of two things she was very passionate about. Before she knew it, she was off to a very fast start in the real estate industry. Debbie attributes her success in the real estate industry to hard work and having proven real estate coaches. "I have always known that education is important in any business."

A little over five years ago she started researching coaches in North America and stumbled across Craig Proctor, who is a top agent and coach in his field. Through Craig Proctor she was introduced to Todd Walters. With the help of her two real estate coaches, she quickly became recognized as a top agent in her area. She holds several designations, as well, making her one of the top teams in New York State. Today, she is the CEO of "The Renna-Hynes Team," and is consistently ranked high for her accomplishments on the local, state, and national level. She has received numerous awards, including her most prized accolade: REALTOR Associate of the Year 2007.

Debbie has always been a leader and a teacher. According to Debbie, "I am a passionate people person! I've taught for over 25 years, and loved learning from my students as they learned from me. Buying and selling a home requires the same kind of passion and dedication as everything we pursue in life." Her love for sharing knowledge is not only what brings her closer to her clients, but it helps spread the word, as she has shared the stage with many of the top speakers in the industry to tell her story.

Her first book, which she co-authored with her real estate coaches, *Death of the Traditional Real Estate Agent: Rise of the Super-Profitable Real Estate Sales Team,* says it all! With the addition of *Ignite Your Life*, she has taken another step to reach out to others and inspire them to their greatest potential.

Debbie has resided in Rochester, NY since 1978. She and her husband Jim, who is also a realtor, have proudly raised three sons. When she's not selling real estate or coaching mega agents she volunteers her time with the Rochester General Hospital, TWIG Association, Veterans Outreach Center, and Children's Miracle Network, and various other organizations that continuously inspire her. Some of her greatest joys come from reading, writing, cooking, and painting.

You can connect with Debbie at:
Debbie@thedrhteam.com
www.debbierennahynes.com
https://www.facebook.com/debbie.rennahynes

CHAPTER 14

SEVEN STEPS TO SOCIAL MEDIA BRANDING FOR NETWORK MARKETING SUCCESS

BY JATAYA WILEY, PhD

Network Marketing is a great opportunity to build a business that will create prosperity and wealth for generations to come. As someone who has been very successful in Network Marketing, I can say from experience that branding yourself as opposed to the company you are with is crucial for long-term success in the Direct Sales industry. When you brand your company your company gains exposure, gains the credibility, you link yourself to the credibility of the company and you have to rebuild your entire network if you decide to switch companies or if the company closes. If you brand yourself you become your brand, you build credibility, your network develops loyalty to you instead of your company, and you can take your brand anywhere.

Social Media gives you the opportunity to get your brand in front of a world-wide audience and an unlimited number of potential customers. In an industry that thrives off of networking, branding yourself online is a major asset. Achieving this through social media is very effective if it is done correctly. Every post you make and every piece of content you share is building your brand. Your social media personality should be a reflection of your business personality, and that should stay consistent across the board. It takes time and effort to build a phenomenal social media brand. Follow the 7 steps outlined in this chapter for your ultimate success.

1. BE CONSISTENT

The most important step in any social media branding strategy is consistency.

What does it mean to be consistent on social media?

- Consistently representing yourself and what you're about.

- Sticking to a schedule – don't post twenty times one week and then go silent for months.

- Posting in the same voice across all networks.

- Knowing your audience and consistently posting the kind of information they are following you for.

Posting on a regular basis does not mean that you have to be signed in to all of your social media accounts all of the time. HootSuite and Buffer are tools available for scheduling posts in advance.

Creating Consistency on Social Media Profiles
Being consistent on social media starts with creating profiles that look the same:

- **Avatar:** Choose one avatar or profile picture and use it across all of the social media platforms that you use.

- **Colors:** Use the same color scheme across all platforms.

- **Background Images:** For Social Media platforms that allow you to use a background image or cover photo, use the same basic design according to the image dimensions set by that platform.

- **Username:** Your username – or "handle" – should be as similar as possible across all networks. For example, if you use @yourcompanyname on Twitter, don't use Facebook.com/yourname.

- **Profile Information:** Make sure your "about" section remains current and consistent on all your social media platforms.

2. DEVELOP YOUR SOCIAL MEDIA VOICE

Branding is *not* all about your logo, your avatar, or your design. Everything you choose to post on social media is building your brand. What you post, and the way you post it, is ultimately going to stick in people's minds more than your design or tagline.

What Makes You Unique?
There are many Network Marketers in the industry. Think about your social media voice and what makes you stand out. Why should someone partner with you, instead of another sponsor, team or business opportunity? If you want to set yourself apart from the thousands of other sponsors, teams and companies, you must find a way to be different and unique.

Think About Your Tone
How do you want your posts to come across? Do you want to be seen as kind, helpful or inspirational? Or will you differentiate yourself by bringing some humor to the industry? You could use a combination of many different tones; however, you'll find that one will become more common and work best for you.

3. KNOW YOUR AUDIENCE

Although a lot of your social media branding strategy is going to be about attracting the kind of followers you want for your business, it's also important to think about what your audience wants.

Choosing the Right Social Media Platforms
Although you might want to be active on "all" the social media platforms, the truth is that it's better to master one platform than to do ten inadequately. Facebook, Twitter, Pinterest and Google+ are trending right now. You can also use additional sites like Instagram, Periscope and YouTube as part of your social media strategy, and by sharing them on sites like Facebook and Twitter.

When making posts it is important to remember that in order for people to start following you on social media, you need to be relevant to their lives in some way.

4. MAKE THE RIGHT FIRST IMPRESSION

For many prospective customers, social media could be the first impression of you and your business. You want to make sure that their first impression is a good one. Here are a few ways to accomplish that goal:

1. Stay Professional: It's a given that brands will get some form of negative feedback; however, the way in which you deal with it is what other followers will notice.

   You can choose whether to respond in a simple, yet polite, manner, and direct the customer to your support team. Whatever you do, never respond back to a customer in a rude way, and make sure that you do take the time to respond to public complaints.

2. Don't Leave Your Profile Empty. It's not a good look when a visitor to your website clicks a link to one of your social media profiles only to see that it hasn't been setup and you are never there. Make sure that there's a good mix of content, by including informative and promotional posts, texts and images. Remember that it is best to be consistent in your posting schedule, or don't bother at all.

3. Use Professional Images: It is a good idea to get professional headshots and social media graphics created. This isn't as important to your followers as your posts will be, but it still helps shape the first impression they get of you and your business.

4. Be Seen as Someone who Interacts: Being seen as someone who interacts on your profile can also make a great first impression. Not only does it show that you have followers who like to interact with you, it also shows that you're a "real" person. People will always prefer to follow real people, and engage in real conversations, as opposed to following brands who simply talk at them and try to sell products.

5. DECIDE WHAT TO SHARE

When branding yourself as an expert, it's important to decide the kind of things you're going to share. It's also crucial that you decide what NOT to share on social media.

Types of Content to Share on Social Media

Questions: Asking on-topic questions is a great way to build up engagement on your profile. Even if people like your posts, you'll get more of a reaction if you directly ask them a question.

Useful Information: Sharing useful industry information or news is a great way to get followers to see you as an authority.

Inspiration: Lots of people use social media as a place to escape from the daily grind and get inspired. It obviously depends what niche you're in, but inspirational quotes can be extremely successful when spread out amongst your regular content. Being seen *as the* place to go to get inspired could become a key part of your brand.

Photos & Videos: Photos and videos tend to get more response than plain text on social media. It makes sense, since they're quick to digest and will stand out on a social media timeline. So make sure you include plenty of these in between text updates.

Your Own Content: Don't forget to share links to your own blog and promotions, just be careful not to overdo it. Some followers won't ever bother subscribing to your blog or mailing list, so sharing the links on social media is a good way to make sure they see what you have to offer.

What NOT to Share on Social Media

Constant Promotions: Although people do love a bargain, and they will love that you're offering them something special just for being a follower, then won't love being sold to constantly. Keep the promotions to a minimum and opt for posts that add value to their lives. This is what is ultimately going to build your brand and help create more loyal customers.

Customer Disputes: There could be some exceptions to this rule, but even when you're being authentic it's important not to air your dirty laundry in public. This means not publicly naming and shaming customers who have unreasonable complaints, or post something inappropriate on your page. Instead, delete any offending public comments and leave things be. Your reputation should always remain professional.

6. WORK ON BUILDING TRUST MORE THAN ANYTHING

People do business with people that they know, like and trust. See every post you make as a way to build trust with your target audience. Every image you post, link you share or quote that motivates this target audience brings you one step closer to being trusted. And with trust comes loyalty, support and, ultimately, sales.

Always Add Value

Every time you post, ask yourself this: "Am I adding value to my follower's life?" It doesn't have to be anything really profound. It could be as simple as bringing a smile to their face. Regularly asking yourself this question will ensure you're doing your very best for your followers.

Don't Forget Your Current Customers

Many business owners think that social media branding is all about getting new customers, but it's also about connecting with your current ones. A loyal customer is far easier to sell to than a brand new customer, so don't forget current customers in your social media branding strategy.

7. KNOW YOUR GOALS (AND MEASURE YOUR PROGRESS)

Social media can be powerful, but for some it can end up being a complete waste of time. That's why you should never jump into your social media strategy without having clear goals, and measuring your progress towards those goals. Here are a few ways to help measure your branding efforts on social media:

Search for Yourself: Regularly search for your name or your business name across the various social platforms to see what people are saying about you.

Keep an Eye on Engagement Levels: If you're doing things the right way then you'll see more people sharing, liking and commenting on your posts.

Website Tracking: Use tools like Google Analytics to see how many people are visiting your site from your social media profile links.

Use a Tracking Tool: Ultimately it's a good idea to invest in a social media tracking tool. HootSuite is a very popular option for both scheduling and tracking the success of your social media posts.

Revising Your Social Media Strategy

So what do you do with all the information you've gathered? You use it to tweak your social media strategy to bring even better results. Here are some things you might want to change:

- The time of day you post

- The number of times a day you post

- The number of photos/ videos you share

- The types of content you share

- The ratio of promotional to useful posts

- The number of personal posts you share

Keep tweaking and tracking until you feel you've hit the "sweet spot" that seems to really resonate with your social media followers.

CONCLUSION

When it comes to branding yourself as an authority in the industry, you will be looked to as a leader and an expert. People care more about the value that you can provide and how you can help them become successful more than they care about your company or product that you have to offer. You are the CEO of YOU.Inc, and branding yourself will help you to succeed in any Network Marketing business. You have something that no one else on this planet can provide, and there is someone out there waiting on you to show up and change their life.

About JaTaya

Dr. JaTaya Wiley has spent most of her life inspiring and motivating others to step forth and walk into their greatness. JaTaya has always had a passion for learning and has earned a Bachelor's Degree in Technology with a concentration in Web Design from Kent State University, graduating *Magna Cum Laude.* She continued her education at Kent State, where she earned her Master's Degree in Technology. JaTaya has also received a Doctorate of Philosophy in Human Letters from CICA International University & Seminary.

JaTaya is a vibrant speaker and served as the Executive Director of the Greater Cleveland Public Speakers Association. She has years of speaking experience and has spoke before audiences of thousands. She also has over 15 years of professional network marketing business experience. JaTaya has combined her speaking ability with her leadership skills and has become the dynamic driving force behind her nationwide team of over 6,000 distributors.

JaTaya's business success is due to her ability in leading her team in areas, such as developing strong personal and business relationships, while providing solid training and mentorship opportunities. Helping others to achieve success and to live the lives of their dreams by creating substantial streams of income is what drives JaTaya to remain focused on her business goals. JaTaya has helped many of her team members accomplish monumental achievements and promotions, earning financial gain on their journey towards financial freedom.

JaTaya's expertise in network marketing, social media and her unrelenting passion have afforded her success with connecting people and products through technology. With over twelve years of technical work experience, she thrives in the dynamic and fast-changing field of Information Technology and Computer Science.

JaTaya has a heart for service and is passionate about giving back. JaTaya served on the board of the Aldersgate-Zimbabwe Well Project as the Marketing Director. There she led the development and execution of a comprehensive strategic plan, with a focus on social media and webpage management, community partnerships, fundraising and volunteer development. Her efforts helped in leading the team to raise enough money to build a well in Zimbabwe, Africa.

JaTaya served as a Loaned Executive for the North Coast Combined Federal Campaign, the government sector of The United Way. During her three years, she raised over three quarters of a million dollars in charitable contributions. She was honored at the White House as one of the recipients for the North Coast Combined Federal Campaign's Innovator Award for extraordinary contribution through hard work and dedication to the campaign.

JaTaya is also a plus size model and is currently signed with Pro Model Management & Talent Agency out of Akron, OH. Her most recent work includes clients such as Nike, Rue 21 and Humira. JaTaya currently holds the title as Ms. OH Plus America 2015. Her platform is Alive On Purpose, a non-profit agency dedicated to the promotion of life by finding help for people struggling with depression, trauma, and suicide.

For more information about branding yourself for network marketing success, please visit: www.jatayawiley.com or contact: info@jatayawiley.com.

CHAPTER 15

IGNITE YOUR LIFE WITH BUSINESS TRIBES

BY TONY PARK

There are many ways to *Ignite your life*, and this book from some of the leading authors, mentors and consultants from around the world, outline many of them. One of those strategies is to use the power of networking. Now you have probably heard all about networking and anyone can do that – but we are talking about super networking – using the power of Tribes to change your life.

Tribes – I hear you say, have been used by other authors and commentators, however only for a limited way – some look at consumer tribes, some at employee tribes and others confuse what a tribe really is. Very few truly understand what hidden power can be unleashed by understanding the full range of Tribes and how you can turbo charge your circle of influence and Ignite your life.

This chapter will outline a range of tribes, using my experiences over the last 40 years in business and life (see Bio) to explain and show what power can be unleashed by effective use of tribes and a few errors I have made along the way. Along with this understanding will be an outline of a 5-Step program that can assist you and your business to grow and develop.

WHAT IS A TRIBE

A tribe is created as an individual grows from being self-centred and starts to form groups to act together, however with no real purpose. If the group wants to grow and develop, they form teams, with leaders and followers creating a more efficient working unit. However the outcome is focused on the team, and not all the followers gain a positive outcome from its actions. A tribe is a more mature stage, when people and things work together so everyone wins, even though they may have at times different or conflicting positive outcomes. Tribal members have at their core something that binds them, as if there are invisible rubber bands between them. These bonds or links, between what academics call actors or nodes, are specific to the tribe. It may be a family, school, sports team or work tribe, with these two-way links – respect for each other, a want-to-do or act to help each other and a feeling of wellbeing when others achieve from the tribe.

In turn, you will achieve more by that positive support from the people in your particular tribe. The development of the links between actors is more important than the actor or nodes themselves. Most business owners make a sale, that's terrific, and use marketing activity to get the best sale they can. (My node is important.) However, a focus on tribal marketing creates positive linkages so you can get a second, third or lifetime sales by a change in the manner of the sale. (Our nodes are important.) Further, you can sell to the tribal members of your tribal members – turbocharging your business to more lifetime sales.

Various stages of businesses and organisations © Tony Park

142

To try to understand what tribes are, let's look at some of my tribes:

Personal Tribe, Family Tribe, Friends Tribe, School Tribe, Old Boy Tribe, Employee Tribe, Supplier Tribe, Membership Tribe, Political Tribe, Purchaser Tribe, Consumer Tribe, Virtual Tourism Tribes . . . to name a few.

However, there are also industry-specific tribes:–

Tourism: Agent Tribes, Referral Tribes, Trip Adviser Tribe, Regional Tourism Tribes

Franchising: Franchisee Tribe, Loyalty Card Membership Tribe, other Franchisee Consumer Membership Tribes.

Agriculture: Influencer Tribes, Chef Tribes, Neighbour Tribes

Industry organisations: Member Tribes, Government Tribes,

Not-For-Profit: Donor Tribe, Direct people benefit Tribe, Support Tribes

. . . and many more, showing that you may have a huge range of Tribes, directly and indirectly, that you can influence by caressing them, romancing them, making them feel important. This then gives you a base to show solutions to their problems – not to what you want to sell.

FIVE STEPS

There are Five Steps to understand, engage, maintain and make extra profit, that will Ignite your life and turbocharge your business or organisation.

Step 1: Understanding your Tribes
So how can you understand your Tribes? I have found one method is to use an Excel spread sheet, using a tab for each separate tribe. With each Tribe Member of a specific tribe down the page, and then across the page in separate cells, write other tribes to which you may think they also belong. Making another tab for these new tribes, you can link the initial Tribe Member by a hyperlink to the new tab. Once you have an indication of your tribes, you then can take the next steps to engage them, to understand what their problems are and what solutions you

have to satisfy them. This also can prioritise who and how you should engage them. Social media, face-to-face meetings, group talk, there are many methods to engage – all should be subtle in that the important person is the Tribe Member, developing **respect** that will turbocharge your business.

Takeaways

1. List your Tribes and how you can engage them.

2. List the Tribes that they may belong outside your tribe.

Step 2: How you engage your tribes

Tribe members feel engaged when they feel special and respected, not unlike a marriage. These things happen slowly and are built on the understanding of what the other party is looking for in their lives. A foundation to build this tribal relationship is communication. The best communication is two-way; methods include social media feedback and communication and face-to-face discussion and reflection. Another method is to give relevant information to assist them in business and in life, using blogs, Facebook, Instagram and other social media. Some "sellers" use email campaigns, however, this needs to be managed so you are sharing information, gaining respect rather than just trying to sell something. There are many examples of people sending out information by email or blogs, sharing on many social media platforms, having free webinars or personal forums, sometimes for 6 to 12 months, before you may sell a product or service. However once engaged in a positive way, you then can see the power of Tribes and engage with their tribes, with recommendations and advocates to their contacts, based on the respect that has been generated by you. This way 100 tribal members you know, could finally engage say 10,000 people; 9,900 who you don't directly know, but they know you through their contacts of your tribe. Now that's the power of the tribe.

Takeaways

1. "Romance them."

2. Give before you sell.

3. Two-way conversation to understand their problem and your solutions.

Step 3: Maintenance

Once you have identified who your Business Tribes are and have been able to engage with them to understand what problems they have and the solutions you have to satisfy those needs, you need to maintain that relationship. A quick sale is just that – a quick sale that is based normally on price, not quality or value for money. Once the sale is completed, you have to spend more time and effort to make another sale, again normally based on price that may have a minimal profit. The importance of maintaining that relationship of the Tribe, is not only for a future sale to your Tribal member, but more importantly for the other members of their Tribe – turbocharging your business. You need to keep up the activities that you used to engage them: blogs, presentations, speaking to forums and groups, updates to products and services, new methods, etc., and setting up online forums, especially "secret" groups on Facebook and LinkedIn, so you can get discussion across tribal members so they feel special and respected. This development of Virtual Communities cements your tribe together, and develops a desire to be part of the "inner circle." However, you need to both keep on giving and also creating a culture of sharing across tribal members.

Takeaways

1. Maintenance of your Tribe is for future sales.

2. Use the super power of a tribe to have your tribal members as advocates for you – to their tribes.

3. Continue the activities you used to engage your tribes – as you are now engaging indirectly your tribal members' tribes.

Step 4: How to make extra profit

Keller, in his 1993 paper on Brand Marketing, had major attributes of a good brand, representing brand values that develop positive perception of the good or service, leading to purchase and loyalty to purchase and recommend. The major brand value of a tribe; mutual respect, further increase loyalty, with the price/sale process being reduced in importance between buyer and seller, and increases the expectation that the seller will provide the best value for money solution for the purchaser's problem. The purchaser will not focus on the price as the main reason for purchase, but is satisfied with a value-for-money solution from a friend. The culmination of that process is a greater profit on the individual sale/

purchase process, based on the respect generated by these activities, as well as more sales to others. With the Supplier Tribe, understanding the challenges of suppliers to your business and working with them on their limitations could reduce your inputs without putting pressure on the profit margins of the supplier. Similarly, with Employee Tribes, working with your team can reduce the wage increase pressures while developing loyalty that leads to higher and better sales and production. Membership Tribes suddenly start to expand as they become more relevant to outside potential members and they become fashionable to join.

Takeaways

1. Creation of a tribal culture creates loyalty and a higher yielding sale.

2. Understanding of input Tribes like suppliers and employees can reduce costs, while increasing efficiencies of supply.

Step 5: Turbo Charge your business
How to use this new culture to turbocharge your circle of influence, for profit? Using the power of this mutual respect for tribal members across all of your tribes, creates advocates for sales and cost reduction. Sales are increased as tribal members start to talk to their contacts and other tribes – contacts that you don't know and who may not know you and what you can do for them to satisfy their problems and challenges – and then want to become part of the main tribe, with price pressures being reduced. An example would be having 100 various tribal members that you have now engaged in a positive way to become advocate for sales and supply of goods and services. Say each of them has 100 personal tribal members, potential sales and suppliers who you have not engaged yet, but now 10,000 new potential sales – with your 100 tribal members selling for you in that most powerful medium – word-of-mouth. Similarly, suppliers of your supplier tribes will want to supply to you as you are prepared to work within their limitations, allowing them to supply at a better price and in a manner that makes your business more efficient.

Takeaways

1. Tribal respect creates advocates that sell to the tribes of your tribal members.

2. Price is secondary and value for money and membership of the Tribe become more important.

WHAT IF YOU DON'T RECOGNISE AND ENGAGE?

The standard business practice is to focus on one sale at a time and take them when you can, with price as the main determinant. While this seems to be easier, with little activity to engage and maintain your customers other than marketing and advertising, you have to keep on finding new customers with increased costs per customer over time. With suppliers, trying to put pressure to reduce price all the time just ends up moving from supplier to supplier, creating inefficiencies of supply and increasing costs. Similarly with Employee Tribes, not understanding their needs and wants creates discontent, increasing pilferage, pressures for increased wages and turnover of staff, all increasing costs to the business. To understand, engage and maintain a tribal culture is not easy and in the short term may seem to increase costs, however, without it the development of a business can only be at a linear level and limited growth. In the medium and longer term the costs per sale and costs for product and services are reduced, while increasing the efficiencies of the business. In every business, there is a hidden potential that can be unleashed only by the use of Business Tribes.

CONCLUSION

For over 40 years I have used Business Tribes to develop organisations and business all around the world. I have seen some organisations grow, while others have closed. I have had businesses become super successful and lead the world in their sectors and had others fail by not concentrating on all their tribes that influence them. This short chapter is inadequate to show you all the power tips of Business Tribes, I have outlined them in greater detail in my book, *Business Tribes, Turbocharge your Circle of Influence, for profit.*

About Tony

Tony Park, born and raised in Tasmania, Australia and living in his community of Sorell with his family tribe, has a passion for assisting people, businesses and his broader community.

Tony's understanding of tribes started at a young age when he became a cub scout in 1965. His understanding of the stages people must go though in their personal development continued to deepen. Since then, Tony has taken personal and business development to the next level – *Business and Community Tribes*, where the focus is on teams becoming tribes. This tribe mentality creates a stronger two-way linkage within teams that benefits the individuals, the business and their communities.

All through life he has used the power of people networks – the power of tribes – to help people and business operate at their maximum potential. Tony is the recipient of many business and community awards on a local, National and International level, including from: Scouts Australia, Junior Chamber International, Telstra Small Business Awards, Tasmanian Tourism Awards, and Academic awards at the University of Tasmania.

Tony has been directly involved in many community and not-for-profit organisations for over 40 years, including Scouts Australia, Rural Youth, Young Liberals, Junior Chamber of Commerce (Jaycees), Chamber of Commerce - local, National and International levels, industry organisations in construction, tourism, transport, agriculture, education and aged care – as well as assisting many organisations like Rotary, Lions, Heart Foundation, Cancer Council, Make-A-Wish Foundation, Hutchins Old Boys, Athenaeum Club and Cystic Fibrosis.

Tony Park has been successful in developing businesses in Transport, Retail, Tourism, Construction, Agriculture, Aged Care, Franchising, Consulting/Coaching and IT, using the theory and basics of *Tribal and Network Theory* to develop some of the major brands in these sectors in his community. Currently with consulting and coaching businesses at: www.businesstribes.com.au and www.businessgardener.com.au, he also has developed an online market place for business animation: www.anyymate.com and a world-leading tourism package booking system: www.ecotemptationholidays.com.au.

Park is the author of a number of books and academic papers, including *Business Tribes - Turbo Charge your circle of influence for profit*. Tony has a large range of qualifications as a Fellow to a number of Australian Organisations, National and

International coaching and mentoring qualifications, and a large range of University qualifications, including an MBA(Mktg.), Masters of Marketing, and currently he is a PhD candidate. Tony has been a speaker and coach across 24 countries around the world, an academic with a number of Universities across Australia, with published papers on networking and developing tribes, he is working and advising people all over the world, in what they can achieve when they harness their Tribal Power for themselves. It does take time, it does take planning – it does take a start.

Tony has a number of programs designed to assist you to understand, create and maintain the tribes in your life. Contact him at tony@park.com.au to start your journey to engage your tribes and *Ignite your life.*

Visit: www.businesstribes.com.au and register for the business tribe blog and coaching, and become part of his tribe for success.

CHAPTER 16

KEY SUCCESS PRINCIPLES: MASTER THE INNER FIELD

BY SINCHAN PATIL

We first make our habits and then our habits make us.
~ John Dryden

Why are some people more successful than others? The answer is simple. Successful people have success habits. They do what other successful people before them have done and follow in their footsteps. Success leaves a trail. It doesn't matter where you were born or how you look or whether you are male or female, if you do what other successful people have done, by following their success habits you are bound to become successful. It's just a matter of time. I have boiled down everything I learned about success into *Ten Key Principles*. Times will change, technology will advance, cultures will vary from place to place but these Principles of Success remain constant. They apply irrespective of the industry or business. And I want to assure you that these principles can be learned. Some are easier to understand and apply than others, but each one of them can be acquired.

Here are the Ten Principles:

Principle 1: Have Clarity of Intention

Principle 2: Take Responsibility and Practice Positive Thinking

Principle 3: Embrace your Fears

Principle 4: Work the system ruthlessly each day

Principle 5: Always give back

Principle 6: Take massive Action

Principle 7: Be the best in your field

Principle 8: Build harmonious relationships

Principle 9: Never give up!

Principle 10: Enjoy the journey

The game of success is played on two fields - the inner field and the outer field. The outer field represents what's visible – the results and actions. The inner field is what's invisible – your thoughts and emotions. In this chapter we will focus on the inner field. Master the game in the inner field and your life will take off like a rocket.

PRINCIPLE 1: HAVE CLARITY OF INTENTION

When you have Clarity of Intention, the universe conspires
with you to make it happen.
~ Fabienne Fredrickson

The very basic and the most important question of them all is - What is it that you want? It is so surprising that many people have never thought of this question. Most of the people that I meet are not happy where they are. They complain about their job, about their boss, about how unfair life has been to them. And when I ask them what they want, they invariably tell me what they don't want.

It is a well-known fact that you become what you think about most of the time. So it is absolutely crucial that you are clear on what it is that you want and put all your focus on it. For example, if you want to be financially successful, then it is not enough to just say "I want to be rich." That in itself is just a dream, a wish. It is not enough. To have clarity of purpose, you should start by imagining every aspect of how your life will be after you have achieved your goal of financial success. What will you drive? Where will you live? How big will your house be? What will you do when you have financial success? Where will you travel? What clothes will you wear? Also think about what other people will say to you? Who will you interact with? What will your family and friends say to you? How will you feel when people admire you or when you become a role model for others? When you can provide anything you want for your loved ones? Feel the feelings of pride, joy, self-confidence, happiness and freedom that you will have when you reach your goal. When you can clearly see and feel all these things, then and only then you will have clarity. It is this clarity that will drive you to success. As Dr. APJ Kalam said, "A dream is not something that you see while sleeping, it's something that does not let you sleep."

The interesting thing is once you have complete clarity, new doors and opportunities will start opening up to help you get to your goal.

Exercise #1:
Write down 50 goals. Include everything you want, places you want to travel, people you want to meet, things you want to do. Review this list to ensure you have goals from all key areas: Relationships, Health, Personal Development and Finance. Then against each goal, mark whether this is a 1-year, 3-year, 5-year or 10-year goal. You may notice that you may have lot more 1-year and 5-year goals, but not enough 3-year or 10-year goals or vice versa. After adding enough goals for all timeframes, pick the four most important goals in each timeframe and start working on them.

PRINCIPLE 2: TAKE RESPONSIBILITY AND PRACTICE POSITIVE THINKING

Whether you think you can, or you think you can't, you're right.
~ Henry Ford

Taking responsibility is one of the hallmarks of successful individuals. Unsuccessful people spend most of their time in the old habit of blaming. They will blame their upbringing, their family, their circumstances, their luck, their company, their boss and worse yet, themselves. They assume they are the victim, and as a result they say to themselves, "I will never be able to succeed because ...".

Blaming others, yourself, your past or your circumstances will only assure you continued agony and frustration. Victim mentality is like a self-fulfilling prophecy. Because you are in that state of mind, every action you take ensures that you continue to remain in that state. If you want to succeed, then you need to immediately snap out of the victim mentality and take responsibility. Once you assume responsibility, you will realize that you have a choice to make decisions and change your circumstances.

Many people let fear and doubt rule their lives. They will have a great idea, a wonderful vision. But they have doubt in their own abilities and they give up before they even start. A key essential to success is that you must completely, without a shred of a doubt, believe in yourself that you will be able to achieve your goals towards success. This is achieved by practicing Positive Thinking.

Your thoughts lead to your feelings; your feelings lead to your actions. Your actions lead to your results. The one thing in this universe that you have absolute control over is your thoughts. You have the ability to choose if your thoughts are negative memories from your past, or positive reinforcement for your future.

When your mind starts to wonder and you slip back into your old negative thought patterns of worry and doubt, interrupt that pattern. Say "STOP", see a big red Stop sign, and think of your clarity of intention which you want to achieve. Practice this all the time. Do this enough times so that it becomes a habit. Pretty soon you will see that your mind will unconsciously interrupt the negative patterns and solely focus on the task at hand that will take you towards success.

Exercise #2:
Write down a list of all things, people and circumstances that you currently believe are holding you back or causing you not to achieve your full potential. Then, against each item write down what are YOU now going to do about it. As a responsible individual, list down the steps you will take to change your circumstances.

PRINCIPLE 3: EMBRACE YOUR FEARS

Everything you want is on the other side of fear.
~ Jack Canfield

All fear is learned. We are born with only two fears. Fear of loud noise and fear of falling. These are ingrained in our DNA as survival instincts. Every other fear is learned over the course of our lifetime. And the great thing is that all these fears can be unlearned. Courage is a habit. And it needs to be practiced to develop unshakable self-confidence. A courageous person is not someone who does not feel fear. A courageous person feels the fear and moves forward in spite of the fear.

The two primary fears that prevent a person from achieving success are the fear of rejection and the fear of failure. These fears have their roots in childhood conditioning. It indicates lack of self-confidence and low self-esteem. When you face your fears, take steps to move towards it, the fear diminishes. Your self-confidence and self esteem grows. Similarly, when you avoid the thing that you are afraid of, fear grows and your self-confidence decreases. Sometimes ignorance and lack of information leads to uncertainty and fear of the unknown. The act of gathering more information will give you more confidence and courage. Although remember, you will never have all the information. After a certain point you need to take action. Never be afraid to step out of your comfort zone. As your comfort zone expands, so does your success potential.

Another key point to remember as you start your success journey is you will come across situations which will have you question your integrity and core values. Your values and principles are your core, your center. Standing by your values and principles during difficult circumstances takes courage. When you stand by your values, you are true to yourself and ready for unlimited success.

Exercise #3:
Write down a list of five things that you are currently fearful of, which are holding you back. Then for each one of them write down what action you will take immediately to overcome these fears.

PRINCIPLE 4: WORK THE SYSTEM RUTHLESSLY EACH DAY

Success is never owned; it is only rented – and the rent is due every day.
~ Rory Vaden

The single most important quality of successful people is self-discipline. The price for success has to be paid upfront and it has to be paid every day. The difference between successful and unsuccessful people is that successful people do what must be done even if they don't feel like doing it. This may mean missing a big game; this may mean not

IGNITE YOUR LIFE

watching hours of television every evening. Instead they focus on doing things that get them closer to their goal. Remember to do things today what others won't do, so that you can have things tomorrow that others won't have.

Imagine you own a farm. You cannot expect to work on it only in the last two months before the harvest and expect that you will reap anything. For the farm to produce plentifully, you have to sow the seed, water it daily, remove the weeds and care for it every day. Then and only then you can reap the benefits at harvest time. The same applies to achieving your success goals. You have to work at it every day. Procrastination is your biggest enemy. If you are procrastinating, it only means that you don't want success bad enough.

Part of success is when opportunity meets preparation. Successful people are always investing in themselves. They are lifelong learners. They read books, listen to audio programs, attend seminars and network with other successful people. They always do more than what they are paid for. They are excellent time managers. They plan their days, their weeks and their months. And they always work their plan. Every day.

Exercise #4:
Refer to the list of the top four goals that you have from the first exercise and create a plan for the next day, next week and next month. Ensure that everything you are doing is aligned with your success goals. Then every night before going to sleep, write your reflections in your journal. What were you able to achieve today per the plan? What did you miss and why? What did you think, feel, say or do? Once you start this habit you will be able to look back and take a different action for the tasks you missed and reinforce the actions for the tasks you achieved.

PRINCIPLE 5: ALWAYS GIVE BACK

The meaning of life is to find your gift.
The purpose of life is to give it away.

~ Pablo Picasso

Dr. Wayne Dyer talks about scientific research around kindness. Whenever someone engages in acts of kindness, no matter how big or small, the serotonin levels increase in both the giver and receiver of an act of kindness. And to make things even more interesting, anyone who

156

witnesses an act of kindness also has an increase in serotonin levels. Serotonin is a "feel good" neurotransmitter. So this means the giver, receiver, and those who witness the act of kindness experience a boost in happiness.

Whatever you give is going to come back. It's a universal law. Some people hesitate to give because they come from a mindset of scarcity, but in reality life is abundant. The more you give the more you will get in return. Another key to remember is that you should start giving now, irrespective of where you are financially. I always hear people say, I will start giving when I have more money. But the fact is if you find it hard to give 10% to charity when you are making $50,000, it will be incredibly difficult for you to give away a $100,000 when you start making a million dollars. The habits need to start early.

Imagine you were on an island and there was room for only a handful of people. Imagine there was a tribunal held tomorrow and you were asked the question what did you contribute to the world? What value did you bring to this world? Why should you be allowed to live the next year? Wouldn't it be great if you could stand there proudly with your head held high and talk about all that you have given back to the world and show them the lives you had touched?

Exercise #5:
Every morning in your journal write down the question, "What am I going to give to my friends, family and community today?" At the end of the day you write down your answer. Find a charity or an organization for a cause that is close to your heart and start contributing to them today.

If you have followed the previous Success Principles, you now have a clear purpose, you take full responsibility for all your actions, you have a positive mental attitude and you have overcome your fears. You always give back to those who are less fortunate. Remember the more you give the more you get. You will find that new doors of opportunities start opening for you. Even ones that you were not even aware existed before. And very soon you are in an upward spiral towards Success.

These first five principles form the foundation of success. Once you have mastered these principles you can start focusing on remaining five principles of the success game. Take immediate and massive action and always strive to be the best in your field. Build harmonious relationships with others on the basis of strong values and high integrity. Never be fazed by any intermediate failures and keep going everyday till you succeed. And lastly and most importantly, remember to enjoy the journey.

As Sir Richard Branson once said, "You are not happy because you are successful. You are successful because you are happy!"

About Sinchan

Sinchan Patil is an India-born, U.S.-based Leader and Entrepreneur who specializes in success habits, leadership skills, and management. Sinchan has worked for numerous Fortune 500 companies providing them with consistent, high quality service which produces significant cost savings via superior project and portfolio management.

Sinchan writes a success and leadership blog. He is also co-founder of PM Alternative (www.pmalternative.com), a company that provides clients significant cost reductions by providing an alternative to conventional project management services.

You can follow Sinchan on: twitter @patilsinchan or read his blogs at: www.sinchanpatil.com.

CHAPTER 17

THE POWER OF MEANING

BY SNEZHANA-SOPHIA ZAMALIEVA, PhD

Man is a being in search of meaning.
~ Plato

I want to share with you how the power of meaning can be used for achieving a fulfilled life. But first, here is the story how a world-renowned philosopher, Victor Frankl, has influenced my life. He developed his concept in the 1930s, and tested it in the 1940s during almost three years in German concentration camps. Dr. Frankl wrote a book, *Man's Search for Meaning*. It has sold more then three million copies in the United States. The book was translated into more than twenty languages and has brought change and comfort to many people.

Frankl believes the key to a positive view of life is awareness that life has meaning under all circumstances, and that every single person has the capacity to find meaning in life.

Logotherapy translates as "therapy through meaning" – we could also say **"health through meaning" or "personal growth through meaning."**

Ten years ago, I started on a new path in my life. I was successful in my business career and I thought it was a good opportunity to fulfill my dream. I went back to University and received a Masters Degree in psychology and psychoanalysis. I was eager to find an answer to two important questions:

- What is man?
- What is the meaning of life?

My dream came true. I was on my way to becoming a mental health professional. I literally plunged into the study - it was almost 24/7. One of the fantastic courses we had was an observation of the main Personality Theories. At the end of the course we had an exam, and to get ready for the exam we had to do quite a lot of independent study; among those topics was Viktor Frankl's **Logotherapy**. Before then, I had never been introduced to this psychologist.

So, I searched the Internet and the first thing I found was his book, *Man's Search for Meaning*. The more I read, the more fascinated I felt. This was exactly what I was looking for – support for my inner discussion regarding human kind. I couldn't agree more!

Logotherapy teaches that life doesn't owe us happiness but instead, it offers us meaning.

Logotherapy helps us objectively appreciate our imperfections and be aware that the challenge lies in our incompleteness: our opportunity to grow, possibilities for change and to evolve. It focuses on an individual's unique, step-by-step path forward.

It's impossible to change our past, but we are neither slaves nor victims of it. Our responsibility is to change our **present**. By doing so we are simultaneously influencing our future. Each of us has limitations, but we also have a certain **freedom** within our limitations.

It's important to remember that happiness, peace of mind, satisfaction, and success are only by-products of our pursuit of meaning.

Logothearpy teaches us how to use the power of meaning to live in the face of inescapable uncertainty, and to bear unavoidable suffering in our lives. I read the book *Man's Search for Meaning* in TWO DAYS! I even canceled some meetings because I couldn't push myself to close the book. I said to myself that I must study Frankl's approach, because I knew that it would be an incredible gift to use his method in my counseling and coaching work.

To make a long story short, I worked really hard and now I am a Diplomat Clinician in Logotherapy and a Faculty member at the Victor

Frankl Institute of Logotherapy. I earned my PhD and published my first book on logotherapy in the Russian language – *The Freedom to Decide: Viktor Frankl's Logotherapy and Existential Anthropology*. And using my education, clinical and research experience, I have developed my own method – LOGOCOACHING.

WHY MEANING?

It is official – the search for meaning is a megatrend of our time! There is a growing desire for meaning!

Most of us would agree that nowadays *the existential query* is fairly common. We hear people talking about:

- ...lack of purpose
- ...lack of direction in life
- ...lack of meaning in life
- ...emptiness and meaninglessness

Many people would say they feel that something is missing in their lives; they feel lonely, overwhelmed and unfulfilled. The level of stress is increasing due to health and relationship issues, financial challenges, job insecurity or long-term unemployment. Not knowing where to turn for solutions, many people escape from such meaningless experiences through different forms of addiction, depression or aggression.

There are two types of people: the "Yes"-Person and the "No"-Person. The first type says yes to life despite all the challenges they might have, and the second type generally sees life in a negative way, despite the good things they experience. As a result a "YES"-Person feels mostly happy and fulfilled, while a "No"-Person is usually frustrated and disoriented.

A lot of people fall between these two extremes. The important thing is that it is possible to make a shift from a negative to a positive attitude. Only we are responsible for it! Logotherapy is a great tool for making this shift happen! It helps people to say yes to life whether the suffering they experience comes from difficult human relations, job trouble, illness, guilt or self-made problems. *You can rise above ill health and blows of fate if you see meaning in your existence.*

Meaning can be found in our responses to life. Once we realize that we are unique and have necessary resources available in the form of talents, capabilities and inner strength, we are no longer totally at the mercy of fate. Realizing that we have areas of freedom (however small they may be) and that we have choices in response to the demands life places upon us, we cannot remain in the victim stance any longer.

Just think how often people wonder about the meaning of life? Do they know the difference between the meaning of life and the meaning in life? How would we feel knowing that meaning can always be found? Would knowing that not be easier for us to cope with life's greatest challenges?

The answer is "YES!"

Here are seven benefits of living a **meaningful life**:

1. *Be motivated by the search for meaning.*

2. *Deeply know and appreciate your value system.*

3. *Be able to keep positive and courageous attitude towards life, despite challenges and difficulties.*

4. *Be able to accept past mistakes and turn regrets into tools for personal growth.*

5. *Be aware of the meaning of the moment.*

6. *Be connected on a deeper level to others and yourself.*

7. *Be able to transform your attitude and thinking.*

Lets say you decide to search for meaning in life, then you certainly will question yourself:

- ***What is Meaning?***
- ***How do I find meaning?***

WHAT IS MEANING?

If we take care of the moments, the years will take care of themselves.
~ Maria Edgeworth

We must distinguish two types of meaning: Ontological and Existential. In other words *meaning* **of** *life* and *meaning* **in** *life*, or *global meaning* and *meaning of the moment.*

When you search ***Ontological Meaning*** you are mostly aware that there is an order in the universe and you are part of that order. Scientists see this order in the laws of science or evolution, humanists see this order in the laws of nature and ethics, artists see it in harmony and religious people will see this order as divine.

The **Ontological Meaning** is inaccessible for us. We can compare it with the horizon – you can strive as much as possible toward it, but it is not possible to reach. It is important that you still pursue Ontological Meaning, even if you can never attain it. It is a matter of faith, of hypothesis, of personal experience. Only you can make an important choice – either to live as life has meaning and you are a part of the chain of life, or you can live as if life is chaos and you are a victim of its caprice. This choice is yours and you are responsible for it, nobody else!

This might sound discouraging that you cannot reach the Ontological Meaning, but the good news is that there is a second meaning – the **Existential Meaning** which you can and must reach to live a fulfilled life. The Existential Meaning is the meaning of the moment. The important question you should ask yourself is – What is life asking of me now? And your response to this question will determine what kind of person you will become.

Frankl believes that you are a unique human being who goes through life in a series of unique situations, and each moment is offering you a meaning to fulfill it – a chance to act in a meaningful way! In a moment, I will teach you how you can do that.

The understanding of the meaning of the moment is a skill. And like any other skill, it needs to be trained for and practiced. By practicing, you will experience an interesting change in your life. The following questions will help you to train for the new skill in challenging moments. This is a writing exercise. You can type these questions into your smartphone, that way you always have them available:

- *Name the situation which is challenging you* _____

- *What is life asking of me?* _____

- *What is my respond to the situation?* _____

- *What are my feelings about this situation?* _____

- *What was the lesson this situation provided me with?* _____

- *What will I do to grow and develop myself from this situation?* _____

- *What is my first step?* _____

Your first step will be a meaningful response to the challenging situation or meaning of the moment.

HOW DO I FIND MEANING?

This is another important question you will face eventually.

Some philosophers such as French existentialists Sartre and Camus, support the pessimistic idea that there is no meaning in life but that a human being has to lead a meaningful life – therefore you should create the meaning. The German existentialists including Victor Frankl are convinced that meaning exists, and we have to search for it! We have a will to develop meaning! This is the strongest motivation for living and taking action. Humans are beings in search of meaning. Seeing meaning in our life allows us to develop our capacities and struggle against difficulties in life. If your will to find meaning is ignored or repressed, you will feel empty.

There are three ways to discover meaning. I call it the **"ECA" Method.**

1. *Experience*

2. *Creativity*

3. *Attitude.*

The first way: (**E**) is for Experience (experiential values).

It could be encountering relationships of various kinds or experiences

THE POWER OF MEANING

with nature, culture or religion. For example, think about a beautiful sunrise, or traveling to your favorite destinations, or someone you love deeply. Those are meaningful experiences, and by being aware of them, we fill our lives with meaning. Victor Frankl recalls how once, in the horror of the concentration camp, he heard a melody, played by violin. This music reminded him about his beloved wife. He didn't know where she was, nor if she was alive. But that little melody brought back all the special experiences he shared with his wife. It lifted him beyond the misery of his struggle to survive one more day in the concentration camp. This moment had great experiential value for Dr. Frankl. It was a treasured gift life gave him that day.

Now here is a question for you. What have you received from life through experiences that were deeply meaningful? Think, reflect and write down the answer!

Developing Mindfulness:
> *There is only one moment in time when it is essential to awaken.*
> *That moment is now.*
> ~ The Buddha

We live in the now not in the past or future. Living in the now means acknowledging and accepting the flow of time – the past is the past and the future is hypothetical. Mindfulness means being fully awake and alert - these are obviously necessary qualities for experiencing the meaning of the moment. Why not practice Mindfulness Meditation? Learning to be in control of your own mind instead of letting your mind be in control of you.

Lots of ideas for mindfulness meditation - mindfulness breathing, mindfulness walking, mindfulness in thoughts, even mindfulness eating. Choose what you like more and develop your own mindfulness practice.

Here are seven tips:

1. Practice what you preach.

2. Do one thing at a time – when you are eating – eat; when you are reading – read; when you are cleaning – concentrate on that activity.

3. Let go of hindrances.

4. Focus your attention on what you are doing (again, again and again).

5. Set the scene for your meditation.

6. Protect your meditation time (5 minutes in the morning) and have a special reminder to do so.

7. Commit to it.

I love mindfulness breathing. I do it throughout the day. My reminder is a red light. When the traffic light is red – great! I do my mindfulness breathing!

The second way to discover meaning: (C) is for Creativity (creative values).

This is the best known way of course. We experience fulfillment from goals reached, tasks mastered, and a job well done. This way to meaning is as readily available to us as we are willing to respond to the tasks life places before us. When using our creativity, our unique talents and strength, we can be vitally engaged in life and find life well worth living – or in other words, meaningful.

Utilizing this way leads us to deep fulfillment as well as to a discovery of our innate endowments and to the development of their potential to the fullest. Think about your talents. Make a list. Are you using your talents in your life?

Now think about what you give to life through your creativity? What creative gifts have you have offered to others through your talents, your work and your goals that held meaning for you? Write it down.

The third way is: (A) attitude (attitudinal value).

This unique contribution of logotherapy to mental health is that it enables you to be a "yes" sayer in the face of tragedy, to find meaning in meaningless situations.

Even when creative or experiential ways of finding meaning are not possible, a person still seeks to find meaning in the midst of suffering – bearing it courageously rather than feeling degraded because of it. Meaning ensues from the attitude brought towards the blows of fate.

Frankl referred to the capacity for finding meaning in the face of human suffering, guilt, and even certain death. We have the potential to transform suffering into human achievement and guilt into meaningful action. By that, we can become more than we were before, by facing the challenges life presents to us. South African dissident, Nelson Mandela, is an inspiring example. He tolerated 30 years of imprisonment with dignity, because his imprisonment symbolized the struggle for equality.

MEANING CAN GIVE US STRENGTH AND COURAGE!

What is your meaning and have you defined it in every area of your life? If not, I hope that this chapter will help you get started in finding your meaning.

About Snezhana-Sophia

Snezhana-Sophia Zamalieva, PhD is a certified expert in psychology, logocoach, speaker. Born in St. Petersburg (Russia), Snezhana-Sophia graduated from Saint Petersburg State University with a master's degree in Sociology. In 2003, she received her MBA degree in the Presidential programme on training managers at Saint Petersburg University of Management and Economics.

Snezhana-Sophia supports the idea of life-long education and implements it in her life. Later, she graduated from the East European Institute for Psychoanalysis with a master's degree in psychology and psychoanalysis. She continued her education attending the program at The Center for Group Studies (Modern Leadership), New York and Victor Frankl Institute of Logotherapy, Abilene, Texas.

She is now a Faculty Member and Diplomate Clinician at Victor Frankl Institute of Logotherapy, and she is an Associate Professor of the General Scientific Studies Department at the East European Institute for Psychoanalysis.

In 2012, she was awarded her PhD degree from the Philosophy Department of Saint Petersburg State University with a thesis on the Meaning-centered Philosophy of Viktor Frankl.

Snezhana-Sophia is also an experienced sportswoman; she has a black belt in martial arts and is certified as TDI diver.

Snezhana-Sophia is President of the Maestro Temirkanov International Foundation for Cultural Initiatives from 2004. This is a non-profit organization with the mission to preserve, develop and enrich Russia's national musical heritage and to share their legacy with the world.

She was awarded the Vernadsky Silver Medal for contribution in the development of science, The MBA Cup – 2006 International Prize for non-profit Foundations contribution in the development of culture. In 2015, she received The Statue of Responsibility Award in grateful recognition of distinguished leadership in promoting the work of Victor Frankl throughout the world.

Snezhana-Sophia is a certified specialist of the European Confederation of Psychoanalytic Psychotherapy and Association of Cognitive-Behavioral Therapy. She is an active member of the Russian Psychological Society. She is the author of numerous articles, courses and master-classes. Her monograph *The Freedom To Decide: V. Frankl's Logotherapy and Existential Anthropology* was recently published and is considered to be the only research on Victor Frankl's Philosophy in the Russian language.

Her life philosophy is: "He who has a why to live for can bear almost any how."

Her services include: Coaching, Counseling, Speaker, Lectures, Seminars, Workshops

Snezhana-Sophia helps clients to transform their thinking, become more resilient, apply and use the meaning philosophy in day-to-day life and work.

Recently she was invited to speak at the XX Jubileum World Congress on Logotherapy "Humanity's Search for Peace and Purpose." She was one among respected speakers such as Dr. Arun Gandhi (grandson of Mahatma Gandhi), Dr. Steven Southwick (Yale University), and Dr. Stefan Schulenberg (University of Mississippi).

Contact Snezhana-Sophia at:
- szamalieva@gmail.com
- www.zamalieva.ru
- skype: snezhok-sophie
- FB: https://www.facebook.com/szamalieva

CHAPTER 18

ACCELERATE YOUR WISDOM

BY TAD BRISTOW

True wisdom comes to each of us when we realize how little we understand about life, ourselves, and the world around us.
~ Socrates

Have you ever found yourself at crossroads in your life? Sure you have. Recently I found myself in just such a spot. It's not the first time. It probably won't be the last time.

I am a retired PwC Partner and IBM executive. Upon *retirement* I traveled a bit. I played a bit of golf. I worked on home projects. I played a bit of golf, okay, I played a lot of golf but there had to be more. I bought into a franchise business. I learned a lot. It kept me busy but there had to be more. When the opportunity came to sell the business, I didn't have to think twice. I sold it and here I am, at another crossroad.

Then came the expected questions from family and friends and my lovely bride. So what are you doing now? What are going to do? You know, the usual.

I not so jokingly told them, "The good news is: I can do anything I want. The bad news is: I can do anything I want!"

STARTING A NEW CHAPTER

As the ink dried and another chapter came to a close, I began searching for a new path. In this self-evaluation journey, I found myself praying that the Lord would help me find wisdom and knowledge to guide me toward the next chapter of my life.

I decided to go back to the beginning, diligently exploring my spiritual library and revisiting some of my favorite authors: Edwards Deming and his essays on knowledge and systems, Stephen Covey and his books *The 7 Habits of Highly Effective People* and *First Things First*, Wayne Dyer and his multiple works, and interestingly enough, my co-author Brian Tracy.

I met Brian in 1991. He was professionally speaking in the area of sales achievement to my employer, Computer Assistance. At the time, there were only about 50 of us in the room. Today, he addresses audiences of 500 to 5,000! I still vividly remember him and his flat screen projector – regaling us with the accomplishments and tactics of Alexander the Great. He left a lasting impression. So much so, that I continue to read and listen to Brian's works.

GETTING WISE ABOUT WISDOM

As I prayed for wisdom and knowledge, it occurred to me that I might want to investigate in-depth those two words. If you are truly, earnestly asking for something, you had better know what it is. *Be careful what you wish for, you just might get it, ran through my mind.*

Let's explore these elemental words.

Wisdom: (Noun) The quality of having experience, knowledge, and good judgment; the quality of being wise.

Synonyms: sagacity – intelligence – sense – common sense – shrewdness – astuteness – judiciousness – judgment – prudence

Antonyms: folly - stupidity

This definition struck me as lacking, and I was puzzled by the circular reference. Wisdom points to wise and wise points to wisdom? I started my career as a programmer and I know an infinite loop when I see one!

Knowledge: (Noun) Facts, information, and skills acquired by a person through experience or education; the theoretical or practical understanding of a subject: what is known in a particular field or in total; facts and information: Philosophy - true, justified belief; certain understanding, as opposed to opinion. Awareness or familiarity gained by experience of a fact or situation:

Synonyms: understanding – comprehension – grasp – command – mastery – expertise – skill – proficiency – expertness – know-how – education – scholarship – schooling - wisdom

The philosophical definition piqued my interest. More research required!

Continuing with my reading, in particular, the works of Mr. Deming - I discovered that he was a keen scholar of epistemology, the study of the philosophy of knowledge. While exploring epistemology, I found reference to an interesting article written by Edmund Gettier in 1963. He proposed that "knowledge is justified true belief." The following diagram depicts his thesis.

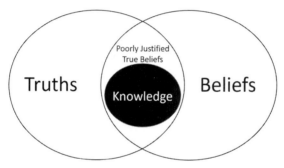

This definition resonated with me. More importantly, the picture itself held me captive.

Truth is most often used to mean being in accord with fact or reality.

Belief is the state of mind in which a person thinks something to be the case, with or without there being empirical evidence to prove that something is the case with factual certainty.

A simple analogy: I **believe** the bridge will support my weight. I cross over the bridge. It is now a **fact** or **reality** for me. I now **know** that the bridge will hold my weight. Subtle, yet significant.

There is great deal more to this philosophical framework, but it will suffice for our discussion.

So where is wisdom? Could it possibly fit into this framework? Why, throughout millennia, in almost all religions and spiritual discussions, are the words wisdom and knowledge inseparably linked?

THE CHORD OF WISDOM

I propose that wisdom is the intersection of knowledge, truths and beliefs.

Wisdom lies at the nexus of our personal knowledge, beliefs, and truths. We experience wisdom when we intuitively acknowledge this correlation.

Think of these three domains as bells in our heads. If we read, experience, or witness something in our world and it does NOT fit with our current knowledge, truths, beliefs we might surmise it to be interesting or discount it all together. However, if it passes all of our tests, we say, "Yes!" We deem it to be wise. It's almost like we discovered something that was long hidden.

 I call this harmonious ringing of the bells the chord of wisdom.

We can probably all agree that wisdom is difficult to define – yet, we know it when we see it. This is not a trivial statement. For us to deem something as wise, we will filter the statement or the act through our body of knowledge, our truths (facts), and our own personal belief system. When it passes this personal litmus test in all three areas we hear the chord of wisdom. We intuitively say, I agree. That is the essence of wisdom.

The key here is to understand that wisdom is personal. Everyone's body of knowledge, beliefs, and truths are different. They are also continually evolving. Have you ever discovered a piece of wisdom in a book that you perhaps have read many times, and suddenly, a statement that you've read before takes on significant new meaning? It now strikes a chord. Perhaps you said to yourself, "How did I miss that!" What changed is that you expanded in some or all areas that now allows it to resonate.

As I thought about this, more questions came to mind: So if this is wisdom, how and when is wisdom acquired? Why do I surmise one person to be wiser than another? Is wise, the use of a person's collective wisdom? If so…

CAN WE MEASURE WISDOM?

Is it possible to empirically measure wisdom? If you read a wise saying and agree with its wisdom, could you articulate why you think it is wise? It's very difficult. However, could we entertain that an individual's **degree** of wisdom can be measured by his or her **appreciation** of wisdom?

To test this theory, I took a sampling of several hundred people from different demographics. This demographic data capture was fairly simple—Age, Education, Spirituality, Economic Security, and Reading Habits. The simple exercise of the survey was for the individual to read quotes and have the reader answer if they deemed the statement wise. No reference to the author would be made to prevent any bias.

In discussing the survey with a friend, he asked me a simple question. As the author of the survey, wasn't I deeming what was wise by including it in the survey? Wise friends will do that to you. So in order to remove my bias, I propagated a database with a thousand quotes and had a program randomly select them for me.

The key point was to ascertain if wisdom is bound by socio-economic boundaries or constraints. I wondered if, and, or how, it might be influenced by age, education, spirituality, or economic stability?

Highlights from the survey showed the following:

- *Age would appear to have the most impact on recognition and appreciation of wisdom.*

- *Formal education is a differentiator when viewed by age group. Without continuing study and reading, it has less of an impact later in* life.

- Homeschoolers showed up as outliers within their peer group. The differentiating factor upon further review indicated a higher degree of spirituality and a broader range of literature in their studies; particularly, the humanities and classic literature.

- People of similar ages, similar education differentiated based on their economic stability and spirituality.

- At the college senior level, wisdom appreciation was somewhat higher with those studying liberal arts than those in science and engineering fields of study.

- Spirituality surfaced as an outlier indicator in formative years and continued throughout all age groups.

- Within each age group, a higher degree of spirituality and reading lead to a greater appreciation for wisdom.

As you might have already suspected, George Bernard Shaw was right: "Youth is wasted on the young."

A simple case in point. We have all encountered a brilliant person who is an expert in their field of knowledge. We may have witnessed that this person can be uncomfortable, perhaps even confused, when moved from their comfort zone of collective knowledge. Perhaps we say, "He certainly is smart but he doesn't have much common sense." Well, common sense isn't!

Given the context as depicted in my diagram, I formulated my personal definition of wisdom.

WISDOM IS THE RIGHTEOUS APPLICATION OF KNOWLEDGE.

Righteous or righteousness, like wisdom and knowledge, seems to go hand-in-hand across all religions and philosophies. The notion of righteousness is articulated by philosophers as a grounding in morality and principles.

I propose that **righteousness** is the glue or bridge between our truths and our beliefs.

Application implies that we not only agree but deem to act in accordance with what we understand to be wisdom. It also corresponds to the conscious mental act of testing the world against our knowledge, truths, and beliefs.

We can and do go about our lives gaining additional wisdom. We organically grow in our knowledge, truths, and beliefs and hence our wisdom. That said, we need not simply grow old to expand our wisdom!

ACCELERATE YOUR WISDOM

When viewed in this context, it is quite feasible that wisdom can be accelerated. In order to achieve this, we must congruently expand our bodies of knowledge, our understanding of our truths and our beliefs.

I propose that one can accelerate this process. My autobiographical study of "wise" individuals in history (Ben Franklin, Thomas Jefferson, Edwards Deming, and others), leads me to believe that they conscientiously or intuitively accelerated their wisdom.

The Aperture of Wisdom

Volunteer
Mission Work
Research
Citizenship

Spiritual Reading
Prayer
Meditation
Self Reflection

Professional Study
Self Improvement
Autobiographies
Curious Reading

This intersection then, is really an opening. It can be expanded. I call this opening the aperture of wisdom.

We can accelerate our wisdom by conscientiously being ever more curious about the world we live in:

- Dedication to your spiritual knowledge to establish and expand your principles and understanding.

- Curiosity for knowledge above and beyond your necessary daily boundaries, such as reading the classics, exploring philosophy.

- Expanding your experiential knowledge by seeking out experiences outside of your traditional norm like volunteering, travel, or mission work.

- Always continuing in your professional studies.

- Doing what I call curious reading. Like chasing down the meaning of knowledge and wisdom.

- Reading self-improvement books like this one.

- Reading autobiographies of people who fascinate or inspire you.

- Learning more about a period of time that intrigues you.

All of this moves you outward and opens wider your aperture of wisdom.

As our Knowledge, Beliefs, and Truths are actively and aggressively expanded and with it our aperture of Wisdom, we will find ourselves experiencing the chord of wisdom with greater frequency in our lives. Perhaps something about this chapter struck a chord with you. Perhaps you will find other chords of wisdom in this book. It is my hope and prayer that you will take these words and apply them and that your life becomes a symphony of wisdom chords.

Socrates was right. "True wisdom comes to each of us when we realize how little we understand about life, ourselves, and the world around us." Could that lead to humility? Yikes!

Welcome to your next chapter.

Cheers!

About Tad

Tad Bristow is the Founder and President of Pilit Consulting and the Owner and President of BriFolz Enterprises, LLP. He consults with organizations at the executive level in Information Technology with a concentration in IT strategy, organizational effectiveness, project rescue, outsourcing, mergers and acquisitions, and IT startups. He helps executives and their organizations start or restart a business or critical project.

He enjoys speaking to audiences in the areas of Wisdom, Project Rescue, and Mergers and Acquisitions.

Tad is a recognized entrepreneurial information systems executive with a proven track record of developing and leading successful service and software businesses on a local, national, and global basis. Through his strong leadership and motivational skills, he has recruited and developed high performance teams that focus on bottom line results.

He is known for his ability to concurrently direct strategic and operational initiatives while managing multiple "first of a kind" client delivery projects.

A graduate from the school of hard knocks, Tad attended the University of Illinois studying metallurgical engineering. Working full time, he continued his studies at Richland Community College and DuPage Community College focusing his studies on business administration. It was during this time that he discovered his true life calling in the area of computer science and programming.

In 1994, Tad was accepted into Partnership at Coopers & Lybrand, LLP. In 1998, Coopers & Lybrand merged with Price Waterhouse becoming PricewaterhouseCoopers, PwC. At PwC, Tad was the Midwest Lead Partner for Emerging Technologies and the Global Partner Champion for Enterprise Systems Management. In 2002, PwC Consulting was purchased by IBM. As a Partner, he was a member of the merger and integration teams for both the Price Waterhouse and IBM Consulting mergers.

In 2009, Tad retired from IBM as a Partner and global executive. At IBM he was responsible for all of IBM services in the areas of Portals, E-Commerce, and Content Management. Under his watch, his practice developed a number of familiar websites and technologies. Hallmark, Home Depot, Lowes, Harry and David, LL Bean, NCAA are just a few of the websites his teams developed. On the technology side, perhaps you've used a Sony Blu-Ray player. Tad and his global team helped develop the authoring system used by the major motion picture studios for the creation of the all Blu-Ray discs.

Married to Peggy Folz and the proud father of three children, Tad enjoys Golf, Travel, Snow Skiing, the Arts, and exploring the rich history of Mobile, Alabama and the deep south. He is a proud Rotarian and enjoys serving on various non-profit and community organizations.

He is currently working on two books. *Accelerate Your Wisdom* (The righteous application of knowledge) and *Land the Plane!* (A humorous story about the serious business of project rescue).

- https://www.linkedin.com/in/tadbristow

- Tad@PilitConsulting.onmicrosoft.com

CHAPTER 19

FIGURE OUT YOUR GOAL AND FIND A WAY TO ACCOMPLISH IT

BY SAINT JAMES LIMOGES, PhD, CHSA, RELO, ALHS, ABR

As Early As I Can Remember, I Wanted To Know Why Some People Are Rich And Others Weren't.

~ Dr. Saint James

My mom's name was Johnetta she was a butcher's assistant, my step-dad's name was Lee Doll and he work various jobs – bartender, bus driver, etc. My grandmother's name was Maryetta, she was a maid for a family in the Park Cities area (wealthy and very exclusive area near Dallas, Texas). I was born and raised in sunny, south Dallas, near the state fair of Texas. Looking outside my bedroom widow, I could see my Granny's veggie garden, small chicken coop and the area where she raised rabbits. (All inside the city limits.) We lived in a small whitewood framed 3- bedroom 1- bath home, no bars, no security alarm. My family wasn't poor, they were working lower class.

I have never missed a meal or went without any basic necessities, but my parents had a very interesting way of paying their bills. First was the mortgage, then food, then the car payment, then utilities, ...and all other items were place in a hat and paid or not paid. I saw my mom tear up more bills than I can count every month (mostly medical, because we had no health insurance). I remember hearing her say often: "money doesn't grow on trees; can't get blood out of a turnip; rich people are greedy and thieves."

One day I was outside playing and a sharply dressed man was going door to door selling encyclopedias (which no one bought). I watched him go all the way down the block and back up to my door, when he asked if my parents were home and I answered, "No sir, but my Granny is home."

Back then we didn't worry about stranger danger, so I took him inside to talk with my Granny. He introduced himself and my Granny offered him some sweet tea. They sat in living room, he pulled out two books, one Granny opened, and I sat on the floor with the other one. Oh what beautiful bold pictures it had, with such sleek smooth shiny pages. I don't have a clue about their conversation because I was lost in my new world. All I know is that my Granny put volumes 1 through 5 on a payment plan. (Looking back today, that just blows my mind because she didn't money for anything except bills and home stuff.) It took her almost two years to buy the entire set of Britannica encyclopedias. Every other day we would read, and I dreamed of traveling the world and being rich. My Granny would just laugh and say, it's more important to be happy, not rich. She would always say being rich is hard, and not for all people, but everybody can be happy.

In the summer, I would always beg my Granny to take me to work with her and she would say when you get older, you can go and help me. Next day same story, I would stomp off mad and was dropped off at neighbor's house to be watched until my parents came home. Summer time rolled around the next year, I got the same old story, you can go when you're older. Well, one day the neighbor was sick, and both my parents were at work so guess who finally went to work with her Granny? Me, ... boy, I'm bouncing up and down like a kid who ate a whole package of chocolate chip cookies with a milk shake chaser.

I hopped into the front seat still bouncing and ready to roll (no seat belt requirements back then). Seem like she drove forever before we arrived in Park Cities area, homes just kept getting bigger and bigger plus a lot of expensive cars. I thought my eyes would pop out. My Granny just laughed and said, close your mouth before your teeth and tongue fall out.

We arrived at Mrs. Cohen's home who greeted us at the back door, and to my surprise called me by name. "We finally get to met you, Maryetta talks about you all the time." (I reply… really she does, giggling)

Granny put her apron on, made me a snack, then Mrs. Cohen said I should go out to play with her daughter and son (both were a little older than me), so Granny took me to the backyard, introduced me then went inside to work. That summer changed my life, every summer afterwards Granny would take me for two or three days with her. I never really cleaned, just played and talked with Mrs. Cohen's kids.

One year I asked my Granny why some people are rich and other people were not rich. She said all she knew was that white people were born rich, die rich, and black people were born broke and die broke. "Baby girl, I don't want you cleaning nobody's home, mending nobody's clothes like me. Study hard, do good in school, and get yourself a real good job and be happy."

Granny had limited education, yet she was the smartest woman I knew. But something seemed wrong with her thoughts of wealth. I never heard her say a bad word against anyone, never a racial slur, nothing negative. This has always, always bothered me. How can I, a black child, soon to be a black teen, become wealthy black adult?

Several summers passed by, but the thought never lefts my mind. One year all the parents in my area were given a choice for the kids the stay at the current middle school or be bused to a better white school. Most parents said "no" and were very anger about it. My Granny told my mom it could be a good thing, so on to the next school I was bused in a different school district. Boy, it was different alright, I saw upper class black and white parents dropping their kids off in very nice cars; black and white people in big lovely homes. Right now I'm craz-e-e, craz-e-e-e confused about who, when and why some people are wealthy.

Fast forward my life to adulthood. I'm married to a truck driver with kids and we live in a house at Lakeland and down the street from Doctors Hospital. I'm reading everything I can find about money. I bet I read over 500 books before I was 30. I remember being made fun of all my life for being different, and my Granny saying, "Baby, people talked bad about Jesus and he is the son of God, so you're in good company." (This didn't make me feel any better, though.)

One day my girlfriend pissed off her boss and about a week later or so, she was transferred from working days, 7am to 3pm, to working 11pm to 7am, the overnight shift at Doctors Hospital. She needed a babysitter BADLY or would lose her job, so I agreed to watch her son, next day, she needed me again, so a week passes by and she ask if I would babysit him permanently for a few bucks a week? I said sure, since he just slept the whole night. A few weeks later my friend gave my number to some other single moms and before long, I had several kids sleeping at my place.

Seeing a business opportunity, I went to community college and became certified in child development. Then I applied to the State of Texas for a registered group home, and hired my mom and auntie Shirley to work with me. I read everything I could about day care, food prep, accounting, etc., and went from babysitting to an in-home day care business, because I wanted and desired to be wealthy. Granny use to talk about being equally yoked (she was very religious). I didn't have a clue what she meant. She would say, "Just keep living, you will figure it out."

I start attending seminars on wealth, reading about self-improvement, and still watching kids in our home. At this point, I'm starting to understand the equally-yoked comment my Granny spoke about. I have discovered that my husband and I have two totally different views on the world, personal growth and wealth, but love conquers all. Right??

Fast forward dreaming of being rich and thought to myself, "I will never become rich caring for twelve kids in my home." About two weeks after having that thought, I'm driving through an economically-challenged neighborhood and I see a white one story building for lease on Dolphin Rd in East Dallas. I write the number down, but didn't call. A few weeks go by and I drive by again, it's still available. (A little voice inside said "call," the other voice said "Are you stupid, you have no money saved, no credit.") I arrive home battered and bruised mentally, call my Granny and she said (her voice so sweet), "You have nothing to lose." My mom agreed. Damn it, not what I wanted to hear. Now I'm mad, but I don't know why.

Next day I call the number and a mature man answered and invited me to meet him at the building, which I did. He drove up in a big black Mercedes-Benz. He was wearing a leisure suit, had gray hair and shiny glasses. Before we go inside, he asked, "What are your plans for my building?" "Sir. I have a day care in my home and I want to expand so I can be rich." He laughed and said, "Really??"

He told me the monthly lease amount, the amount needed for deposit, and also that I needed good credit. My eyes were as big as a plate. We walked through the building and it is dirty, to say the least. I thanked him for his time and went home – thinking internally to myself, over and over again, "How can I get this money? What are my options???" I was literally obsessing over this building and how to get the money. (This is how I began to understand the universal law of attraction.)

Next day, I asked him to meet me again, this time I came with measuring tape, pen and paper. I walked through every room, marking and talking to myself. ("Baby beds will go here, toddlers there, kitchen okay, great.") He said okay, let's talk money. (I said "Oh shit!" to myself.) My mouth opened and words start flowing out completely on their own. It was like I was having an out-of-body experience.

Long story short, I got the building with very little out of pocket. The Landlord told me he has never ever given a three-year lease, with one-half deposit for cleanup and half-off rent for the first six months."

I immediately talked with my current clients and raised my fees, borrowed money from my mom, Granny, saved money from household bills, and signed the lease for my first Daycare. Back to that 'equally-yoked' thing my Granny spoke about. My husband and I separated and have an on-again and off-again relationship for years, then finally divorced. I am a student of life, learning then applying what I have learned, to grow and earn more—he was not!

I went from a 12 kid in-home Daycare to a 32-kid center. Later, I opened three other locations; the largest center was licensed for over 228 kids. All were 24-hour centers and earning over six figures a year. Between opening my first and second Daycare, I met my current husband and love of my life, Johnny.

Over the last 40 years I have read and listened to over 5,000 books, and attended hundreds of seminars regarding money and personal grow. I would earn lots of money and spend it all but $50K, or lose it all, get depressed, cry, get mad and cuss, then start over again. I fully understand

187

the law of attraction, visualization, etc. But I could never get everything working together in my favor or understand what exactly I did to make good things happen.

Now, I do know the definition of insanity, but I was still the cat chasing my tail in a circle, until I discovered something one day that changed my freaking life forever. We were painting a room in the house from a bright red color to a white color. So we went down to the local hardware store to get the paint and brushes. We get home, give it two coats of white paint and let it dry. We wake up to find that the darker color bled through, so back to hardware store and the guy in the paint department says, "Oh yeah, you should prime the wall with a special primer, then apply the new paint."

At this point, I'm still in the hardware store thinking to myself, now I understand why some people (myself included) go to seminars, read books and magic happens, while others have very limited success.

Primer makes new paint adhere to the surface better, and makes it possible to paint over darker, bolder colors with a single stroke. Having a limited belief is like bad paint on a wall, if you try to repaint it with a new color, the old color just bleeds through.

It took me a few more years, but I began to put all the pieces together and developed the 90-Day challenge that completely change my life and the lives of others. Then Mind-TKO.com was created, so anybody who wants true change in their lives has a simple system to follow. Now that I've told you my story, let me tell you how you too can change direction and achieve the life you want.

Here are two things you should do to get started:

1. Figure out what you want.

This in my opinion is the hardest thing to do, because most of us were never taught how to follow our passion, to do what we love, to follow our dreams. We spend more time planning for a vacation than we do planning for life. Try this process:

    A. Get a glass of wine, turn on music that inspires you, and remove all distractions.

B. Take out some paper, write down all the thing you love to do for fun.

C. Out of that list pick 2 or 3 things.

D. Take a few really deep breaths, close your eyes, place your hand over your heart.

E. Now ask yourself this question, "Which one would you do every day for free?"

Once you have identified want you truly love doing, that's half the battle. This process can be used for almost any situation

2. Discover your "why".

Most likely there is a reason why you have been stuck or not doing what you really want to do in life. So let's find out why. Growing up, most of us heard or saw things in our childhood that left some type of permanent mark (both good and bad); these shape part of our reality. Who we marry, careers we choose, what we believe to be possible or impossible, etc. (Limiting beliefs.)

Ask yourself this question. What was the first three or four negative thoughts that popped into your head when you did the exercise above? Write down your answer and examine the feeling behind the thought.

In closing, remember all things are possible, you just need the right tool.

About Saint James

Saint James, Ph.D., CHSA, RELO, ALHS, ABR is a passionate Life Coach and Motivational Speaker with various talents who resides in Dallas, Texas. She is also a Certified Neuro-Linguistic Programming Life Coach and holds a Certification in Child Development. Additionally, Dr. Saint James is a Licensed Insurance Agent, Financial Coach, and Realtor with multiple designations. Throughout the years, she has been featured on the Brian Tracy show and has appeared on prominent channels, including ABC, NBC, CBS, and FOX affiliates around the country.

In addition to being the creative mind behind "The 90 Day Overhaul", Dr. Saint James is the proud Founder of Mind -TKO Academy and Mind -TKO Coaching. Furthermore, she is an avid writer of numerous self-development articles and has been featured in a multitude of publications. She has been named as a TRENDSETTER in *Fortune magazine*, and been featured in *USA Today*, as well as *YAHOO! Finance*, *Wall Street Journal's MarketWatch*, and over a hundred other media outlets. Dr. Saint James is an author and speaker. She has also been featured on America's PremierExperts in Life Coaching.

Dr. Saint James' primary passion is to help others unleash their limitless potential and create the life of their dreams, all while overcoming challenges and improving the overall quality of their lives. When she's not immersed in her diverse career, Dr. Saint James loves to read great books. (She has read over 5,000 to date.) Most importantly, she enjoys traveling, cooking, hanging out at the beach and spending quality time with her family. Dr. Saint James is happily married to her husband Johnny and together, they are the proud parents of five sons.

Whether you're looking to earn more money or would like to re-invent yourself, Dr. Saint James is your go-to Life Coach and Speaker. For more information, please visit: MindTKO.COM

Total life transformation awaits!

CHAPTER 20

THE FUTURE BELONGS TO THE YOUNG...AND AMBITIOUS

BY GREG ROLLETT

I'm very optimistic about young people. I'm optimistic about what young people are doing today, and what they will continue to do in the future. However, with all the advancement and good being done across the world, I see young people heading in two very different directions— two very clear, distinct directions.

Moving in one direction is the young person who is glued to their phone. They are literally watching the world pass them by. They're looking at other people's Facebook and Instagram feeds and saying, *"That looks fun. That looks like a great dinner. That's a great vacation."* They're living through the lives of others and having none of the adventures themselves.

Moving in the opposite direction is the person who is creating their present and their future. They are taking a hands-on approach to their life. . . they're living! These are the ones traveling. . . exploring. They're creating families, businesses and jobs. They are leveraging and using technology to change their world, and ultimately the world everyone else will live in. These young people are taking an active approach in shaping the future that they want to live in.

These are two very distinct groups that young people are merging into.

It is the second group that we need to pay extra-special attention to. We need to foster, coach, mentor, market to and watch this group carefully.

How do I know? I'm part of this group.

One of the earliest memories I have of myself with grand and ambitious dreams was sitting in my bedroom at 8 or 9 years old. I remember the bed was to one side of the room and my makeshift posters, which I ripped out of Sports Illustrated, lined the walls. I also had a huge, full-length mirror in my room. Every single day I would grab my mini baseball bat, which I got at a Florida Marlin's game, and stand in front of my mirror poised and ready to swing.

I would hold my bat and I'd pretend it was the bottom of the ninth, World Series, Game 7, two outs. Everyday I visualized hitting home runs. Everyday I saw myself playing baseball in the majors. I was going to stand in that diamond and hit home runs alongside the greats, there was no doubt about it.

In high school though, I decided to be a rapper. It was obviously a great career choice for a little, skinny white kid. But, you know, I had big dreams and ambitions. This might sound strange, but at the time I was modeling my rapping career after, and trying to emulate the business model of, New Orleans rapper and record label head, Master P.

Master P, whose real name is Percy Miller, was a guy living in an innercity, a troubled area in New Orleans, Louisiana. At the time, it was the murder capital of the world. It was in this environment that Master P started his record label, No Limit Records. He took everyone from his neighborhood and essentially said to them, *"You are going to put out an album, and so is everyone on our block. We're all going to come out of this bad situation and get ourselves out of the hood. We're going to create lives for ourselves."*

I thought that was incredibly ambitious. Using this formula, *No Limit Records* released 23 albums in 2008, collectively selling millions of copies in the process.

Taking this model, I used a loophole in the senior program at my high school to start my own record label. During my senior year, I was released from school at noon everyday to start a senior project. It was during this time that I signed my first artist, myself, along with my best friend at the time. Late in our senior year, we released a self-funded, self-produced and self-published album, *Ballin On 82*, under the moniker of The Burglazz. The title paid homage to the street we were both born and raised on in South Florida. (The real ironic part of the story is my old friend is now a SWAT team member of a south Florida police unit.)

With my newfound ambitions to be a world famous rapper, I set the bar high for what I wanted to accomplish, much like playing in Game 7 of the World Series. Dreaming should never get smaller, only larger as you continue on in life.

In the early 2000's, the pinnacle of the music industry was being on featured on TRL, in Time Square, or getting interviewed by Carson Daly. That was the big dream and the big ambition. It gave me something to strive for, something to continually work toward. Having a big dream also helped me make decisions. I had to consciously decide whether the choices I was making were moving me closer or further away from my goal.

Now, sad to say, I wasn't able to get on TRL. However, I was able to perform at Madison Square Garden at the New York Music Festival back in 2003. Performing inside that iconic arena – walking down the same hallway where the Knicks walk in, where all the great players look to shine, and all the great musicians hope to get their names in bright lights – was incredible.

I got to walk onto that stage and perform a couple songs in front of fans, industry professionals and other artists as part of the festival. It was amazing. It was as cool as you could imagine and then some.

I always had ambitions to do something grander. I never wanted to just work at McDonalds. I wanted to own thirty McDonalds. I wanted to skip the lines and the red tape and get there as fast as I possibly could.

If you listen to mainstream media, you frequently hear stories about companies speaking about their Millennial employees and their ambition like it's a bad thing. You hear things like, *"He's worked here for two weeks and he thinks he owns this place."*

Why is this a bad thing? Why can't we look at this as a positive character trait versus a negative one? Why don't you want employees who want to take ownership in your company working for you? Why not encourage Millennials who want to help your company grow? Why not give them the tools, guidance, and nurturing required to help them grow and get into a position where they can run the company someday?

Not every young person has these ambitions. In fact, I see a big gap between the ambitious and the un-ambitious. I believe those with drive, motivation and ambition should be celebrated, and I'm not the only one. Every year, there are magazine covers that tout the "30 Under 30," or the "40 Under 40," lists. From *Inc. Magazine* to *Forbes* to *Fortune*, these young and ambitious leaders are being recognized, and they help to sell a lot of magazines. You see young guys like Zuckerberg, gracing magazine covers and mainstream media, who have rapidly amassed billions of dollars.

Then, on the other end of the spectrum, you have student loan debts that outnumber credit card debts in the United States. The student loan debt has grown to more than $1.2 trillion. How can you inspire a generation to be ambitious when they can't even afford the cost of living on their own? They can't afford food or gas.

These young adults are sitting in their parent's homes with the most expensive pieces of paper they've ever owned, and receiving none of the benefits their college education promised them. Since the age of twelve, they've been hearing from parents, grandparents, teachers, coaches, and everyone else willing to offer them opinions, that the key to a good life was working hard and getting a college degree. Yet, there they sit, disheartened that all the doors are still apparently locked before them. No job. No budding, prosperous career.

So, I ask again: How can these young people be inspired to become ambitious? The short answer: technology!

Someone with whom I've been able to spend a lot of time with recently, New York Times Best-Selling Author, Peter Diamandis, says that technology will be the X-factor in many aspects of the future. Technology is the force that will continue to give us abundance, because it allows us to do so many incredible things. Technology allows the millennial generation to have multiple passions. Millennials will not be defined by one thing.

My good friend, Best-Selling Author, and International Speaker, Pa Joof, talks a lot about the concept of identity. Gen X and Boomers typically self-identify by what they do, not who they are. You commonly hear them say, *"I'm a dentist. I'm a real estate agent. I'm a financial advisor. I'm a teacher."*

For Millenials: That is not who we are. That is what we do.

This young group doesn't identify themselves as being one thing. They have multiple interests and multiple things that define them.

When I look at myself, I do not just see a writer, marketer, or a business owner. I'm also a dad. I'm into fitness and being healthy, I'm a CrossFitter. I live in the music world, in the marketing world, in the nonprofit world, in the media world, and in the fashion world. I do adventure races. I like food. I like cooking. My job does not define who I am.

This young group doesn't define themselves solely by the actions they partake in at the office between the hours of nine to five, or any other hours or situations for that matter. These young kids are doing some really, really cool things. They're starting companies. They are creating unicorn companies – a term venture capitalists use to describe startups that are valued at more than $1billion.

For example, Evan Spiegel, the 25 year-old founder of SnapChat, has one of these unicorn companies. SnapChat is now worth billions. All Evan did was simply take advantage of the technology and communication trends of the young and ambitious.

Then you have an entire group that creates what I call the side hustle.

You have the guy working nine to five as an insurance adjuster. However, when he goes home, he's creating statues and comic book figures that he sells on Etsy. He's potentially making just as much money selling these little statues and figurines on Etsy as he is at his nine to five. He doesn't define himself by his nine to five. He has passions. He has outside interests. He's willing to pursue multiple options for income, and not afraid to think outside the standard box.

There's an entire industry emerging where young, stay-at-home moms have created second incomes for their family by blogging about the products that they use, and getting paid by the companies to do so. They write about what they do with their kids and the different products they use to help with the laundry, among other things. This ambitious group has gone from single income families to double income families with only one parent leaving the house out of thin air, and technology. It's incredible the opportunities they have created for themselves.

Then, you have things like Kickstarter. Literally all you need is an idea, and you can have the world fund it's creation before you ever have to manufacture a product. Now, young people can be encouraged to dream big, and then sell that dream and vision to others. They can test their ideas in the real world by having real people pony up the money with less personal risk to make it a reality. This can equate to raising millions of dollars without pitching investors, or giving up large sums of their company in equity shares.

There are young people climbing the corporate ladder faster than ever. Young people are not just at a desk in a newsroom, they are either becoming the newsroom or taking over the anchor positions themselves. These are people like Nicole Lapin, who was the youngest anchor ever at CNN and CNBC before leaving big media to publish her New York Times Best-Selling book, *Rich Bitch*. These are all really great examples of this generation making money, though, as we've already discussed, this group values so much more.

You have young people who are taking care of their bodies more than ever. There's a sport called CrossFit, and more than 209,000 people competed in the CrossFit Invitational in order to compete at the CrossFit Games. There are also wildly popular races and adventures that speak to Millennials. For example, the Spartan Race, an obstacle course race where you pay upwards of $100 to jump over and climb through barbed wire and hop over fences and cars. The Spartan Race alone had over 650,000 participants last year. This year they expect over 1 million people to participate in the Spartan Race, most of them under the age of 30.

You can't go from a nine to five with a side hustle, and multiple CrossFit classes each week, if you're not taking care of yourself. That extends to more than physical health too. These kids are trying to live healthy lives that feed who they are at their core. They want a full life, not just a full checking account.

Millennials are doing things differently on their vacations. They are going to see the world now! They are not waiting until their "golden years" to explore the vast cultures the world has to offer. They're not waiting until retirement to go take the two-week trip to Bali; they're going now while they still want to jump off cliffs or surf the world over. They're walking 10 miles a day seeing the sites, sleeping in hostels, and taking planes, trains, and automobiles all over the continent. They are running with the Bulls in Spain and Shark Diving in Scotland while it's still exciting and cool, they're not waiting until these things become reckless and foolhardy in their minds.

These young adults are forming groups like the Summit Series, a private mastermind group made up of some of the most impressive entrepreneurs in the world. The founders were in their mid-20s when they started the series that would allow them to connect and network with the likes of the Bill Clintons, the Steve Forbes', the Tim Ferriss', and the Arianna Huffingtons of the world. This whole movement started by inviting these types of people on ski trips. They said, "Hey, Bill Clinton, can I just take you on a ski trip?" He agreed. Five years later they bought a mountain right outside of Park City, Utah to hold these gatherings. In the process they have raised millions of dollars for charity. Instead of going on vacation, they own the vacation destination and have the best party guests you could imagine.

This is a generation of people who are looking for more out of life. They're looking for better. They want a career – they just might not want to define it in the same terms as their parents. They are taking care of themselves, physically and mentally. They are doing things that their grandparents never dreamed of as possible. They want to have families and to see the world. They want it all.

Quite frankly, the ambitious ones, the kids who believe in the power of their dreams and continue to create goals that get bigger and bigger, are going to have it. So, what does that mean to you, my Baby Boomers and Gen X's? Well, my challenge to you is to look at these young people in a different light. Do not write this group off. They need your mentoring and they need your guidance.

Whether you like it or not, they're going to be the leaders of this world quicker than you can imagine. They're going to be the bosses someday, whether you like it or not. We, the Millennials, are the ones who are going to take over and control this world.

Knowing this, over the past few months, my team and I have decided to give a new voice to this generation. We've created a brand new media network called The Ambitious Network at ambitious.com.

We're going to give young people a place where they can not only see other young people doing these things, but we are going to give them the path, the blueprint, and the resources they need to actually live these lives. When they want to go take that vacation they'll know where to go, how to book it, and what is out there to discover. They're going to know how to invest. They'll know how to go out and get that first mortgage. They'll know how to go out and find the ambitious careers that are available to them.

We're really trying to create a young generation that lives a life full of ambitions, not regrets. There are a lot of people who lie on their deathbed with regrets. But, the thing is, it's always the things they didn't do they regret way more than the things they actually did.

What I want to do is help that person who is sitting at home on a Friday night binge watching House of Cards on Netflix. I want to help that person get up off the couch and start living their life.

Ambitious.com will inspire that person to want to be Kevin Spacey, not just watch Kevin Spacey. That is what we're trying to do, and it's what I think will shrink the gap between the ambitious and the un-ambitious. It's my contribution toward a better future for my generation, a future filled with potential, dreams, and a life that's completely and utterly full.

[This article has been adapted from Greg Rollett's speech at the UN Headquarters as part of the Global Economic Initiative.]

About Greg

Greg Rollett, @gregrollett, is a Best-Selling Author and Marketing Expert who works with experts, authors and entrepreneurs all over the world. He utilizes the power of new media, direct response and personality-driven marketing to attract more clients and to create more freedom in the businesses and lives of his clients.

After creating a successful string of his own educational products and businesses, Greg began helping others in the production and marketing of their own products and services. He now helps his clients through two distinct companies, Celebrity Expert Marketing and the ProductPros.

Greg has written for *Mashable, Fast Company, Inc.com, the Huffington Post,* AOL, AMEX's Open Forum and others, and continues to share his message helping experts and entrepreneurs grow their business through marketing.

Greg's client list includes Michael Gerber, Brian Tracy, Tom Hopkins, Coca-Cola, Miller Lite and Warner Brothers, along with thousands of entrepreneurs and small-business owners across the world. Greg's work has been featured on FOX News, ABC, NBC, CBS, CNN, *USA Today, Inc Magazine, The Wall Street Journal,* the *Daily Buzz* and more.

Greg loves to challenge the current business environment that constrains people to working 12-hour days during the best portions of their lives. By teaching them to leverage marketing and the power of information, Greg loves to help others create freedom in their businesses that allow them to generate income, make the world a better place, and live a radically-ambitious lifestyle in the process.

A former touring musician, Greg is highly sought after as a speaker, who has spoken all over the world on the subjects of marketing and business building.

If you would like to learn more about Greg and how he can help your business, please contact him directly at: greg@dnagency.com or by calling his office at 877.897.4611.

CHAPTER 21

BELIEVE IN YOURSELF! 7 LIFE LESSONS LEARNED THE HARD WAY

BY ANNA NIKACHINA, PhD, MD

As a physician specializing in rehabilitation and pain management, I work with people facing tremendous difficulties. Some patients have recently survived a tragic event, such as a physical abuse, a major trauma, or a stroke. As a result, many of them suffer from chronic pain. Pain and depression come hand in hand, so more often than not my patients are overwhelmed and depressed. My department serves these patients in a multi-disciplinary approach, dealing

with the current medical condition, recovery, and mental state.

Often, when I try to help my patients who seem stuck in one of these difficult health situations, and corresponding difficult personal or financial situations, I hear back: "You are a doctor. What do you know about hard times to teach me there are no 'dead end' situations? What do you know about financial instability? How do you know how difficult it is to raise a child by yourself? Doctors have a perfect life, lots of money and ideal relationships. You have no idea what a real life is!"

This is when I usually smile and say, "Oh believe me, I know." Despite my reassurance, I can still see doubt in their eyes. After one too many of these conversations, I decided it was time to share my story, to share life lessons I learned the hard way in order to help others overcome their obstacles and build successful lives.

I was born in Russia and raised by wonderful parents. I had the ideal, happy childhood. I completed my early education, university, and then medical school without any problems. I graduated with honors. I got married young and by my early twenties I was raising two children, my seven-year-old step son and my newborn son. Despite the challenges of parenthood, I became an MD and PhD by the age of 26. I secured an academic position at a medical school and life seemed pretty much settled. Still, I knew it could be better...especially after I visited the United States. After that visit, my perspective on possible opportunities for my family, and myself, broadened.

The criminal and economic situation in Russia was worsening every day. Without a doubt, I felt (despite objections from some of my family) the best thing to do for my career and my family was to immigrate. I knew I *just had to go for it*! After doing some research, I quickly figured out that immigration to the United States is almost impossible unless you are a minority, a refugee, or have relatives already living in the county. None of this applied to my family. Immigration to Canada, on the other hand, seemed to be a realistic option and to some extent even more attractive because of the strong immigration support system. Surprisingly, the entire immigration process did not take long, only six months from the first step to my arrival in Toronto, Canada.

Upon arrival to Canada, I discovered I would have to go through a long, painful process to confirm my medical credentials. I was very fortunate to meet people who helped me understand the entire process. *I surrounded myself with positive people.* They gave me valuable tips, became my mentors and close friends. Within a year, I passed my United States Medical Licensing Examinations (USMLEs), and a few months later my Canadian licensing examinations. I completed a few months of clinical observership and began applying to residency programs.

While my professional life was doing well, my personal life began to unravel. Shortly after we moved to Canada, our family started to grow apart. I was making progress towards my goals to become a physician but my husband could not find himself living in either Canada or the U.S. He couldn't adjust culturally. He had to go back and forth between

Russia and Canada for business purposes, which just made it harder to adjust. Because of his work in Russia, he spent most of time there.

I basically became a single mother, taking care of two kids, house chores, studying, and working nights part-time in order to provide additional income. After I went through hell with all the stressful exams and doing everything around the house and for my family, my husband announced our family would be moving back to Russia.

I had to make a tough decision, as I could not see myself going back to Russia. After a few unsuccessful attempts to convince my husband to stay in Canada, we decided to separate so I could continue my medical career and he could return to Russia. He left quickly and left me financially devastated. The situation was far from optimal: no job, two kids, no money to feed them, no family to help, unpaid bills, and pending interviews for residency, which I could not even attend because I had no money for travel. It was all such bad timing, but I knew the decision to pursue my career was a *risk worth taking*.

I found a job at a beauty clinic. The money was barely enough to cover food and gas, and by no means would cover a mortgage, car insurance, or utility bills. I was having nightmares from constant collection calls and letters from creditors. I was driving without insurance, having palpitations every time I saw police cars. Pretty soon my house was without TV, Internet, phone, water, and electricity.

Thankfully it was still warm weather, and I was able to cook food for my kids on a grill outside. I picked up a second job and was basically working days and nights. I was even able to go for a couple of interviews, but did not get a residency position at that time. Eventually I found a smaller, more affordable house and started to pay off creditors. My personal life was starting to look up. I met someone new and began a relationship. Awhile later, we were excited to learn we were expecting a baby girl. Just when I thought that the crisis in my life was over, devastation struck.

On the day my daughter was due to be born, my 19-year-old stepson was tragically killed in a car accident. We were very close. The pain of his passing was unbearable. I delivered my baby girl the day after his funeral and all I can remember from that time is endless physical and emotional pain.

That was not the end of tragedies in my life. Within just a few months I lost my father, both grandmothers, and a great-aunt—all of whom were very close to me. At some point, the pain of losing the dearest to my heart people made me feel numb inside. But life was moving on. I still had two kids - a 12-year-old son and a newborn baby girl. I realized I had no choice but to *stay positive and persevere!* I pulled myself together and continued to work on my goals.

Finally, I was able to find a residency position in one of the busiest hospitals in New York City. Unfortunately, my second relationship did not work out and I was once again a single parent. I now had to make the transition from Canada to the U.S. by myself. I moved to a small apartment in the Bronx with my 18-month-old daughter and 13-year-old son. I had to find a school for him, babysitter for her, and did not have a single friend or family member in this new country. I had only a $1,000 in my account, no credit history to apply for a loan or credit card, never received a penny of child support, and only had an old car, which I brought from Canada without insurance. Despite these financial hardships, I was extremely excited because I realized that the residency was a major step towards my career goals and a brighter future. I knew that the *hard work would pay off* and I would eventually fulfill all my dreams.

Step by step, working long shifts as a resident, and working a second job to earn extra cash, all the while caring for my baby and my son as a single parent, I continued to maintain healthy habits. I didn't bother with excuses about not having enough time. I prepared healthy meals for my children and myself and exercised in whatever free time I found. Often, this was in the time between the end of my second job and the beginning of my first, between one and four in the morning.

My hard work did payoff. I graduated from residency and became a fully licensed physician. Now, however, I had to move from NYC to a "medically underserved area" in order to obtain status as permanent resident in the U.S. After growing up in a very large city in Russia, then living in Toronto and NYC, the transition to a small rural place was quite painful for me and my children. I once again decided to stay positive and hold faith that *if you believe, you shall receive.*

While my heart is in a big city, I have made the most of being in a small area. I considered the situation of working and living in a very small, rural town as a unique opportunity to grow personally, develop professionally, and build a network of professional connections. I became certified by two boards, Physical Medicine & Rehabilitation and Pain Management. I had an amazing clinical experience as the only Physical Medicine and Rehabilitation specialist in a radius of 200 miles, working as a Medical Director and managing very challenging cases. I was also able to spend more quality time with my children and developed a stronger connection with them while overcoming the difficulties of the transition together.

Despite the difficult move, we made it. I received my green card. I am now in the process of a new exciting step towards my career and personal goals…steps to a better overall future. Given all I've been through, I truly believe if you remain positive, plan each step of your life and work hard, anything is possible. I truly believe these seven lessons can help anyone reach their goals and dreams, despite any obstacles that may exist.

LESSON 1: JUST GO FOR IT!

If you truly believe there is a better future for you and your family, do not be afraid to leave your comfort zone. Just go for it! Create a plan. Know why you are doing it and do not listen to people in your life who offer discouraging comments dictated by their fears, doubts, and insecurities. The most important thing is to simply take the first step. Just go for it!

LESSON 2: SURROUND YOURSELF WITH POSITIVE PEOPLE!

Be prepared to deal with multiple challenges on your way to future success. No one promised it was going to be easy. Stay determined, be open-minded, and think big!

Do not be afraid to ask for help. Create a network of friends and positive people to help you achieve your goals. If you believe in yourself, others will as well. The right people will not only believe in you, but help you reach your goals.

LESSON 3: TAKE RISKS!

Do not be afraid to take risks on the way to YOUR success. Risks may create temporary difficulties but facing them is the right decision on the ultimate path to achieving your goals. Once you have made a decision - stick with it! Do not waver. Stick to one vision, one mission, and the road will become clear. If the road is truly worth traveling, it is worth taking risks.

LESSON 4: STAY POSITIVE AND PERSEVERE!

No matter how hard life hits you, stick to your values. Persevere. Remain positive. Stay strong. This is especially important when you are raising children. You are their role model. It is your job to show them how to respond to stressful situations in a constructive and positive way.

Do whatever it takes to keep it together and maintain a positive, presentable image. Breathe. Exercise. Meditate. Use your stress to reinforce healthy habits - not to create the unhealthy ones! Remember - no matter how bad your situation seems - there is always a way out and it is up to you to get there. Be who you want the world to see when you achieve your greatest success, not who you are during your lowest points.

LESSON 5: HARD WORK PAYS OFF!

It doesn't always seem clear, but the doors will open eventually. Never give up! You are the only one fighting for your success. No one knows what you are going through but you. The only way to make success happen is to take charge of your own life by working hard. Make it happen!

LESSON 6: SAVE YOUR EXCUSES!

We hear it all the time. There is not enough time for personal or professional growth, beauty routines, or exercises. It is simply untrue. There is time, if you plan carefully and multitask every way you can. For example, your mind is not occupied when you are doing household chores, so use this time efficiently. Wear wireless earphones and listen to audio programs, educational lectures, affirmations, motivational speakers, or even learn a new language. Do a few sets of push-ups or squats while cooking or cleaning. Instead of completing one task, by the time you've finished you will complete several. There is no such thing as lack of time, only lack of motivation and proper planning. Save your excuses!

LESSON 7: IF YOU BELIEVE, YOU SHALL RECEIVE!

Everything is possible as long as you believe in yourself. America is truly a country of endless opportunities. Many immigrants came to this country just like me, without money, relatives, or friends, without knowing the language or traditions. They made it to the top by simply being persistent and working hard. If you are not happy with who you are and where you are now, only you can change it. Create a vision of your ideal life, set goals, outline a detailed plan, and work tirelessly to complete the plan. If you believe in your vision, in yourself, you shall receive the greatest rewards of personal success.

About Anna

Anna Nikachina, MD, PhD is a physician specializing in rehabilitation and pain management. Dr. Anna is helping patients to manage acute and chronic pain associated with musculoskeletal and neurological conditions. She strongly believes in a power of mind-body connection and implements approaches oriented on treatment of the whole patient and not just separate symptoms, concentrating on restoring patients to their highest level of function and improving their quality of life.

Dr. Anna was born and raised in Siberia, Russia, in a large industrial and academic city, Novosibirsk. She earned her Bachelor's degree in Psychology from Novosibirsk State University. She graduated *Summa Cum Laude* from State Medical Institute, Novosibirsk, Russia. During those years she learned not only Western approaches, but also principles of Eastern Medicine. She received training and became certified in Acupuncture and micro acupuncture (Su Jok therapy). Dr. Anna became an MD and PhD in her early twenties. After completing a post-doctoral fellowship, she worked as an Assistant Professor of a Department of Integrative Medicine at Novosibirsk State Medical Institute.

She then immigrated to Toronto, Canada, where she confirmed her medical credentials allowing her to enter a residency program in NYC, NY. She finished one year of internship in General Surgery and then three years of residency in Physical Medicine and Rehabilitation in Montefiore Medical Center, Bronx, NY.

Dr. Anna is a Diplomate of American Board of Physical Medicine and Rehabilitation and a Diplomate of The American Board of Pain Medicine. After her residency training she worked as a Medical Director of an Acute Inpatient Rehabilitation Unit and outpatient Rehabilitation Services at The Aroostook Medical Center in Northern Maine, where she gained a unique experience building up a flourishing practice starting from zero, and being the first and the only physician in her specialty in a radius of almost 200 miles. In 2013, her Acute Rehabilitation Unit was ranked by Uniform Data System for Medical Rehabilitation (UDSMR) in the top 10 percent of nearly 800 rehabilitation facilities across the United States.

Dr. Anna is the proud mother of two wonderful children: son Igor, a very driven young gentleman who is now studying Business and Psychology at the University of Maine, and adorable daughter Katerina, a 3rd grade student, who enjoys dance and gymnastics and loves participating in beauty pageants.

In this book Dr. Anna shares her personal inspirational story of making the way to personal and professional success by overcoming obstacles in a series of unfortunate events—as an immigrant, a single mother and a foreign-trained medical doctor.

You can connect with Dr. Anna at:
- www.twitter.com/DrAnnaNikachina
- www.facebook.com/AnnaNikachina
- email: annanikachinamd@gmail.com

CHAPTER 22

"IT'S NOT OVER UNTIL I WIN!"
— How to Design your Profitable Business or Career That Supports Your Lifestyle, Honors Your Dreams and Desires, Unlocks Your Authentic Powers and Magnetic Image that Has Powerful Impact!!!

BY ASHA MANKOWSKA, MA, ESQ.

Today I want to inspire you to live your dream life that you design on your own terms. The life I am living now was always my dream. I was able to design my life and international business based on my true passions. Traveling, being a published author and speaking in many countries allow me to share my mission and message with many successful leaders and entrepreneurs, and help them design their powerful, magnetic branding and profitable business based on their dreams and higher purpose in life.

I hope sharing my story and some of my strategies will help and inspire you to get where you want to be.

Trust me, it doesn't take unattainable skills or genius. All the skills I will mention are LEARNABLE. I am just a regular person like you! I just had a deep faith that I can do anything I put my mind, heart and enough effort into.

I always had a passion for being fearless, unstoppable, and courageous.

I am passionate about designing life and business, based on honoring our true passions, desires and unlocking and reclaiming our powers, discovering our true voice, leading our life with HIGHER purpose, and true VALUES, and designing the magnetic, powerful branding, that will leave a lasting impressive impact and legacy by having a business that supports dreams and lifestyle.

I mentor my clients to release their passions, live their dreams, and begin a new chapter in their life by designing a meaningful, exciting business, and impact that is based solely on their true deepest values. That can include travel, time with family or anything else that makes them happy, so they can truly SHINE and have impactful lives.

HOW do we accomplish it? I use powerful formulas and business tools I developed over decades of study, personal and business development, and experience with my clients. Thanks to those proven formulas my clients experience breakthroughs, followed by immediate, massive, inspired action and implementation, and I hope you will too.

I always had a gift for recognizing people's strengths, callings, or as my clients like to call it: "their million-dollar value." I could see clearly what held them back. I could identify the gaps, fears or blind spots that they were simply unable to see by themselves. But even with all those skills I wasn't able to see my own blind spots. To uncover them I had to completely leave my comfort zone and challenge myself beyond anything I ever expected. It turned out to be the beginning of the life journey that I was destined to take.

HOME, COMFORTABLE HOME

Respecting my parent's wishes, I walked the traditional path. I got a solid education in law school and landed a good job as an attorney that I absolutely hated. Listen carefully, I will tell you something that you don't hear often. Yes, I am a born entrepreneur. But I won't feed your mind with the idea that I dropped out of high school, and I achieved phenomenal success thanks to my brilliance and hard work. I worked very, very hard for my education, and it was worth it!

At the age of 24, I had actually achieved everything I wanted. I was on the top of the world, I had an education from the best universities, with my additional MA degree in Journalism and PR, that I finished in secret, and I finally had the career of my dreams. I was published in several countries, had a successful business, parents and friends that loved me, success, money, happiness, significant achievements and a complete comfort zone.

What else I could possibly want? Why was I feeling that there was more waiting for me out there? Do you sometimes hear this little, irritating inner voice, nagging you? Well, I did. I found myself in a most dangerous place – content in my comfort zone. Change and growth starts outside of a comfort zone. When you stop growing, you stop living.

Something inside me believed that I was meant to do something special in my life and leave a legacy, even though at the moment this picture was completely blurry, and it looked like a million pieces of a puzzle.

I decided to try something completely new and discover who I am at a deeper level and continue to a higher level of success. Unexpectedly, I moved to America.

What is outside of Our Comfort Zone?
I've left behind everything I built and achieved and I've started from ground zero. I found myself in a completely different country, culture, language, legal system, and all by myself, without any support system and only enough money to last me for a month. I decided to take a leap of faith; I believed that failure was not an option. Not in my book. The future was about to challenge all my beliefs.

My life in the U.S started pretty rough, holding down three jobs, going to school full-time, and experiencing a new relationship.

One year after moving to the U.S., I broke off the relationship that was supposed to last the rest of my life. I had a job I hated. As an attorney, I was overworked and unappreciated, going to school full-time and working full-time. With my family so far away, I was completely alone. I felt like my life had completely ended.

Even though I felt like a complete failure, I still wasn't able to quit. I was too stubborn to do what perhaps a normal, rational person would do.

Facing this failure put me at another turning point in my life. I could take the easy way and go back home, or I could face my reality and stay. Again I had to start from ground zero, with wounded ego and without any guarantee that I would be successful. So far it didn't look too promising. But remember, I was stubborn beyond imagination and I couldn't JUST quit.

I discovered that there is one thing I wasn't scared of, that most people are: COMMITMENT. I always was and I remain fully committed to achieving success in anything I do.

Turn Struggle Into Strength

Sometimes we experience adversity and even hostility, people are trying to treat us poorly, wanting us to give up. Do you know the best way to silence your critics? Become very successful, significant and influential, with a powerful and respected Brand/Identity! Treat this as a time that you show what are you made of. The challenges can be different but the principles to overcome them are exactly the same.

Honor your struggles; they made us who we are today! The more you honor your hardship and yourself, the more powerful fuel they become to your strengths.

When facing hostility we can easily become frustrated and angry, and stay at this stage... many people do. How about turning your negative emotion into FUEL and source of motivation? You are the only one who can conquer your frustration, so don't give them control over you.

Muhammad Ali said in the face of adversity: "I am gonna show you how GREAT I AM..." Big influencers and achievers never followed the status quo and many times they rubbed others the wrong way. You don't have to be loved and liked by everybody. It takes courage to confront and challenge the status quo or others' fears and mindset, but people will respect that more. Be proud of where you are from; be brave, courageous, and controversial.

My decision to quit law after eleven years was very controversial. People thought that I was crazy. But becoming a business coach, author and keynote speaker, was the best decision of my life.

THE POWER OF A STRONG BRAND IN LIFE AND BUSINESS

Phase 1: Clarity

Whatever happened doesn't define you. You define yourself, create your reality and design your IMAGE, BRAND, and IDENTITY!

Do you want to enjoy the full impact of your life, recognition, significance, and financial freedom that you deserve? Then start creating yourself in a way, so you can have anything you always wanted. Discover your authentic gifts and superpowers. This is a foundation to transform and start from where you are RIGHT NOW. Fortune rewards the brave!

This is what makes YOU unique, influential and powerful. It makes your brand respected and authentic; people can relate to you, feel the integrity, get truly connected and fall in love with your brand. That's HOW in life and business you stand out above the crowd, and that's WHY people LOVE YOU and choose YOU over anybody else.

Phase One of creating your IMAGE/BRAND/IDENTITY is to GET CLARITY on:

- Your True Dreams, Desires and Passions

- Your Strengths, Gifts and Authentic Superpowers

- The Transformation You Provide for Others

- The Best Way to Design your Business that suits your Lifestyle

The One Law of Success

Why is it so important to identify and follow your true passions and dreams? When you are creating your life by honoring YOUR true desires then you never compromise your priorities and highest values. True success and happiness are just natural consequences of this fact.

I've realized that the life I was living wasn't my own. Sometimes we create endless goals or projects to try and accomplish so much, but in the end, we are still NOT fulfilled. Instead, I decided to set up higher standards based on MY values, dreams and passions!

I want to inspire you to DREAM BIG. Never let anyone convince you that your dreams are NOT realistic! The moment when I saw the tears of happiness in my parents' eyes was absolutely priceless and worth everything I went through. So don't let anyone feed your mind with his or her fear, and tell you that you can't afford something you want. You CAN'T afford NOT to follow your true passions. Discover your gifts and powers that make a difference in people's lives. Dare to be extraordinary and live an extraordinary life! If I can do it, you can too!

Impact of Your Powerful Story

My story, struggle and transformation made me survive and thrive!!! It allowed me to create my branding that is in alignment with my identity and became very appealing to many of my clients, because they could relate to my transformation from burned-out attorney to fulfilled business coach. Having this powerful branding resolves MOST difficult CHALLENGES. It allows my clients to connect with others with authenticity and integrity, and removes the struggle of VISIBILITY, MARKETING and SALES.

To design Your *Magnetic Branding* in life and business we identify:

1. Your POWERFUL STORY, an essential part of designing a strong BRANDING.

2. Your Mission Statement.

3. *A bulletproof promise* to Your Ideal Client/Romantic Partner.

4. Who is the Ideal Client/Ideal Partner, what are their needs, struggles and where they can be found.

5. What's Your WHY.

Phase 2: You are your Brand

Our Image or Brand has to mirror our true passions, values and powers. The next step is to recognize how you show up in the world?

Are you making the right impression that you want, so you can have the powerful impact you desire? Is your branding clearly communicated with the world: your clients, your employees, your boss, your friends, and your loved ones?

Elizabeth Talerman's definition is exactly what I want you to keep in mind: "... *for an individual, it starts with integrity, authenticity, a clear and consistent message, and a true understanding of what you do in the world that is of benefit to others. Whether we're talking about a massive*

Fortune 500 brand or an individual, it's all the same."

The impression of YOUR BRAND and how others can relate to it creates your IMPACT in the world, not the other way around!

If you want to know what kind of brand you have, you need to look at the RESULTS:

1. Do you have a relationship, business or career of your dreams?

2. Are you feeling truly appreciated and valued by your clients, boss, employees or significant other?

3. Do you create the exact amount of financial success, wealth and abundance that you want and deserve?

4. Do you know that you are happy with the place you are at right now, but you know that there's MORE out there for you?

SOME OF MY POWERFUL BUSINESS TOOLS

No. 1: Vulnerability is Sexy

My parents set this wonderful example for me: working hard, being tough and resilient. It means to honor my promises, keep my commitments, and show up even when I don't feel like it, or when it is "inconvenient."

There's the other side of this equation. We strong and successful people ARE there for others, but we don't want to accept help or refuse to ask for help. Since we are expected to always be strong, we don't want to appear or feel WEAK. This is our Achilles' heel. It might be quite CHALLENGING TO MANY OF YOU, but I am about to show you an even more powerful way to success.

In 2013, Brené Brown had an outstanding TedEX talk about *The Power of Vulnerability* that confirmed everything I deeply believe.

"In American culture," teaches Dr. Brown, "we associate vulnerability with emotions we want to avoid, such as fear, shame, and uncertainty. We too often lose sight of the fact that vulnerability is also the birthplace of joy, belonging, creativity, authenticity, and love." She dispels the cultural myth that vulnerability is weakness and reveals that it is, in truth, our most accurate measure of courage. The word "courage" comes from Latin *coraticum* - heart!!!

People value, respect and trust the most: integrity, authenticity and transparency. Being vulnerable is an attractive asset that allows you to be truly authentic, charismatic and captivating. Strengthen your courage muscle; voice out loud your opinions, emotions, hurt or pain. Have courage to be assertive, fight for your values, dreams, needs and desires. Don't be afraid that others might think that you are weak. THIS IS NOT A CURSE, IT'S A PRIVILEGE THAT WE WERE DENIED FOR TOO LONG. If you meet any criticism, it's from those that are living in fear that they are, in fact, human.

No. 2: Knowledge is Power

Education and a great support system give you an extra edge and advantage. I believe that a great, solid education and support are the key elements to a fast and phenomenal success. It prepares your brain for constant learning and challenges. It makes you CONFIDENT, knowledgeable, curious, and wanting to know more. It leaves you with the great habit of educating yourself, whenever and however you can. That's why the best leaders and athletes invest in coaching or mentoring. It helps them achieve success faster, strategically and easier.

No. 3: Be the Ideal Client/Partner You Want to Attract

We hear this a lot: "The world reflects back to us how much we value ourselves." When we respect and appreciate ourselves and others, people treat us with respect and appreciation.

When you are confident and strongly believe in yourself, you will have a certain aura about you that will demand reciprocity from others. When you start adding lots of value, people tend to stick around. Having this proven value that you are adding to the world will give you CREDIBILITY.

Some people think that their titles will define them. There's nothing more powerful then the experience that you provide for others and their testimonials about it. This creates your REPUTATION!

We need to be conscious of the fact that how we act gets mirrored right back to us. The people, partners, friends or clients that we attract might go through the same challenges or are dealing with the same issues that we do or did in the past. We attracted each other because our vibration was in alignment at some level. So if you are dealing with some challenges right now: perhaps your clients are not taking the action steps you are recommending, or you cannot get a clear "yes" from them, look at what you are doing yourself. Do you want to attract more decisive, nurturing, determined, positive, committed and successful people? Be one yourself.

CONCLUSION

There's obviously more to this that I would love to share with you. Achieving what we desire, our greatness, is a process. It takes commitment, perseverance and resilience through all those challenging situations, and good or bad moments. Be grateful for those trials, even if it sounds ridiculous right now, they will mold you into the person you need to become to achieve your dreams. We look up to those who seem tough and successful, but we really admire those who have the courage to do what most people think is not possible and thrive.

About Asha

Asha Mankowska, MA, Esq. is a fearless Business and High Performance Coach, Consultant, Trainer, Branding Expert, Author and International Motivational Speaker. She is a born entrepreneur, launching her first business at the age of 21 when she was in her second year of law school, successfully building three companies in Europe from the ground up. She knows for a fact how difficult and frustrating any type of transition can be. Asha teaches clients from around the world how to achieve a healthy balance in their professional and personal lives.

In addition to being a recognized journalist (MA degree in Journalism and PR), published in several European countries (including Poland, Germany and Sweden), and running very successful consulting and educational businesses, she was an attorney for the past eleven years. Asha is Founder of the "Speakers Bureau" for dynamic women entrepreneurs, the Radio Host of *Crush Fears with Asha* and host of the video podcast, *Interviews with Asha: How to grow your business*. Her book, *The Change 4: Manifest Your Greatness Today*, where she was a co-author, was published in April 2015 on four continents.

In addition, Asha is a Founder and creator of IMPACT IMPRESSION; powerful branding training for coaches, consultants, experts, entrepreneurs and business owners.

Asha Mankowska, Esq.
www.AshaMankowska.com
www.YourFavoriteBusinessCoach.com
www.yourfavorite-lifecoach.com
Asha_Mankowska@yahoo.com

Contact:
Facebook: https://www.facebook.com/AshaMankowskaTheBusinessCoach
LinkedIn: https://www.linkedin.com/profile/view?id=173194011&trk=nav_
responsive_tab_profile
Twitter: https://twitter.com/AshaMankowska
YouTube: https://www.youtube.com/user/YourFavLifeCoach

CHAPTER 23

SEVEN NUGGETS OF WISDOM
—On How To Transform Your Life from Average to a Rich And Famous Lifestyle. 100% Guaranteed.

BY JAYANT HUDAR

I always believed in Magic and that some people have magical powers to transform other peoples' lives. I believe this because I have been helped by such people all through my life.

In my quest to find magic in life, I accidentally kept stumbling upon somebody who had amazing magical secrets of health, wealth and just about everything. From then on, life has been an adventure. I learnt a few secrets of the ancient masters, which can almost immediately get you what you dream of—be it a Mercedes Benz car, a sea-facing apartment or Farm House Land. You name it and it manifests. The Law of Attraction works!! *You only have to know how to use the secrets properly.*

The problem in identifying these extraordinary people with such superpowers is that they look just like us. I am blessed to have met such life-transforming people who have ignited my mind and catapulted my thought-process from ground level to a higher space.

I will now share a few of the scientific ideas and wisdom-nuggets from wise men which took me to the next level in life and business in quantum leaps:

1. IDEAS - ONE GOOD IDEA CAN CHANGE YOUR LIFE.

A good idea has the power to transform life. It has changed my life positively time and again.

Ideas are the starting point of all fortune.
~ Napoleon Hill.

Books are the best place to find great ideas. They have made my life more meaningful, interesting and exciting. I attribute much of my success in life to the great books I studied and continue to read.

A person who won't read books, has no advantage over
the one who can't read.
~ Mark Twain.

The greatest gift my father gave me was the love for books. Very early on, he taught me to develop myself by reading self-help books and making books my guides. I remember a few of the good books he gifted me were, *How To Win Friends And Influence People* by Dale Carnegie, and *The Lazy Mans Way to Riches* by Joe Karbo. I feel everybody should read and study these two books.

You discover you have wings when you open a book.
~ Unknown

A good book or even a "quote" is a device that can ignite your imagination, motivate you to take action and inspire you to jump to the next level in life. I collect "quotes" that I like and stick them all over my place. I have been telling my kids since they were two years old, showing them my book shelf, that those books carry the secrets of wealth and happiness in life. My kids love reading and I feel blessed.

Suggested Action:

1. Prepare a list of 100 good books to read – buy them, study them, invest in yourself and develop yourself.

2. Teach your kids early on to read books and develop the passion to read.

3. Collect good quotes and keep them close and read them often.

An investment in knowledge pays the best interest.
~ Benjamin Franklin

Search for one good idea; decide on your goal today – one that will fire your imagination and motivate you to take action.

If you are not into reading books, seriously rethink and start today. You are losing too much and too many things to mention here. Reading books is a Super Highway to becoming Rich and Famous.

2. GOALS - LIVE ONE HUNDRED LIVES IN ONE

Life is a series of experiences - small and large. Why not experience everything that your mind desires? Who says you can only live one life? Don't limit your life experiences to only one.

Read the biographies of great people and you will live their lives'
experiences in the shortest time period.
~ Mahatma Gandhi

People live their whole life and write one autobiography. You can learn from their experiences in a few days. Read one hundred autobiographies of the 'Greats' and you would have literally lived one hundred lives and learned from them.

This idea fired my imagination. It made sense to me, I wanted to live more in my one life. Why limit my life and career to only one field? Just because I studied in one field did not mean I had to work in the same field for the whole of my life. I later got into multiple business lines. The pivotal point was, "Explore and reach your potential!" for which God gave you this life.

I made up my mind to experience as much as I could in this lifetime. I made a list of things I wanted to do and experience: to travel to at least a hundred countries, go bungee jumping, visit and swim at the Great Barrier Reef, visit the Eiffel Tower, the Taj Mahal, the Egyptian Pyramids and a long list of such experiences to feel like I was experiencing a hundred lives.

As of writing this article, I have travelled to twenty-six countries and still counting. Travelling the world can have a magical effect on your living experience. You have to get out of your comfort zone and see the grandeur of God's beautiful creation.

Life shrinks or expands in proportion to one's courage.
~ Anais Nin

Have you made your list of life goals?

Actionable:

1. Make a list of goals/dreams you wish to achieve, things to do and experience.

2. Plan detailed steps how you can achieve and do all this in one life.

What do you want to experience and what memories do you want to collect? Write it down and do what it takes to achieve it. The drive to ACHIEVE things with passion will somehow lead you towards greatness, and that in turn will make you Rich and Famous.

3. GO TO THE NO.1 EXPERT - LEARN FROM THE BEST IN THE FIELD

When my father had a heart attack, relatives and friends gave suggestions and advice on what to do. However, it is so difficult to know what's the best thing to do. There is always a question in the mind, is there something better than what I am doing? Am I missing something? I can't forget Dr. Arun Mehra's advice, a renowned heart surgeon himself. He said, go to the No. 1, topmost, renowned heart specialist available in India, because only then will you have peace of mind. Anything less than that will leave you guessing and anxious. We did as he said and it helped. It reduced my father's anxiety *and* ours too. This is so true for everything in life. If this can be applied to a situation of life and death, why not in our career and life?

Learning from the best and most successful in a particular field gives you a feeling of surety that nothing else can replace. Because you KNOW that nothing better is available. It actually FREES you.

I applied the same logic and searched and found the best-of-the-best authors and experts in business, marketing, management and consulting. I decided to read everything they wrote, and watched and listened to their audio/video seminars and courses. I travelled halfway around the globe many times to attend their seminars, to meet the experts in person and learn from them. A good coach shortens your learning curve and helps you to reach your goals very fast. The top experts have a fire in them. When you meet them in person, some of the fire rubs off on you.

Actionable:
1. Find the TOPMOST and the best-renowned experts in the field you are interested in, and buy their books and courses. Attend their seminars and workshops in person and new opportunities will magically open to you.

2. Find a way to talk to these Experts. Ask intelligent questions. Pick their brains and be prepared to pay their price to get the advice.

4. DO BUSINESS - DECIDE TO BE RICH – DO WHATEVER IT TAKES

If you are born poor it's not your mistake,
But if you die poor, it's your mistake.

~ Bill Gates

In his book, *Rich Dad Poor Dad,* Robert Kiyosaki says " when you are young, work to learn not to earn." He also goes on to say that most rich people did not become rich by earning a high salary, but by having a business. Hard work may not make you rich, but "leveraging" in business systems can. Along with specific domain expertise and knowledge, *your attitude will decide your altitude in life.*

Acquire Valuable Skills:

As Brian Tracy says, "Your greatest asset is your earning ability." Increase your earning ability by learning the required SKILLS to become rich. Find out what talents you are born with and build on those.

The Currency of Business is Words not Numbers.
~ Ted Nicolas

Words are the most important and the greatest asset humans have. Words can make you rich. Your choice of words while speaking or writing will decide how well you succeed in life. It's the "words" that will close your sales, fetch you an order or negotiate a better deal for you. In the list of skills to acquire, I would rate speaking skills along with copywriting skills on the top – copywriting so that you can study the language which sells or convinces. Study NLP (Neuro-Linguistic Programming) and use it in every sphere of your life, relations and business and you will see a huge impact in your life. It's a secret not many people take seriously. However, you should.

Align your Life purpose with your Business or Job:

I aligned my business to my life's dreams and goals. A normal business requires your presence in the office regularly, I shifted to online and Internet-based businesses in such a way that I could work from anywhere. This made it possible for me to travel and see the world. I stopped doing the things that got in the way of my life's goals. My business and my life's goals are aligned.

Actionable:

1. Acquire the additional skills required to add value to yourself and your business.

2. Improve your earning ability by investing in yourself.

5. OVERCOME LIFE AND BUSINESS HURDLES – BUILD A MENTAL EDGE

Fortunes come and fortunes go. You are only really financially self-sufficient if you can make it again from scratch. The self-confidence that can come from knowing you can repeat your success gives you a terrific mental edge.
~ Bradley S. Jacobs

In life, sometimes plans do not pan out the way you intended. Situations may change for the worse. It happened to me 2004. In an attempt to expand the business I had nurtured and grown, we attempted a joint venture and merged with a bigger company. The idea was that the bigger company was going in for public issue and would get listed on the stock market, thus giving us the leap we wanted. It didn't work out as planned, and I lost my baby - my business - along with the brand name. We lost good people and a huge amount of money and goodwill. So many years of hard work went into somebody else's lap . . . leaving me high and dry.

My family was a constant source of motivation and support for me, which inspired me to start again from scratch, a business based on my previous experience. I started a Business Growth Consulting company called "School of Business Wisdom" and made it back. It was not an easy task. However, now I know what to do to start again from scratch and I use that knowledge to teach others too.

This experience of losing almost everything after almost fourteen years in business and then starting all over again - the thought that I can do it again from ground zero - gave me the mental edge and tremendous confidence.

Actionable:

1. Keep in mind that, like the weather, times and technology can put you out of business. Build your mental edge by developing new skills for which people will pay.

2. Never lose your hope and keep fighting. Persevere to grow in life.

6. PRODUCT AND SERVICE – BUILD A PRODUCT OF QUALITY WHICH YOU CAN SELL EVEN TO YOUR MOM

If you want to be rich, you have to do some business. The biggest leverage in your life is your business. And marketing is the leverage of your business. If you learn to do this properly, you can transform your business, and in turn, your life and lifestyle.

I learnt the concept from Jay Abraham of "being the best advisor or Fiduciary to your customer" and to "build a product or service which you can sell to your own mom." Your offerings have to be good. Once you take this "MOM" angle, you will never go wrong.

Make it risk-free for others to do business with you:

In this concept of "Risk reversal," you take away all the risk from the customers' side and make it easy for your customers to do business with you. Offering customers a risk-free money-back guarantee with your product or service makes it easier to sell and also keeps your customers happy.

At the same time, see that you avoid energy drainers in your life. These are people who sap your energy and pull you down. They are not happy with anything you do. Identify them in your life and stay away. Life is too short to waste time with such people In your business and life, select people who you like and who you would like to work with. Select star performers, they will make profits for you and add value to your life.

Money has the power to transform lives. Build a "system" to earn money as fast as possible.

7. MOST RIDICULOUS AND "THE GREATEST MONEY-MAKING SECRET IN HISTORY!"

This book by Joe Vitali had great impact on me and my whole business. In this book, Joe and many other authors share the concept of "Giving away Money" to make money. I call it a ridiculous way to make money. I tried it and it worked.

I used the same concept in various forms and it worked without fail. I made lots of friends by giving away things. I gave books away; I received more books. I gave away money and I received money from somewhere else – much more in quantity. You should try it.

I have found that appreciating what you have and having gratitude towards life is the easiest way to attain happiness. Prosperity in life is easy to come by when you and your family are at peace spiritually, when you learn to be happy with what you do with passion and gratitude, and you give away what you desire—the universe gives it back to you ten times over. Just try it, you will be amazed!

Actionable:

1. Start giving away money with gratitude and a happy mind.

2. Learn to appreciate what you have and feel the gratitude.

Live a life of action, excitement and make a difference in others' lives. When you help make a difference in enough people around you, you are bound to become famous. *Money follows fame.* Make a good name for yourself.

All the best! Have a Wonderful Life !

About Jayant

Founder and CEO of the "School of Business Wisdom," Jayant Hudar is a Business Growth Consultant and a Seminar Speaker. He is known for his practical advice to business owners to transform their "not-so-profitable business" into profitable ventures in a short span of time using "Marketing without Money" techniques. His Seminars and workshops have helped thousands all over the world.

Jayant has also co-authored a book, *The Prosperity Factor,* with Best-Selling Author Joe Vitale, famous for the movie, *The Secret.* Jayant has been a student of the topmost names in the business and marketing world including Jay Abraham, Scott Hallman, Chet Holmes, Mark Victor Hansen, Martin Howey and Brian Tracy.

Jayant was featured in the Top 25 Business Consultants in India and USA in *Siliconindia* Magazine, and in the Top 20 Consultants in *Consultants Review* Magazine in 2014.

Jayant is a serial entrepreneur and he started his career in 1992 after graduating in Engineering and then went on to do his Postgraduate Diploma in Business Management. Since then, he has owned fourteen different businesses, including Information Technology, Restaurants, Power Generation, Education and Training, Sales and Services and Brand and Reputation Management amongst others. He is part of the TopLine Business Solutions consulting network in more than 56 countries.

Jayant has been interviewed numerous times on national television as well as on local TV and radio channels for Internet Marketing and Business Growth Consulting. Many of his interviews are on YouTube – giving away lots of ideas to small business owners.

Jayant also works as a Virtual Marketing Director for his clients, working with a limited number at a time. They get his international business expertise at a much lower cost to their companies. He is an Internet Marketing Specialist – which makes him a special combination of an offline and online business expert. His Guerilla Techniques of Marketing and Promotions have doubled or tripled his clients' business turnover in a very short time. Some have made phenomenal growth of 100 times or more within three years.

Jayant now consults with celebrities and high-profile individuals as an Advisor where confidentiality and privacy are most important.

Jayant Hudar lives in Navi Mumbai, India with his family.

You can reach him at:
Mobile: +91-9321812220
WhatsApp: +91-9322812220
email: jayanthudar@gmail.com or info@schoolofbusinesswisdom.com
Websites : www.jayanthudar.com
www.SchoolofBusinessWisdom.com

CHAPTER 24

THE REAL REASON THE SUCCESS YOU DESERVE IS ELUDING YOU

BY JOHN HINE

- Is there an area of your life you feel is stuck?

- Do you have a feeling that you are intended for something greater?

- Have you tried, but never seem to get what you want?

- You've taken massive action, said affirmations till the cows come home and visualised them till you're cross-eyed, and nothing seems to work?

Don't worry you are not alone; it's not your fault! It is reckoned that 97% of all people who use these sorts of techniques alone do not get the results they had hoped for. The 3% are the lucky naturals who would have probably succeeded anyway.

So what do the rest of us have to do?

Well, I am about to show you, in a relatively few, simple steps. If you put what I'm about to teach you into action, success will follow. It might take you time, depending on how big your goal is. However, by putting the work in, you should achieve all of your goals.

Can I guarantee this? No, I can only do that with my clients who guarantee to put our plan into action. As I can't look over your shoulder, *only you can do that* by consistently following through with each one of the steps.

Overview

You know you can do better – you're smart and intelligent, everyone says so. But, that being the case, why is it sometimes you find it difficult reaching your goals? In some areas of your life everything seems to flow, but in other areas that you really want to expand, not so much.

So, what is holding you back? Why do some things work so easily and others seem impossible to achieve? If you've been goal setting, taking action steps, saying affirmations night and day, visualising and it's still not worked, then the problem is in your subconscious mind.

Taking massive action, visualising and saying affirmations is under the control of the conscious mind, and your willpower. However, the real power lies in the unseen, in your own subconscious mind. This is the powerhouse that has helped you to achieve all the things you wanted to. Unfortunately, it's also stopping you from achieving the other things too. It is not that it is wilfully working against you; it's just that the blueprint in your subconscious is stopping it from working.

Every time people try to move forward towards their heartfelt goals, something stops it from happening. That something is a piece of bad programming in their subconscious blueprint.

So where did this faulty programming come from?

Limiting Beliefs

From the moment we are born, up to approximately six years old, the subconscious mind was completely open. Our little mind was like a sponge, absorbing everything around it. Our brain was generating theta waves, which made us very suggestible. At that age we are completely dependent upon everything around us. Powerful figures, like our family, their friends, neighbours and the environment left a deep impression. They didn't do it deliberately, they were just not aware that we were taking in everything they said, and did, literally.

Those offhand comments were taken literally by us, and the constant worrying about money, security and relationships, left a deep impression. This formed the blueprint that your subconscious mind has been operating on for all these years, as seen through the eyes of a little child. Does it reflect reality? Of course not! We are no longer three years old, but these are the limitations our subconscious has been operating under. This is why people don't achieve some of their goals; our blueprint won't let us.

THE THREE LEVELS OF CONSCIOUSNESS

I. The Conscious mind - simply sorts and is a form of pattern recognition. It's that bit of us we call us, but in reality it's only the bit that makes us aware of who we are. At any given time, masses of information are flowing up from our subconscious minds, allowing us to do, and not do, certain things. For the most part, we are totally unaware of this going on as it's happening so fast.

An Unfair match:

It is reckoned the conscious mind is capable of handling seven pieces of information a second. On the other hand, the subconscious is estimated to be able to handle, literally, billions of pieces of information each and every second. Therefore, if we are going to make changes, it has to be on a subconscious level. The conscious mind's job is to set up tasks and problems for the massive power of the subconscious to solve. Unfortunately, we have all fallen into the habit of trying to solve these problems consciously, and quite often, fail miserably to do so.

II. The Subconscious mind - the subconscious mind has been described as a giant three-year-old who takes everything on a literal level. When you have something which is billions of times more powerful than your conscious mind, but that doesn't rationalise, care has to be taken in our communication with it. It can either be an immensely powerful friend, or your worst enemy. When you've done anything successfully, it is your subconscious that has helped you to do it.

All those exams you passed at school and university were with the co-operation of your subconscious mind. It is true that you consciously thought about the problems set in your exam papers, but it was the subconscious that pulled all the information together and presented it to the conscious awareness.

The subconscious remembers everything that has ever happened, including all those negative things from your impressionable childhood. If we want to make a really important change, it's going to have to affect the blueprint in your subconscious mind.

III. The Superconscious mind – operates through the subconscious. The word 'subconscious' simply means we are not aware of all the actions it has taken. There is also an element within you called the Super Conscious Mind, this is where all your aspirations, dreams and lifetime desires come from. It is that still, small voice within that comes in dreams, flashes of inspiration or heartfelt desires. It is literally that genius part of you.

The superconscious mind causes you to aspire to something, the conscious mind becomes aware of it and the subconscious makes it happen.

Thought-Feeling-Action

This is the process we all use to do anything in life, whether you want it or not.

Something happens around you, a thought comes up from the subconscious and we experience a feeling and behave in a certain way. If we are to change anything, it has to be in one of these three areas. We will have to change the thought, our reaction to that thought, or the way we behave, once we have it.

(a) **Thoughts** - in the end a thought is just a thought, it has no reality of its own. We can choose to ignore it if we do not like it. However, so many of us feel compelled to do something about it, because it came into our heads.

(b) **Feeling** - this is where our subconscious blueprint comes in. When the thought passes through our subconscious blueprint, it is decided how we are going to react. By changing our feeling associated with that thought, it causes us to act in a different way that leads to success.

(c) **Actions** - simply by taking continual action won't guarantee success for 97% of the population because of the limiting beliefs in our subconscious blueprint. There is nothing wrong in taking massive action once you have changed that limiting belief in your subconscious mind.

So, how would I achieve this change with a client? We would construct a plan together to reach the goal in life, or business. I would then use a powerful tool, such as PSTEC, hypnotherapy or NLP, to break the unconscious link between Thought-Feeling and Action, in addition to what I am about to teach to you below.

If you do what you've always done, you will end up with what you have.

It is a very trite thing to say, but it's also very true. So let us find a different, more effective way of doing things. Now it's time to give you a real solution that will work 100% of the time, if you apply yourself.

THE SOLUTION

Whenever we have a goal, or heartfelt desire, that we can't seem to achieve, it causes a reaction. As we have already discovered, our first thought is to struggle and try to make it happen. But, unless we change our limiting belief, and its blueprint, it will only end in frustration.

Your subconscious is ultimately trying to protect you – by stopping you doing what you want to do. Unfortunately, you are no longer three years old and needing protection! The simplest way forward is to make a plan of action of how to achieve your goal, and take small steps towards reaching it.

1. Make a plan.
Make a realistic plan of how you're going to reach your end goal.

Break that plan up into daily, weekly, monthly or yearly steps.

By taking little steps each day causes no negative reaction from your limiting beliefs and the subconscious let's it happen. This is simply because it doesn't appear to be going against your blueprint. However, by taking tiny steps slowly, but surely, this changes the blueprint and allows you to achieve your heartfelt goals. It sounds too simple, but it works. At the end of each week's successful steps, have a small celebration to imprint that success in your subconscious.

It doesn't have to be lavish, just give yourself a small treat that sends a message to your subconscious, that you are going in the right direction. If you do this each week it will begin to have a deep impression on changing your life's blueprint for the better.

2. Being present (mindfulness)

Remember earlier on we talked about thought-feeling-action? By being totally present, and conscious, throughout your day, you can stop those negative thoughts from having their effect. When a negative thought comes up simply look at it and say,

"I choose not to react to it."

. . . and replace that thought with another one, which is more positive and agreeable.

It will then dissolve away the negative thought. It will probably return later on, but you will simply do the same thing all over again. Fairly rapidly that thought will cease to appear and no longer have the effect on how you feel. You have then broken the chain, the thoughts and feelings, which have kept you from achieving the life of your dreams, simply by being aware of what's going on in your head. Up until now, thoughts have been streaming into your head so fast and you have been reacting to the feelings, without being even conscious of them.

3. Aspire, visualise, choose to be great and ACT

There is nothing wrong with visualising the end result you wish to achieve, just so long as you put it into action. Simply visualising and saying affirmations will likely not allow you to achieve the goal you so much desire, without a physical action.

Professional sportsmen/women, performers, great achievers in life and business, all visualise in some form or other. Last thing at night, before going to sleep, and first thing in the morning upon waking, visualise the end result you want to achieve. Feel yourself in the situation being successful. Actually feeling what it is like in that instance, and achieving your goal. Do not try and force yourself to make this happen while you do it. That part of it will be done as you begin your day and start taking action. By choosing what thoughts you react to, creates your greatest future. You are no longer the puppet of negative past programming, but the master of your own future.

Expect the best and know that you can conquer any obstacle.

You have a choice – what's it to be?

About John

John Hine is a Life and Business Strategist who is passionate about people and works closely with professional high performance business owners who want to grow their businesses and improve the quality of their lives. John has a long-standing career in the arena of professional martial arts, business and personal development. Through his 1-to-1 coaching, classes, workshops and presentations, he has impacted in excess of 120,000 people to live more successful and happier lives.

Through working with John, his clients learn how to not only *significantly increase their income*, but also develop a *powerful success mindset* required to achieve their dreams and goals.

As founder of 4 Steps to Success (johnhine.net), John creates simple-to-use programs for high performance entrepreneurs, runs seminars and workshops, 1-to-1 consulting and presentations.

John Hine's agent recently acquired a publishing deal with CelebrityPress® to co-author a book with world famous Personal Development guru, Brian Tracy.

John is also an author of two books, five eBooks, and his psychology and health-based coaching articles have been published in over 30 national and international publications. These include *Psychologies, Start your Own Business, Winning Edge, Business Now, Better Business magazine, Making money, European CEO, Health & Fitness* and many more.

John has also taught leading politicians in the Houses of Parliament in London "Mindfulness in Movement."

John's ability, training and background has enabled him to learn, not just about himself, but also about life and how to survive and thrive. Using his extensive training not only in High Performance Business, Life Coaching, Hypnotherapy, NLP and Mindfulness, but also Martial Arts and Tai Chi, he manages to bring humanity, practicality and integrity to his people-centred solutions coaching.

John has the ability to simplify and reduce problems down to their component parts. He fuses together both his formal training and personal experiences to bring clarity and understanding to those he helps. He has spent much of his life studying Tai Chi and Chinese Martial Arts under several masters and experts. John is a Tai Chi and Martial Arts Practitioner and runs a network of schools and academies.

For more information on John, visit:
www.johnhine.net

CHAPTER 25

REVERSE ENGINEER YOUR GOALS – A SIMPLE PROCESS

BY JOSHUA DUBIN

It is the set of the sails, not the direction of the wind, that determines which way we will go.
~ Jim Rohn

We are bombarded with countless stimuli competing for our attention. This exposure overload is changing the way we think, keeping us distracted and weakening our attention spans. The world has always had distractions, but it's become harder now to focus single-mindedly with enough concentration to achieve our most important goals.

A detrimental side effect of "multi-tasking" is the lack of effectiveness and timeliness in completing activities. Studies have shown multi-tasking does not exist. Whenever alternating between two tasks, what we are actually doing is switch tasking. When switch tasking takes place, there is a loss of momentum and a portion of time wasted in transition. It is a common occurrence for us to "multi-task" and believe we are maximizing time. This is an epidemic taking over the experience of our lives. By looking around any restaurant, you will find couples out to dinner, both fully engaged in their phones. Unfortunately, we are losing an enjoyment of living in the present.

Most of us can't help but notice what is brightest and loudest, but each of us can condition ourselves to focus on interests and actions more relevant to our goals. People sabotage themselves for a slew of different

243

reasons. This sometimes includes distractions that seem urgent, requiring immediate attention. There's a common tendency to confuse urgent with important. A ringing telephone might feel urgent, but isn't necessarily important. Many distractions are just tasks more aligned with our current comfort zones than the challenge at hand. Fortunately, focusing improves with practice.

It's also pretty common for people to procrastinate. This can even seem productive. Imagine the plight of a new telemarketer hired to make cold calls for a product known to have a low success rate. Maybe he knows this. He might even expect some of the people he calls to yell at him. Can you imagine how many distractions he might develop before making his first call? He might check his email, study his script, sort his database, verify lead information, and sharpen his pencil... Just about anything else that doesn't involve dialing numbers and speaking to a live person. Our friend, the telemarketer, might tell himself he just wants to be ready, to have everything set up perfectly. He's lying. His fear of the unknown is more uncomfortable than his drive for success. He's using perfectionism to procrastinate. No doubt, he would be more successful if he changed his narrative.

There is a correlation between our perspective and getting results. How we define things matters greatly. Two people can have the same experience and perceive completely different accounts of the event. This impacts their actions moving forward. When encountering situations that don't immediately align with your expectations, use questions to shape your account into an empowering one. Here are some great ones:

- *What could I learn from this?*

- *What might I have done differently to achieve a different outcome?*

- *What opportunities do these present that wouldn't otherwise be possible?*

It is amazing! When you use questions to direct your mind's focus, you gain a level of control over everything taking place around you by how you choose to react to it.

ACTION-ALIGNMENT-ENVISION

Our minds only consciously take in approximately 0.00005% of what's happening around us, deleting everything else not deemed relevant. Information only becomes relevant to us in two ways: proactively or reactively. Most people live in a reactive state. Attention is given mostly just when a situation demands it, and then bounces along to the next thing to focus on. Focusing on what is easiest or most comfortable produces mediocre outcomes.

Alternatively, by taking a proactive approach identifying and focusing on our actual goals, we improve our recognition of information relevant to achieving them. Our minds can better decipher between relevant and irrelevant information around us. Being proactive helps you reach your goals.

What we choose to focus our conscious attention on shapes into perception of the world around us. By setting aside a few minutes in the morning and before bed for introspective thought, you become clearer about what you ultimately desire and how to get it.

The first step is to identify your long-term goal and create an alignment with your actions. This a fancy way of saying, figure out what your ideal life looks like. Consider where your values, interests and abilities intersect. What kind of people do you want to surround yourself with? What kind of work stimulates you? What are some ways you take care of yourself, to manage your stress? Consider all the pieces of the puzzle and some first steps to move you forward. Consider what daily routines might help you to further align with your vision.

It might also help to come up with what you don't want first, and by knowing that, consider what the opposite might be. One thing that doesn't work is choosing something just because someone else wants it. Meaning is different for everyone, so it won't be as motivating to just borrow your buddy's. Imagine different kinds of lives you might live. Envision the clearest picture you can for what you want. Nothing is set in stone and you might choose to someday do something different, but the resources you'll gather for this first goal will likely be the bridge to whatever next goal follows, so it helps to be going in the right direction.

SOLUTIONS

You may also benefit from finding someone a few decades older with experience doing what you're considering. Ask lots of questions.

- *What's most important to you today?*

- *What advice would you offer yourself (X) years ago?*

- *What would you have done differently, knowing what you know now?*

These are just a few questions to get started, but older people can offer incredible insight into what we might expect to experience. By knowing what to expect at different stages of our lives, we can best prepare, and fully enjoy, ourselves.

Once you have identified your vision, break it down into manageable pieces. The big picture can be overwhelming, or make you resent the details. Check in on it now and then, but mostly keep focusing on each next smallest step. Keep moving forward.

Write down in detail exactly what you intend for your long-term goal. Start at the end, work back to the middle, and then to the beginning. An easy to understand example of this is when you take a road trip. You begin by figuring out exactly where you are traveling to ultimately. Next, you calculate what route you are planning to use. Then, you begin your trip. You are unable to see all the way from your starting point to your destination, or the majority of your route. But as you start down your route the next portion becomes visible, then the next, and so on until reaching your destination.

You do need detailed directions, or you'll end up in a different place than you intended. For the middle, write out a sequence of events that need to occur to reach your long-term goal. When breaking down my 12-month plan, I break actions down into 3-month segments. It's much easier sprinting micro-races than running a marathon. It also allows for closer monitoring to determine what's working and adjust as necessary. With each three-month plan, work backwards from weeks, to days, to hours until each step becomes obvious.

This next step is extremely important and will make the difference in following through to your goal, or lasting only a few days before falling into old habits.

Establish daily routines and disciplines, and then surrender to them! Release your actions up to choice.

When we don't have a clear outline of specific actions, we tend to stray and develop distractions. People are creatures of habit. Intentional routines help lock in productive habits, whereas unintentional routines leave actions to chance. Create routines that increase your odds for your desired outcomes. Develop daily routines you can ultimately use long term.

As you are getting into a rhythm with your routines, pay attention to what is working and identify areas for potential improvement. Initially, to ensure you are operating as closely to your outlined routine as possible, it is imperative to measure your progress. To do this, rate yourself using a scale of 0 to 10. Place these ratings beside each task on your daily calendar. Yes, you should have a daily calendar. Base your overall ratings on focus, effort, effectiveness and results. When analyzing results, make sure the results are measurable and your desired results are defined. This reduces opportunity for inaccurate interpretation or justification. In weekly planning, it is good practice to schedule time at the end of the week for evaluation of your numbers, to identify areas for improvement and to make adjustments as needed. With the exception of tweaking your daily routine to improve optimization and effectiveness, now it's as simple as just sticking to your plan.

As you cultivate your long term vision, you will have times when you experience easy wins and feel everything is synergistically flowing, as well as times that are perhaps more difficult. It's all part of the process. The trick is to fall in love with the process, not the event.

Let's use Hollywood as an example. Many people grow up loving movies and idolizing the glamorous lifestyles successful stars enjoy. This leads droves of people to decide they want to become movie stars and move out to Hollywood – with high hopes of becoming the next big hit and celebrating success. The actors infatuated with the event of being a big star invariably give up when they don't land the leading role in the first or tenth movie they audition for. The actors most likely to succeed have a passion for learning the script, taking on the role of the character and auditioning - win or lose. Passion for their craft increasingly takes shape in the form of talent, and then opportunity shows up.

One of the best ways to ensure accomplishing your long-term vision is to surround yourself with others operating at a level beyond your current one. When first getting started investing in real estate, I thought I was very knowledgeable until I attended an investment club with members who had been buying and selling homes for 40 plus years. It opens your eyes to what's possible and raises your standards. It also allows you to see what works and model that behavior until you get similar results. You have others to provide guidance and keep you accountable when the going gets tough. Selecting micro mentors who excel in an area in which you wish to improve is an excellent strategy for self-improvement.

Most of us can't help but do it a little, but as much as possible, avoid comparing yourself to those around you. Everyone's path is different, with different trade offs and trajectories. Compete only with yourself, to be better than you were. Learn from others people's successes, but avoid envying them. Constantly comparing only leads to discontent. It is best to visualize your goals and steadfastly stay on your path to a successful completion.

About Josh

Joshua Dubin is among the top Realtors and investing minds in the nation. He relocated to Central Florida in 2001 to attend the University of Central Florida and in 2005 graduated with a degree in Business Entrepreneurship. Since then, he has founded a real estate investment business, as well as a residential real estate sales team that operates in the Central Florida area. Throughout his career he has worked with hundreds of homeowners, investors, and prospective investors to accomplish their real estate goals. Being introduced to the opportunity real estate presents in 2003 at the age of twenty, he attributes his vast knowledge to being fortunate enough to experience significantly different stages of the housing market cycle.

Today, Joshua manages a multi-million-dollar residential portfolio and is actively acquiring investment properties which produce high-yield returns on cash. By recognizing a fundamental flaw in the standard approach to retirement planning that exclusively focuses on building a large nest egg, his strategy focuses on developing channels of passive income through housing. Additionally, he actively rehabs and flips properties to build down payments for long-term investments opportunities.

In his free time, Joshua enjoys spending time with his two amazing daughters, Kailey and Brielle, and his wife Lauren.

Joshua Dubin
Joshua@retireoffcashflow.com

CHAPTER 26

BE FIT FINANCIALLY TO IGNITE YOUR LIFE
—Whether you have $1,000 or $1,000,000 this works for you!

BY MICHELE NAMI-VON HOVEN, RFC®

We Are Made For Happiness.
~ The Dali Lama

Yes, we are made for happiness, those words will forever ring inside my head as I had the privilege to see the Dali Lama speak at Tulane University's Commencement in New Orleans in 2013. One of the most universal issues people have is money. **So why are many people stressed about money?** My theory is that you must take control of your money, don't let it control you. Have you ever stopped to consider how much money people make over the course of a working career? You may not realize it, but you could receive a fortune during your lifetime from earned income alone. Why is it that most people aren't financially independent? Because they fail to plan. Simply stated, there are only two real sources of income: people at work and money at work. Where you will be next year or ten years from now will depend on the decisions that you make today – or the ones you don't make.

When I was young, my mother had investments with a local brokerage firm, I would see mailings come to the house with a big lion on the envelope and that caught my eye. I asked mother what was in the envelope and she said it was reports on her investments in mutual funds. Mother also told me that our Uncle Jimmy owned stocks in companies, and he was able to live off of the dividends from those stocks. This idea intrigued me. Mother didn't have a lot of money, but she knew how to budget and stretch a dollar. Mother was a *"firm believer in investing."*

One day I was in my neighborhood drug store and perusing the magazines and newspapers and saw the *Wall Street Journal*, I was twelve years old and picked up the Journal and started reading through the Journal. Although I had no idea what I was reading, especially all the lists of companies and their financial information, I was captivated that you could own pieces of a company and make money at the same time. *And that is when I was first bit by the financial world bug!* At age 18, I opened my first investment account with Howard, Weil, Labouisse & Friedrichs in New Orleans, I invested $500 in a mutual fund.

My journey in financial services began in 1986. With an already successful tax and accounting practice and Civil Law Notary, I then expanded as a Registered Financial Consultant holding Securities Licenses; Series 7, 63, 65, 26, 6, Investment Advisor, Life, Health insurance and real estate licenses . These experiences make me a unique advisor in the areas of Tax, Retirement, Investment & Estate Planning.

IGNITE YOUR LIFE'S FINANCIAL GOALS AND DESIRES

I want to share with you my passion and expertise, so that you can benefit by living out your financial goals and desires and ignite your life by being fit financially. I have written the book, *Be Fit Financially To Ignite Your Life - Seven Steps to Financial Success for Life.* My goal is to help you reach your financial goals by designing a simple roadmap. I want you to gain peace of mind and confidence that you can attain your desires. Yes, you can be fit financially and win the money game!

PATHS TO SUCCESS

Susan has been a client for over 20 years, as a matter of fact; she was one of my tax preparation clients that I expanded to help with extensive tax, investment, retirement and estate planning. Through the years she followed my Be Fit Financially To Ignite Your Life - Seven Step Plan to Financial Success for Life. Susan paid her home off early, had no credit card debt, adhered to her budget, contributed to her 401(k), grew a nice portfolio, and drove a small SUV. She was the millionaire next door, but you would have never known. Like most millionaires I know, she keeps a low profile.

Susan, who was a widow, called me and was very stressed about her job. I could hear the panic in her voice. She said her manager wanted her to cut her hours but continue the same workload and even add more to it, which would mean more time without extra pay! The company had gone through two takeovers and it wasn't the same company when she started fifteen years ago as a Nurse Case Manager.

She wanted to quit her job, but wasn't sure if she would be able to meet her income needs. She was only 62 and would not qualify for Medicare. She would have to foot the bill for health insurance until she turned 65. How could she replace her paycheck and continue to live the same lifestyle to which she was accustomed? Susan wasn't excessive, but liked to take mini-vacations twice a year to visit family in Texas and a cruise annually.

I told Susan not to panic and we would complete a retirement income analysis, including an exit strategy, which meant going from the accumulation phase of retirement planning to the decumulation phase of retirement income planning on a tax favorable basis. The goal was to give her maximum growth with respect to her moderate risk tolerances. I created her Personal Pension Plan (PPP) and a lifetime of income with a guaranteed Paycheck in Retirement, as I call it – a PIR.

Susan's retirement analysis projected 30-40 year retirement. Now was the real test of all the diligent planning years. Retirement now had a date and a face on it and was very real! When we met to review the analysis, Susan said, "Gee wiz, I have worked 40 years and now I may spend the same number of years in retirement, how can I afford that?"

Because Susan was disciplined and followed the *Be Fit Financially To Ignite Your Life - Seven Step Plan to Financial Success for Life*, she was in an excellent position to retire with dignity that day. And on her own terms! I showed her in detail how her retirement planning would support her lifestyle. And allow her to pursue her goal of doing voluntary counseling for at risk individuals. A huge smile came upon her face and she was so elated that she jumped up and hugged me. You would have thought I gave her a million dollars!

It's moments like this that I find most *rewarding and fulfilling*. Knowing that I helped Susan achieve her financial goals and gave her peace of mind in retirement was my ultimate goal. It was my primary goal to help Susan at this critical stage of her life by relieving her financial stress.

SUCCESSFUL PEOPLE HAVE SUCCESSFUL HABITS

The following week I received a call from Jim, an engineer and his wife, Shelly, a homemaker; he was 58 and she was 55. Jim wanted to retire when he turns 59 in a few months. The oil company he works for has started some major layoffs and he didn't want to get caught off guard. During the previous year Jim had cancer surgery and did not want the mental anxiety of whether or not he could retire early. Shelly and Jim have a son entering college, so they have four years until he, as Shelly so aptly puts it, *"Is off the books!"*

Jim and Shelly have been clients of mine for 18 years and have followed the *Be Fit Financially To Ignite Your Life - Seven Step Financial Success Plan for Life*. They have their home paid off, no credit card debt, drive mid-size vehicles and have a nice nest egg of two IRA's, Roth IRA's, and a 401(k) plan, which I manage for them. Jim has a life insurance plan with cash value for growth that I set up years before; I advised Jim when he left his job he could not take the company life insurance with him. And good thing, since he developed the illness it would be extremely costly to obtain a plan now, if not impossible, due to his illness. Their estate was in order with wills and powers of attorney.

Jim's 401(k) plan included company stock. I explained that there are special tax benefits on company stock and that rollovers of 401(k) plans have some very intricate details and we want it to be done in the most advantageous way to help them, especially tax wise. *There are no second chances when it comes to retirement plans.*

They wanted to be free to travel, enjoy their child-free years, and leave a legacy to their children, not to Uncle Sam (taxes). They wanted to protect and preserve their assets. They were worried about the effects of inflation on their purchasing power, risks of longevity, health care costs and how to support themselves for 30 plus years. Jim said, "Will our money last and will it keep up with inflation?"

A CLOUD OF STRESS RELIEVED

Their comprehensive retirement analysis revealed that YES, they would have enough money to generate guaranteed income in retirement based on their retirement budget and risk factors on their investments. And be able to live in their same lifestyle, even figuring in inflation and taxes.

"Yes, Jim and Shelly, based on all your efforts over the years, you can retire anytime you want," I said to them. Shelly said, "To see the numbers on paper and to know that we are in control of our future, a cloud of stress has been lifted off our shoulders!"

YOUR ROADMAP TO SUCCESS

I feel so proud to know that I played a part in these true life success stories by providing direction, inspiration and capability. I strive to reduce the confusion and frustration out of financial planning. I feel if you have a better understanding and knowledge, then you can make informed decisions. Once you know your whole financial picture, you can take action to assure you arrive at your desired destinations!

You too can accomplish your financial goals with your personalized roadmap to success. You can gain clarity and confidence to lead your ideal life in retirement, or whatever are your financial goals. No matter what age or stage you are in life, yes you can achieve financial independence. You must know the rules of the money game in order to win! With the right tools, techniques and implementation, you will be on track to arrive at your financial destinations. Get in the habit of winning. *YES, you can win the money game!*

IGNITE YOUR LIFE TO WEALTH

I am very passionate about helping people, whether it's one-on-one or in seminar presentations to groups. In order to help more people ignite their life to wealth and win the money game, I wrote the book, *Be Fit Financially To Ignite Your Life – Seven Steps to Financial Success for Life.*

I am honored and privileged to contribute to *Ignite Your Life* to Health, Wealth and Success with Brian Tracy. He has been an inspiration to me for years.

Here are the seven steps, my gift to you:

STEP 1 – ENVISION AND SET YOUR GOALS

You can have a great life when you Identify and prioritize your short, mid and long-term goals. Your goals must be realistic, measurable, and appropriate. And you must put a date and price tag on them! Visualize your desires and crystalize them in your mind. Evaluate your goals and keep them current.

STEP 2 – DESIGN A FINANCIAL LIFE PLAN – ROADMAP FOR YOUR GOALS

"INCREASE YOUR NET WORTH AND YOU WILL INCREASE YOUR SELF WORTH."

This requires some exercise, but it is so worth it! Take a financial snapshot by figuring your Monthly Cash Flow (Income minus expenses) to determine if you have discretionary monthly income that you can use towards your goals. Track your monthly income and your living expenses. Stick to a budget and avoid unnecessary purchases. Remember less is more! Do you need all those cable channels? Try not spending anything one day a week.

By carrying cash you are less likely to want to spend on the small things that add up. Spending should have meaning and purpose. Don't buy what you can't afford. Stop the vultures that have their hands in your wallet; like T.V. Infomercials, friends latest pyramid offering, inflation, taxes, insurances, mortgage fees to name a few.

Determine your Net Worth (Assets minus liabilities). You must know where you are, and then you can determine where you are going. A great financial advocate can take you to the next steps including asset planning and protection, retirement planning; accumulation and decumulation phases, tax planning, college funding, goal planning and estate planning.

The best plan is the one that is implemented!

STEP 3 – KNOW YOUR TAX STATUS - UNCLE SAM NOT YOUR FAVORITE UNCLE?

Identify your marginal tax bracket, take advantage of tax-favored opportunities available today. Taxes may be reduced by deferral, tax free income, asset or income shifting. Are you paying more than your fair share? *Learn what the wealthy know and do!* Learn Savvy IRA planning, 401(k), 403(b), 457, and Self Employed plan options for maximum benefits.

When is your tax freedom day?

STEP 4- PLAN YOUR INVESTMENT PORTFOLIOS

Learn some basic financial terms and techniques of investing, stress test your portfolio. Review your current asset allocations and time frames. Incorporate dollar cost averaging, asset allocation, rebalancing and the Rule of 72, Real Estate Cash Flow Investing.

It's not only what you make, but what you keep that's important. By lowering investment expenses, you may not have to be as aggressive to make higher returns. An efficient portfolio is one that offers the most return for a given amount of risk; or the least risk for a given amount of return. Structure your investments wisely. Put your savings on auto-pilot and pay yourself first.

STEP 5 – ASSESS YOUR PLAN

How is your plan working? You must review your plan at least annually, I recommend quarterly if possible. Is your plan on target to meet your goals and objectives? Determine which indicators to look at in how effective your plan is working. This is critical to the success of the future you.

STEP 6 – LIFE CYCLE CHANGES

Investment goals may change over time as you move from one phase of life to another, such as earning years to retirement income years. Life cycles must be taken into consideration for births, disability, job loss, divorce or death. What effect do these have on your overall plan?

STEP 7 – BE FIT FINANCIALLY & PHYSICALLY

Breakthrough to your highest financial potential by building a better relationship with your money! Take control of your finances and you will take control of your health by reducing stress.

Health is Wealth! If you forget your health, it will forget you.

Be proactive, don't wait until you are in the midst of a financial or health crisis before beginning the planning process, the sooner you start, the more options you will have. You can 'Be Fit Financially' no matter what age or stage you are in life! *Be prepared for success!*

Millionaires don't leave their money to chance, why should you?

I've been called, BFF, Best Friend Forever. Wow, what a great feeling to impact people in such a positive way! Thanks to all my clients and future BFF's. **BEST OF SUCCESS TO YOU!**

About Michele

Michele Nami-von Hoven, RFC®, CEO and President of Be Fit Financially, LLC, a Holistic Financial Advisory Firm. She is a Registered Financial Consultant (RFC), Fiduciary, author, speaker, educator and BFF Coach. Michele is also the Founder of the Women's Financial Solutions Network (WFSN), empowering women to be savvy in the areas of wealth, health and success. Michele's philosophy is when you reduce financial stress, you will be more productive and happier in all areas of your life!

Michele is very passionate about helping people ignite their life to wealth and success. She has been transforming lives and turning people's dreams and goals into reality for over 25 years. She began her financial planning journey preparing hundreds of tax returns a year and saw her clients' hard earned money eroded by income taxes and low-earning interest. She searched for alternative ways to keep more of her clients' hard earned money and investment earnings to increase their purchasing power.

Michele has been a contributor to television and radio. She has sat on many boards including President of business associations and as Director of the Financial Planning Association (FPA) for seven years. She has served on the National World War II Museum Charitable Gifting Committee as an Advisor. Michele was a contributor to the Financial Planning Process Advisory Board in Italy – the process was then adopted by the European Union. She lobbied with great success for IRA reform to increase IRA contributions and equality for spousal benefits in Washington, D.C. She is truly a holistic financial advocate.

She holds the Investment Advisor Representative License (Series 65) and has held Series 7, 6, 62, 63, and 26 licenses. She has completed the Certified Financial Planner programs and is enrolled in the Retirement Income Certified Planner (RICP) program. Michele is a retirement plan investment and rollover specialist with a tax-centric focus on safe money income planning. She has worked for major financial planning firms and has won several awards and achievements for advanced retirement, tax, and estate planning.

You too can be fit financially and lessen your financial stress. Whether you're starting a new career, a family or ready to live an abundant life in retirement, Michele has a deep understanding of the potential obstacles in the way of securing your financial future. She has developed a unique perspective on working through these difficulties to get you to your goals successfully. Michele has a way of reducing the complicated financial jargon gumbo into simple red beans and rice!

Michele enjoys travelling, writing and loves to sing in her church choir. Attend one of her presentations and you may even get to hear her sing a few notes.

Michele is author of the upcoming book, *Be Fit Financially To Ignite Your Life-Seven Steps to Financial Success for Life*. Her book will give you the tools and techniques to reach your financial goals. As a BFF Coach, Michele created the *"Be Fititudes"* to give you the encouragement and focus to take control of your financial world and live a life of financial independence and happiness. Michele says, *"Never settle for less than you deserve!"*

Millionaires don't leave their money to chance, why should you?
~ Michele Nami-von Hoven

You can connect with Michele at:
Website: www.BeFitFinancially.com
LinkedIn: MicheleNamiVonHoven
Facebook: BeFitFinancially

CHAPTER 27

IGNITE NEW BREAKTHROUGHS IN YOUR NONPROFIT
—Winning Strategies to Transform from Bleeding to Thriving

BY MAKARAND UTPAT

Significance: Starting a nonprofit can be a formidable task considering that individuals sharing a common purpose embark on its journey 'on a wing and a prayer.' In many ways, it is quite akin to an entrepreneur launching a for-profit startup company and requires various virtues to succeed – such as having a bold vision, passion, perseverance, learning from failures, keeping the head high, and having a good model (product or service to be sold). However, what separates a nonprofit from its for-profit counterparts are various characteristics such as subtleties of personal beliefs and viewpoints that dominate how nonprofits should function, motivational influences, reward systems, and its unique profit model where no person (owner, member) owns the shares or its property or its assets.

Even when the rubber meets the road, pragmatic challenges remain pervasive such as a shoestring budget, resource allocation and mobilization, team and leadership level conflicts, lack of sound IT infrastructure, donor engagement, marketing, and the social pressure to succeed. Thus, leaders committed to steer nonprofit ships are continually faced with grueling realities and can find themselves in foreign territory.

Background: In my spare time, I play Indian and Western drums with musical bands and orchestras. This passion has allowed me to associate with various for-profits and nonprofit entities. Early on, my involvement took on volunteering, event management, and assisting in fundraising programs. Over the past few years, my manifestations expanded in the form of providing nonprofit IT consulting, co-founding a nonprofit or two, steering nonprofits through crisis situations, fostering nonprofit brand growth, and acting as an advisor in the capacity as trustee on the board of directors or executive decision-making bodies. It is a great feeling to see that the time and energy I've invested in my passion has allowed me to contribute to the nonprofit missions and social causes. As time goes by, it is broadening my horizons and is able to stay with me longer.

High Level Model:

To help simplify complexities, you need to maintain clarity and strike a proper balance between critical components:

- Vision (Why): Vision is about why your Nonprofit is in existence and what is its mission.

- Strategy (Where): Strategy is about determining where your nonprofit currently is (Point A) and where it should be (Point B). It can be short-term or long-term in nature.

- Process or plan (How): Process or Plan is about translating strategy into action via a set of activities, steps, and/or operations to evolve your nonprofit from Point A to Point B.

- People: People are an integral part of your nonprofit and they constitute team members, a volunteer base, supporters, employees, community members, competitors, customers, and donors.

- Product: You are offering product(s) or service(s) to customers or a target audience in order to fulfill the nonprofit's mission.

- Technology: Technology is a set of tools, infrastructure, and technical capabilities.

The game-changing strategies described below are associated with the above critical components:

STRATEGY #1:

Make Bylaws Full-Proof: This could be a missed opportunity since more often than not, nonprofits get founded by zealots who are like birds of a feather flocking together to achieve certain goals but are new to its nuances. You must ensure that bylaws are fool-proof as they act as an important equalizer and safeguard its interests when dealing with unexpected conflicts.

STRATEGY #2:

Embed Governance in the Fabric of Nonprofit: Just like for-profits, the term "Corporate Governance" holds vital significance for nonprofit entities. You must govern financial accounting practices, maintain a code of business ethics, follow public disclosure procedures about donations, implement transparent communication practices, and promote organizational decision-making via roles and responsibilities. It cultivates a positive image in the eyes of increasingly savvy volunteers, members, and donors.

STRATEGY #3:

Instill a Culture of Trust and Make it a DNA of Nonprofit: Trust is the fundamental building block of developing strong relationships. This aspect is so crucial that it can make or break your nonprofit. A few approaches are: being approachable and visible, being a good listener, focusing on problems rather than personalities, remaining fair, ensuring mutual respect between team members, giving each other leeway before jumping to conclusions, taking timely actions to diffuse or resolve situations, and focusing on the big picture.

STRATEGY #4:

Adopt Process for Conflict Management: Conflicts are common phenomena in both young and mature nonprofits. Some examples are:

intra-team relationships, board members power playing battles, the presence of cynics and naysayers, conflicts of interests due to overlap of board members who could also be suppliers or donors, lack of communication transparency, and financial conflicts. They dampen the enthusiasm and stall the progress. You should remain vigilant and must adopt conflict management processes focusing on identification, acceptance, resolution, closure, and education.

STRATEGY #5:

Give Ownership and Accountability to Individuals: I have found General Patton's quote: "Never tell people how to do things. Tell them what to do and they will surprise you with their ingenuity." quite spot-on. Shy or introverted team members, when given ownership, will rise to the occasions. This results in boosting the individual's self-esteem and outlook toward the nonprofit mission.

STRATEGY #6:

Recognize Individuals and Celebrate Small Successes: Recognition and celebrations are great ways to inject a breath of fresh air when momentum seems to be going downhill. Publicly thanking or felicitating individuals during community events results in huge mileage. Individuals repeat rewarded behavior and it serves as the motivation trigger garnering mutual respect. You need to keep track of small successes or quick wins on your radar screen. Small successes signify sense of progression and achievements, clarify direction, and serve as the barometer to measure against nonprofit's strategy and goals.

STRATEGY #7:

Give Your Nonprofit a Social Media Makeover: Nonprofits can grow dramatically by building strong Internet identity. Techniques include: creating mobile-optimized robust website, adopting SEO techniques, generating strong followership through Facebook page/posts, broadcasting updates via Twitter feeds, demonstrating thought leadership via blogs, creations, launching a YouTube channel, having a LinkedIn profile, and a Wikipedia page. Most of these tools can be implemented free or with minimal investment and can have a huge effect in generating greater ROI in the long run.

STRATEGY #8:

Make Marketing a Necessity, not a Luxury: Having a robust marketing plan is a must-have tool in leaders' toolbox and can deliver dramatic outcomes. A marketing plan coupled with social media presence benefits a nonprofit in becoming a brand and restores member confidence. It should be multi-pronged. Methods of marketing: word-of-mouth marketing, direct mailing, e-Mail marketing, and social media marketing.

STRATEGY #9:

Make Fundraising a Forethought, not an Afterthought: Fundraising is the lifeblood, but remains a perennial challenge regardless of whether the nonprofit is in startup-mode or mature state. Because the fundraising landscape is competitive, it is quite crucial to have a proactive strategy. Some ways to achieve: having clarity on what differentiates your nonprofit from other nonprofits and why prospective donors should donate to you, developing a donor database and appealing to them, making community leaders and organizations part of the mission by developing strong relationships, and have them do storytelling, online auctions, celebrity or activist speaking circuits, leveraging marketing plans to raise funds, and gala events.

STRATEGY #10:

Know Thy Competition: Competition remains part of your nonprofit's extended ecosystem. Other nonprofits and for-profits compete for similar things required for your nonprofit's success, such as personnel, resources, funding, etc. You either surrender to it or steadily sharpen your saw. Perform competitive analysis and use it to uncover market opportunities and create disruptions. Some elements: analyzing capabilities with strengths and weaknesses, identifying competitors, geography, understanding what strategies are working right or not, what attracts the donors to them, and what opportunities exist for increasing the market share.

STRATEGY #11:

Establish Success Metrics to Make It Stick: They serve as essential benchmarks in determining whether their strategy has been working or not and how effectively to mobilize resources. They can get overlooked in the midst of the humdrum of life. You must candidly analyze your nonprofit's current state, create roadmap, establish metrics, tie it to its goals and strategy, and monitor the outcomes. They can be qualitative or quantitative in nature. A few examples are: organizational growth, fundraising, marketing, customers, and social media.

STRATEGY #12:

Cross Pollinate with Other Nonprofits: Cross-pollination is a creative way for leaders to engage with broader and loyal audiences earning instant credibility. Developing professional alliances with nonprofits and for-profit entities offers mutual benefits in terms of be able to cross-promote missions, co-sponsor events, learn best practices, and strengthen a nonprofit community in general.

STRATEGY #13:

Remember to Have Fun: Last but not the least, do not miss the boat by forgetting the fun factor. Do not forget the very reason behind the nonprofit's mission. Bring people together in fun ways and build team-bonding. A few ideas are: organizing movie nights, bowling and pizza nights, camping getaways, throwing summer barbeque bashes, annual picnics, golf outings, and karaoke nights.

CONCLUSION:

Most nonprofit leaders struggle with a common challenge: How to make nonprofits relevant? An arduous growth journey with surprises lurking around compels leaders to remain armed with a quiver full of arrows. It requires leaders to go through compelling changes, deliver more with less, constantly evaluate and adapt to shifting conditions, acknowledge that the pace of progress will likely be slower, and ensure that momentum is preserved under taxing circumstances. With the aforementioned game-changing strategies, a nonprofit can propel itself from bleeding to a thriving state. Make your nonprofit relevant again by injecting the above strategies and get your mojo back by igniting new breakthroughs. All the best in your own growth journey!

About Makarand

Makarand Utpat is a crossover leader who has gracefully led for-profits and nonprofits. He is credited with expanding competitive positioning and profitability of many organizations by unlocking their digital potential.

Throughout his illustrious career, he has brought the vision, process, leadership, sustainable value growth, and surefire work tools in the fabric of the workplace to rally teams and deliver results. He is driven by integrity and honesty. Per Makarand, instilling a culture of trust, giving ownership and accountability to individuals, treating them with respect, expecting the best out of them, and rewarding and recognizing them, are fundamental building blocks of what brings out the best in individuals.

Widely regarded as a turnaround expert, Makarand gets called in by C-suite executives to envision and execute game-changing turnarounds on in-flight projects, stalled programs, or new initiatives. A proven ability to foster relationships with C-suite executives, knack for connecting with stakeholders, presenting ideas in an engaging manner, driving change, building consensus, achieving fruitful outcomes, coupled with his work ethic and attention to detail is what sets him apart from his peers.

With an ahead-of-the curve affinity for technology, Makarand has masterminded results through strategic outlook, astute problem-solving skills, negotiation, harvesting buy-in from stakeholders, building partnerships at all levels, and fiscal discipline.

To his credit, Makarand has led best-in-class initiatives in the areas of Sales and Marketing, Compliance Solutions, Customer Engagement Media Strategies, eChannels and eMarketing, Mobile and Cloud Solutions, Social Media, Digital Transformations, and Internet Technologies.

Makarand is a published author with articles, blogs, and white papers to his credit. His work on reusable components has been referenced in designing a patent. He also has had the privilege to co-author and share book space with a "Who's Who" list of CIOs, CEOs such as Facebook CIO Tim Campos, Office of the CIO Dean Lane, and many veteran thought leaders.

Makarand's passion for giving back through social commitment is rooted in his upbringing where he was routinely exposed to burgeoning poverty, malnutrition, youth challenges, and lack of education. Deeply committed to social causes, Makarand is able to proudly apply his leadership skills to many nonprofits in the form of fostering nonprofit brand growth, steering nonprofits through crisis situations, IT consulting, or acting as an adviser in the capacity as trustee, on the board of directors, or executive decision-making bodies.

To top it off, the icing on the cake is that, in his spare time, Makarand is a professional musician who plays Indian and Western drums with musical bands and orchestras.

Makarand can be reached at: (201)-819-0894, via email at: makarandutpat@yahoo.com, or visit him at: www.makarandutpat.com

CHAPTER 28

TEN THINGS YOUR DENTIST WON'T TELL YOU ABOUT DENTAL IMPLANTS, INVISALIGN™ AND BRACES!

BY ALLEN HUANG, DMD, MS & VICTORIA CHEN, DDS, MS

1. YOU'D RATHER HAVE DENTAL IMPLANTS THAN BRIDGES AND DENTURES FOR MISSING TEETH!

It is very common for patients to have more than one tooth missing. Missing teeth can be due to accidents, unrestorable caries lesions, congenitally-missing or severe periodontal disease. When you have a missing tooth or teeth, what will be your best options? If you ask your dentists, they may offer you "several" options, such as bridges, dentures, and dental implants. The decision will depend on "your finance" and "your insurance." Yes, we do agree most dental insurances will not cover, or only partially cover, dental implants, since insurance consider implants "elective treatment!" Therefore, most patients will assumedly choose bridges or dentures to replace their missing teeth because "insurance does not cover it!"

The truth is, if it comes to dentists' own mouths or for their significant others, "dental implants" are the *ONLY* option, and *NO OTHER OPTIONS WILL BE EVEN CONSIDERED! PERIOD!* Dental implants not only give you the best quality of life, restoring your chewing function to almost ninety-five percent of your real teeth, maintain your existing bone level, and the best part is you do not need to grind down healthy teeth to replace your missing teeth. Placed with experienced surgeons, dental implants can almost last for a lifetime. As a periodontist, I often treat lots of dentists, dentist's wives, parents and relatives for dental implants to replace their missing teeth. The dentists not only want dental implants for themselves and for their family, but also the best surgeons to work on their dental implants.

So, what would you rather have to replace your missing teeth? Would you like to decide for yourself or would you rather have insurance companies decide what's best for you? The majority of dentists will choose dental implants for themselves. They don't care if insurance will pay or not! They do not want bridges in their own mouths!

2. YOU'D RATHER REPLACE BAD TEETH WITH DENTAL IMPLANTS, THAN TO SAVE BAD TEETH WITH ROOT CANALS AND CROWNS!

I often see patients proceed to save poor-to-hopeless teeth with root canal treatment and crowns just to simply get out of pain and save their teeth on a short-term basis. They do not realize that eventually these poor to hopeless teeth will fail and they will be at square one again after they have just spent tens of thousands of dollars. With the advancement and predictability of dental implants, the procedure is set to last for a lifetime. Patients with proper advice will save more in the long term if they just simply choose dental implants to replace their poor-to-hopeless dentition.

Lots of dentists are just not brave enough to tell their patients what they would tell their significant other to do, that is, to remove the poor-to-hopeless teeth and replaced with dental implants. Instead, dentists give patients "hope" that the life of these teeth may be prolonged by having root canals and crowns. Most of the them even try to justify their recommendations, even if it is to hold on for the short term. Sometimes, it is the patients who may have unrealistic expectations that their poor-to-hopeless teeth can be saved with treatments—rather than going through the inevitable step of losing them. They might grow attached to them or simply try to buy some time not to spend the money. However, patients often get extremely angry at their dentists when their decision does not pan out. They often argue that their dentist did not educate and convince them sufficiently to choose dental implants.

My honest opinion for you is to choose implants as your restorative option if your teeth are not in good shape and the prognosis is not favorable. It will save you tons of money and headaches in the long run. Guaranteed!

3. YOUR DENTISTS WILL NEED CONE-BEAM TECHNOLOGY TO PLACE YOUR DENTAL IMPLANTS!

Would you let a blind dentist place your dental implants? Without the three-dimensional cone-beam, I consider myself blind when I place implants in my patients. With cone-beam images, I can accurately identify how thick the bones are, how far the implants can go, and the areas to "avoid" where the big nerves and sinuses are. I can even plan complicated implant placements with the "surgical guidance" with the assistance of cone-beam technology. You will hear stories about patients getting permanent "numbness" in their lower jaw, since some facial nerves are damaged during the dental procedures. Damage and permanent numbness are indeed part of the risk for undergoing dental implant procedures. These risks can, however, be minimized significantly by using "cone-beam" images.

Lots of dentists will use traditional x-rays to place dental implants. Traditional panoramic and periodontal x-rays are a little bit better than not having any x-rays, but I consider myself "partially blind" if I use two-dimensional x-rays to place implants. Make sure your dentists can "see" with "cone-beam" images while placing your implants!

4. YOUR DENTAL IMPLANTS AND BONE GRAFTING SUCCESS RATES WILL IMPROVE WITH CGF PROCEDURES!

If you have not heard of the CGF (Concentrated Growth Factors) procedure and you need dental implant or bone-grafting procedure to be done on yourself, you need to find out which surgeon in your city is providing the service. Growth Factors are our own proteins which regulate the complex processes of wound healing and are used to accelerate and enhance tissue regeneration and repair in dental and medical procedures. While you are having your dental procedures, small samples of blood are drawn, centrifuged, processed and prepared.

The benefits of CGF are faster healing, faster recovery, and wound closure. It creates less bleeding, less pain and discomfort. It is a very popular procedure in dermatological procedures, in which Hollywood celebrities such as Kim Kardashian get vampire facials. Sports athletes such as Kobe Bryant and Rafael Nadal also use it to speed up their sports-related injuries.

5. YOU CAN HAVE THE TEETH-IN-A-DAY PROCEDURE TO RESTORE YOUR SMILE AND FUNCTIONS IN ONE DAY!

Gone are the days where it takes 1-2 years to restore your entire smile and dental function. Today, with the Teeth-in-a-day concept, there is no waiting period, and missing teeth can be replaced by dental implants and patients can walk in and out of the dental office with a brilliant new smile. The benefits of this revolutionary procedure include immediate placement of dental implants, no need to show missing teeth after extraction, no waiting period, and no need for temporary removable appliances. It delivers a brand new smile in one day, provides permanent, stable tooth replacement and makes the patient feel good, look good and they can eat well after one dental appointment sitting.

While Teeth-in-a-Day is completed in one appointment, an initial consultation for an implant retained prosthesis is necessary before your tooth replacement visit. During this visit, your surgeon will evaluate your dental health, take a cone-beam radiograph and discuss any goals you may have for your smile so that your prosthesis may be properly fabricated. The procedure is possible due to the strategic placement of a few dental implants, even if you have periodontal disease and have limited anatomical considerations.

6. YOU NEED BRACES FIRST BEFORE HAVING DENTAL IMPLANTS!

I often have tons of patients ask me, "Should I have braces first or implants first?" In ninety-five percent of all circumstances, you will start braces first, and then have implants later after completion of braces. Implants are unmovable objects in your mouth. Once placed, implants will fuse with the bone and nothing can move them. It makes orthodontic treatment challenging since all the teeth now need to move around the implants, and often implants become an obstacle to achieve ideal results for patients. I often see patients who have bucked top front implanted teeth with crooked bottom front teeth. Patients ask me to push their top bucked teeth back and straighten their bottom front teeth. How can I move implanted front teeth backward with braces? In order to push the upper front teeth back, which is impossible for implanted teeth, I have to move the lower front teeth forward to catch up with the upper front implanted teeth. It is such a disaster that patients will never look right! I wish patients' dentists could have sent them for orthodontic treatment first before placing implants for missing teeth.

Make sure you fix your crooked teeth FIRST before you have any implant and bridge work done in the future!

7. YOU CAN HAVE EXTREME MAKE-OVER SMILES WITHOUT EXPENSIVE PLASTIC SURGERY!

Dreaming of a taller nose, more prominent chin and straighter fabulous smile? Most people think improving their looks is mainly the job of plastic surgeons. Orthodontists can actually create similar beautiful facial results without aggressive surgery and at a fraction of the cost! By moving a patient's front teeth back with braces, the lips will typically follow backward, which leaves the nose and chin relatively look more prominent. The end result is an extreme make-over, a new face without rhinoplasty and chin augmentation surgeries. Another bonus is straighter and fabulous smiles, too! The result is truly amazing by having orthodontic treatment only.

#8. WEARING BRACES DOESN'T HAVE TO TAKE TWO TO THREE YEARS. YOU CAN SHORTEN YOUR BRACES TREATMENT TIME TO LESS THAN ONE YEAR!

Most adult patients are hesitant to start orthodontic treatment due to the long length of time required to wear braces. The average orthodontic treatment time averages around a two-year range. There are some procedures and devices for braces to speed up your braces three to four times faster!

The first procedure is a periodontal procedure called Accelerated Osteogenic Orthodontics™ (AOO™). It is a two-to-four-hour surgery performed by a periodontist right after patients have braces placed. AOO™ creates the "bone trauma phenomenon" to increase the bone turnover in a transient six-month period. Orthodontists take advantage of this faster bone turnover window to move teeth and complete braces in three to eight months. Hey, I was an actual patient of AOO™, and it really sped up my braces treatment to less than a year. It however, requires a higher fee and actual surgery for the patient.

The second device is called AcceleDent®. It is a simple at-home mouthpiece device designed to move your teeth up to 50% faster for orthodontic treatment with 20 minutes of use daily. It uses SoftPulse Technology®, which accelerates bone remodel process around your teeth. AcceleDent® also decrease the discomfort associated with orthodontic treatment clinically. Ask your orthodontist to purchase AcceleDent®, which costs you about $750-$1000 per piece.

9. WE SEE INVISALIGN® ADVERTISEMENTS EVERY-WHERE... INVISALIGN® IS NOT FOR EVERYONE!

Invisalign® is truly an amazing and invisible tool to straighten your smile without wearing braces. How does Invisalign® works? Your orthodontists will take impressions or scan your tooth images and send them to Align Company. Upon receiving the images of your teeth, Align Company will use 3-D software to simulate tooth movement to achieve the best final positions. Orthodontists will predict, plan, communicate and instruct Align Company to obtain the "prescription" to correct your crooked teeth and bite. Upon approval by your orthodontist, Align Company will fabricate a series of customized trays ready for you to wear.

The truth is Invisalign® technology has been improved to treat more complicated cases nowadays. However, there will be still lots more complicated treatment that can't be accomplished efficiently and effectively by Invisalign® treatment, such as severe bite problems and extraction cases. I often see patients who have been in Invisalign® treatment with their dentists for two to three years, and their teeth are still crooked and bites are still off. Unfortunately, some cases should be treated with braces performed by orthodontists rather than using Invisalign®.

10. MAKE SURE YOU DO NOT HAVE ACTIVE PERIODONTAL DISEASE BEFORE YOU HAVE ORTHODONTIC TREATMENT, VENEERS, CROWN AND BRIDGE WORK.

Before you decide to spend millions of dollars building your dream house, would you make sure the future foundation of your house is solid and safe? The same principle applies to your dental work and orthodontic treatment. I often see patients who just spent thousands of dollars getting cosmetic dental work done, including veneers, crown and bridges, but their beautiful dental work will not last long, since patients have active periodontal problems that have not been treated first. Take care of your "foundation" first, please! I am also adamant about postponing a patient's orthodontic treatment, and will not start their braces or Invisalign® until their periodontal disease is treated and well controlled.

Remember, your oral foundation has to be healthy and solid before you invest in all the cosmetic dental work.

About Allen

Allen Huang, DMD, MS., co-founder of the Significance Dental Specialists, specializes in Periodontics and Dental Implants. Dr. Huang received his dental medicine degree from the University of Pennsylvania School of Dental Medicine. Following his general dental training, Dr. Huang received a full 3-year scholarship to train in Periodontics and Implant Dentistry at the University of Illinois - Chicago. During his training, Dr. Huang received many academic honors, and was named the first Chief-Resident in program history. Dr. Huang was also involved in the clinical and histological study of platelet rich plasma (PRP) in sinus lift bone regeneration project.

Dr. Huang has been voted "Top Dentist" by his peers for 10 consecutive years since being in private practice. He is a renowned national speaker and lectured numerous dental implant study clubs and companies. Dr. Huang also owns a dental implant company and is the CEO of Altosbiotech, LLC.

Dr. Huang offers cutting-edge technology and techniques to his patients (Pinhole Gum Grafting Techniques, Concentrated Growth Factors Procedure, Teeth-In-a-Day, iTero Computer Scanning System). He was trained under the world-famous Dr. Rosenfeld who is a pioneer and leader of "Computer-Driven Implant Dentistry." All of his cases are planned under Cone Beam Scan in computer software (Simplant, Nobelvision, Vision) for predictable treatment results prior to sitting in a surgical setting.

Dr. Huang is a Diplomate of the American Academy of Periodontology and member of American Academy of Periodontology, American Academy of Osseointegration, Academy of Dental Association, and Southern Nevada Dental Society.

You can connect with Dr. Huang at:
- AllenH@sdsdental.com
- www.sdsdental.com

About Victoria

Dr. Victoria Chen, DDS, MS, specializes in orthodontics. Dr. Victoria has created thousands of fabulous superstar smiles by providing exceptional orthodontic care since 1999. She is the co-founder of Significance Dental Specialists with her periodontist dentist husband, Dr. Allen Huang. Significance Dental Specialists are the most trustworthy and dominating interdisciplinary dental specialty group in Las Vegas, Nevada, with four locations to serve Las Vegas patients and referring dentists.

Dr. Victoria and Significance Dental Specialists were featured on prestigious Las Vegas Women Magazines as cover doctors and voted as Top Dentists for several years. To stay up-to-date on the latest advancements in the field of orthodontics, Dr. Victoria maintains active membership in numerous prestigious professional organizations such as the American Association of Orthodontists, the American Dental Association, the Pacific Coast Society of Orthodontists, the Nevada Dental Society and the Las Vegas Interdisciplinary Study Club.

In addition to traditional braces and Invisalign® and Invisalign Teen®, Dr. Victoria offers headgear-free orthodontics by using the most current technology of Miniscrew Anchorage. Dr. Victoria also offers the treatment of Accelerated Osteogenic Orthodontics™ (AOOT™) – also known as Wilckodontics®, in which she can shorten your braces treatment time from 2 to 3 years to 3 to 8 months.

Outside the office, she enjoys reading, wine tasting, traveling, golfing and tennis. She loves spending time with her husband and two beautiful daughters, Angelina and Cameron.

You can connect with Dr. Victoria at:
- victoriac@sdsdental.com
- www.significanceorthodontics.com

CHAPTER 29

THE POWER OF DECISION

BY GARY DUVALL, CRPC®*

Dark green conifer forests covered the steep mountain slopes towering over the quiet narrow valley as I navigated toward my new home located near the City of Rogue River, Oregon. My car was packed full of my belongings, and at the age of sixteen I had just driven to Oregon for the first time. I had started from my childhood home in Los Angeles, California, the third largest city in the United States at the time. As I crossed over the Rogue River Bridge that late summer morning, I was in awe looking down at the abundant flowing waters below. The Los Angeles River, by stark contrast, was nothing more than a huge dry concrete flood control channel that time of year.

It would take an hour to drive from one side of Los Angeles to another, but I drove through this town in two minutes. As I drove by Rogue River High School where I would spend my senior year and graduate, I was surprised at the tiny size of the facility. I was beginning to experience the phenomena I now refer to as culture shock. As I drove the three miles from town to my new home I was fascinated by the beauty of the open fields and meadows, dotted with livestock and accented with occasional tall stands of fir and deciduous trees. Barns, stables and workshops were as common as houses, with acres of space in between.

---

* Chartered Retirement Planning Counselor℠ and CRPC® are registered service marks of the College for Financial Planning®.

A LIFE CHANGING DECISION!

When I began attending the small town high school in September, I noticed that everybody knew each other really well – except for me, of course. Since nobody knew anything about me, I *decided* I could be whoever I wanted to be! Nobody would know the difference. My *decision* to be a competitive athlete and competent student felt like a sneaky trick on the other students and teachers initially, but to my amazement – it worked! My top performance in the classroom and in sports was such a change my mother cried when she saw my first report card. I accidentally uncovered a success principle and implemented it by having a clear vision of a definite goal, backed with immediate action and powered with persistent determination. I inadvertently discovered The Power of Decision. I learned to act as if I could not fail.

One day at school during the lunch period, a teacher named Mr. Jones stopped me in the hallway unexpectedly to give me an assignment. I became a little worried. He decided a seventeen-year-old like myself should check out a book entitled *Think and Grow Rich* from the school library and read it. I was relieved to be given such a simple and easy assignment. After checking out the book later that day, I took it home and began to read it that evening.

THE MESSAGES FROM THE BOOK - IGNITED MY LIFE!

The words from the book grabbed my attention immediately. As the secrets to success were revealed, one after another, I could not put the book down. The principles of success leapt from the pages into my mind, revealing forces that were already beginning to propel me to success. My definite purpose, backed by strong desire became a tangible reality because I had made the decision to become a studious athlete in my final year of high school. Since I had nothing to lose and everything to gain by trying, I had decided to try by all means. With this new found knowledge I would harness the power of decision for the rest of my life.

A DECISION BASED ON DEFINITE OF PURPOSE

After high school I decided to become a successful businessman. Armed with the knowledge from *Think and Grow Rich*, I knew I would need specialized knowledge and training. So I made the decision to obtain a Bachelor of Science degree in Business Administration from Southern

Oregon University. I possessed strong math abilities as I entered college, because my father had been a standout math teacher and he had made sure I mastered that subject early in life. This aptitude was painstakingly built over a period of years, because math did not come easily to me at first. As I started my college career, I decided to learn all aspects of business management well. I was consciously aware of the power of decision, and knew that my efforts would be fruitful if I kept striving towards a clearly-defined objective with unrelenting effort.

Financial adversity was a constant companion in my first year of college. Fortunately, I had already learned during the previous year that every adversity contains the seeds of an equivalent or greater benefit. I worked various evening jobs while attending classes during the day to earn the money required to cover the costs of tuition and my living expenses. Shortly after I landed on campus I decided to work in the college food services.

Searching for opportunity, I learned to do all the different jobs on the evening shift, and decided to ask to be considered for a management position toward the end of my freshman year. At the age of nineteen, I started my second year of college working as a Student Manager, hiring, training and supervising other student employees. This work enabled me to pay all my college and living expenses without obtaining loans. The habit of harnessing the power of decision had become second nature.

At the beginning of my senior year, I knew the time had arrived to make a decision and select a career. I conducted an in-depth analysis of all known careers listed in the college library. I painstakingly reviewed every occupation from Actuary to Zoologist. I knew by then, I loved working with people every day, was exceptional at math, and particularly liked being able to document my successful achievements so that my performance could be easily verified. Most of all I wanted to make meaningful contributions that benefited others. Early in my last year of college, I focused exclusively on Purchasing, which met all my criteria for a career. Upon graduation I landed a position as a Purchasing Agent with Bear Creek Corporation locally.

Purchasing evolved into my current profession as a Financial Advisor, with a prominent local financial institution. Now, I leverage the specialized knowledge I acquired over the years to help my clients manage their finances, provide retirement planning and investment management services. My driving motivation to become an outstanding Financial Guide occurred several years ago, when I witnessed a remarkable event.

A DARING RESCUE ON THE WILD ROGUE RIVER!

The Rogue River runs through the heart of the Rogue Valley, and many parts of it run slow and easy, suitable for swimming, fishing and picnicking during the summer months. Our stormy season occurs during winter, so when the dry summer days arrive, the water is so clear you can see the rocks at the bottom of the river and the fish swimming by. There are also thrilling guided jet boat rides that are very popular, and these adventures are routinely sold out well in advance. I had joined a crowd of others on the Hellgate River Excursion that fateful day. Like the trips I enjoyed before, the experienced river captain was entertaining us with his great sense of humor, stories about recent events and past historical happenings on the river.

As we approached a treacherous section of river that squeezes through a narrow gorge, our captain explained in detail over the boat's speakers, how the geography creates this phenomenon. He pointed out the perpetual whirlpool to the right that has claimed many lives, while carefully navigating away from its angry swirling waters. As we entered the gorge he explained that this is the place known as "Hell's Gate." Dark gray solid rock walls rise over one hundred feet toward the sky on each side. The boat's massive jet engines were throttled down because only enough power is needed to steer once the powerful current takes over and propelled us forward through the narrows.

The low murmur of the idling engines added to the ominous quietness as we coasted through. To the left on a flat rock ledge, were sitting two couples. All four were wearing life jackets, but with no visible water craft with them. Two were young teenagers holding each other shivering and wet. They were crying. The older couple appeared to be parents and they appeared to be upset, even angry. I remember thinking that maybe the kids had an argument with their parents, and I didn't give the situation much thought. I don't think any of the other passengers of our boat were alarmed either. We were all having so much fun!

THE CAPTAIN MAKES HIS DECISION

But the seasoned riverboat captain assessed the situation in an instant. Without any hint of alarm, he continued narrating his entertaining monologue, but slowly turned the boat around in the first available wide spot in the gorge. With the boat now facing directly toward the raging torrent of water, he calmly stated over the speakers: "I'm going back to see if those folks need some help." His hands gently pressed forward on the dual throttles, and the jet engines roared with raw power and the entire river behind the boat instantly churned white. The boat slowly moved forward against the full force of the river flowing through the crevice created by gigantic rock walls toward the stranded foursome.

As we pulled up alongside the rock ledge, the jet boat stopped moving forward and remained perfectly still despite the jet engines churning the water downstream in an intense display of power. "Would you folks like a hand today?" the captain asked nonchalantly through his loudspeaker. The chilled and frightened river victims did not appear to respond. They were already in shock and now a powerful jet boat filled with 45 people was filling the canyon, hovering over the terrifying current like a motionless helicopter with deafening sound echoing off the steep rock walls. However, the experienced captain had already made his decision and started to inch over to the ledge to initiate the rescue despite the lack of a response from the hapless river goers.

I was on the left side of the boat, on the farthest side from the rock ledge and my eyes were riveted on the vision of these folks coming to their senses and preparing to board our boat. Suddenly, I became acutely aware of the awesome force of the river a few inches away from me blasting against the aluminum sheet that formed the side of the boat. I looked down into water that looked like a thousand fire hoses assaulting the boat from Hell's Gate. The stunning display of natural and manmade forces startled me and I swiveled around in fright to look up at the River Captain positioned at the controls on the elevated pilot's station. What I saw next forever changed my life.

THE CAPTAIN'S FACE WAS AS CALM AS
A MEDITATING GURU

His hands were moving constantly on the controls, as if his fingers were a part of the boat itself. Yet the boat remained absolutely stationary and the stranded four stepped upon the boat one at a time and secured a seat as easily as stepping onto a dock. His hands and arms appeared to be forcefully messaging the throttles, and yet his gaze toward his new passengers never wavered. His mind was in the zone. He patiently waited for everyone to be safely seated. Then he imperceptibly backed off the throttles and gently started floating downstream through the gorge – backwards! As he reached his turnaround point and he rotated the craft around to continue the journey downstream. He picked up his storytelling and joking with the passengers as if nothing unusual had happened.

As I later learned, a local rental shop had provided life vests to these people and told them they could just float down the river that way. The employee of the rental shop evidently did not expect them to stay in the river all the way down to Hell's Gate. These folks got sucked into the whirlpool and survived, only to be shot through Hell's Gate and into the gorge.

THE FAILURE TO GIVE GOOD ADVICE LED TO
A BAD DECISION

Before I got off the boat that day I decided that the financial advice I provide to my clients would be solid recommendations to see them through both the slow shallows and the tumultuous rapids they encounter in life. I would skillfully prepare and guide my clients through the financial whirlpools of economic changes and market volatility. They will be able to trust me to steer them away from the dangerous cliffs of bad decisions and the rocks of fear and greed that wreck many financial lives during the journey down the river of life. I committed to constantly hone my skills through education and experience to enhance my client's financial experience while protecting them from various dangers seen and unseen. This young river captain will never know he became my secret mentor that day.

Fortunately, I learned about the incredible power of decision early in life. On the river that day I had witnessed a quick decision executed with outstanding professionalism, extraordinary skill and without hesitation. He knew exactly what to do and how to do it. He could have radioed the Sheriff's patrol boat that we had passed earlier to perform the rescue. Instead he made his decision and took action to see it through.

ANYONE CAN DEVELOP DECISION POWER!

You make many decisions every day, large and small. It happens so often you can sometimes lose your awareness of this vital component of success. Becoming mindful of your thoughts and decisions is the first step to mastering decision power. Focus your attention on your thoughts when you make decisions throughout each day. By paying greater attention to your decisions your awareness enables you to confidently make more powerful choices. Then you will notice your subsequent actions are having greater results! Take action on your decision quickly with strong desire, persistence and determination. Act as if you cannot fail. Soon you will know you have acquired the amazing **Power of Decision**, and will be able to *Ignite Your Life* at will!

About Gary

Gary Duvall, CRPC® helps his clients try to create, grow and protect their personal and family financial independence. Before graduating from Rogue River High School, Gary had already become an avid student of success philosophy. He turned this passion into a lifetime avocation of learning how to enjoy health, wealth and wisdom, and recently coined the phrase "Transcendental Transmutation" to describe the process of accomplishment. Living most of his life in the Rogue Valley, Gary has served as a Student Manager, VISA Division Manager, Purchasing Agent, Merchandise Manager, Operations Manager, and Sales Manager for various businesses. He reentered the Financial Services profession in 1992, and for over 15 years has served the members of Rogue Credit Union as a trusted Financial Advisor through CUSO Financial Services, L.P.*

Gary is fond of saying, "Money is meant to bring value to your life, not the other way around." The decisions people make should be based on sound logic, and beneficial to their core beliefs and values. Gary has a reputation for making sometimes complex topics, easily understood, and is known for 'not talking over your head.' Gary helps his clients manage their investment portfolios containing mutual funds, annuities and other investment and insurance products.

He is now entering his 30th year of marriage to his wife, Carol, who also graduated from high school locally. They both remain close to their daughter Calley, who turned 27 this year and is employed in the medical field here in the Rogue River Valley. Perhaps because Gary and Carol were born in the greater Los Angeles area and arrived in Oregon with their parents as teenagers, they both love the creeks, streams and rivers that flow through the mountains and valleys of Southern Oregon. The nearby Pacific Ocean coastal area and mountain lakes are favorite vacation spots. They have fountains that run throughout the summer in their back yard. Their three cats and one dog like to drink from those fountains when they are not chasing each other. Even their golf balls seem to find the water on every course. There are others who evidently like the water more, because when Gary goes fishing the fish end up staying in the lake after he leaves.

Gary is a graduate of Southern Oregon University with a Bachelor of Science in Business Administration. He holds the Chartered Retirement Planning Counselor (CRPC)® designation from the College for Financial Planning®. Gary is a Qualifying and Life member of the Million Dollar Roundtable (MDRT), The Premier Association of Financial Professionals®, with 13 consecutive qualifying years.** He is a Past

President of the National Association of Insurance and Financial Advisors (NAIFA) Rogue Valley.

Gary Duvall, CRPC®***
Financial Advisor
CUSO Financial Services, L.P. at Rogue Credit Union
(541) 622-7325 | 541-770-3710 (fax)
gduvall@roguecu.org

*Non-deposit investment products and services are offered through CUSO Financial Services, L.P. ("CFS"), a registered broker-dealer (Member FINRA/SIPC) and SEC Registered Investment Advisor. Products offered through CFS: **are not NCUA/NCUSIF or otherwise federally insured, are not guarantees or obligations of the credit union, and may involve investment risk including possible loss of principal.** Investment Representatives are registered through CFS. The Credit Union has contracted with CFS to make non-deposit investment products and services available to credit union members.

**Membership in the 2015 Round Table is based on production equal to or greater than $92,000 in eligible commissions paid or $184,000 paid premium earned or $158,000 in annual gross income during 2014. An individual becomes a Qualifying and Life member when approved for the 10th year of membership.

***Chartered Retirement Planning Counselor℠ and CRPC® are registered service marks of the College for Financial Planning®.

CHAPTER 30

HEART TRANSFORMATION®

BY ROBERT TORRES

We *all* have points in our lives where we question our worthiness of being loved. We sometimes wonder if love itself even exists. Many end up accepting and falsely believing in a counterfeit version of love and associated abusive behavior as acceptable. It becomes their perceived reality.

Toxic beliefs held in the mind have negative effects on the emotions which results in unproductive, unhealthy and risky behavior. Yet, no matter how each person interprets love, no one is exempt from experiencing hurt emotions, mental confusion, a broken spirit and a sorrowful heart. However, don't despair, there is good news.

I have discovered a spiritual and scientific treatment approach to restoring and maintaining healthy emotions and soundness of mind, and I call it **Heart Transformation®**.

MORGAN'S STORY

Morgan, a 15-year-old girl from a divorced family, was torn between her mother and father. Her father Chadwick was a successful businessman who lived overseas, while her mother Ethel lived in the United States. *Like most divorces, this created hurt and dysfunction within this little girl.* Morgan became very rebellious, continually acting out through dangerous behaviors, such as experimenting with drugs and promiscuity. She had undergone extensive counseling and had been in some of the most elite, costly treatment centers in the country. Yet, nothing was working.

Morgan was desperate for a one-way ticket out of this world. After numerous suicide attempts, she guzzled down from a bottle of bleach. They found her passed out and she was immediately rushed to the hospital. Miraculously, she survived unimpaired.

Shortly thereafter, she stole a vehicle and recklessly drove it on the freeway, then ran into a truck. She spun out of control, also hitting the car of an elderly couple. Miraculously again, she and everyone involved survived the accident. She was sentenced to serve time in juvenile hall.

Her parents heard about our inpatient residential treatment program for children, teens and dependent young adults, which uses the Heart Transformation® therapy. After an evaluation, I called her parents for an emergency meeting. The situation was dire! I said, "Your daughter IS going to commit suicide. It's not a matter of *if*; it's a matter of *when*. Many times kids threaten suicide as a manipulation tactic, but her ultimate reason for wanting to commit suicide is that she feels as if her happiness lies within her ideals of having a stable family. She feels like she got cheated out of having a beautiful family experience and childhood. She has been left longing for those years that she's lost and she wants them back."

Her parents defensively replied with, "She's manipulating. There's nothing we can do about it; she needs to find her happiness in God."

I realize that statements such as this are easy to say, but they are not practical. I continued on. "Let me tell you what she's saying. She genuinely believes that if mom and dad can't get back together, then there is no purpose in her living. So she is going to kill herself."

"Are you suggesting that we get remarried when we both already have spouses? Ethel is also expecting another child from her current husband," Chadwick explained. Of course that wasn't what I was saying and being met with resistance was not surprising, either. They continued trying to make themselves believe that their daughter wasn't feeling the way that she was. *Deep down, it was clear that they knew that Morgan's feelings were very true and very real to her. After all, she had proven that she was very serious.*

At a later time, I took the opportunity to share Morgan's story during a meeting I was holding at an adolescent psychiatric center where doctors, psychiatrists, and mental health specialists were present. I asked, "What would be your counsel?" The range of answers I received surprised me. They talked about the symptoms and labels of the problem. Morgan was accused of manipulation and selfishness. Yet, without one single solution, they were stumped. The only thing that was unanimous was that nobody had any answers. Morgan had already been on too many psychotropic medications and in and out of mental hospitals. Her parents were good people who had tried the punishment and reward system that most parents use. All to no avail. I concluded the meeting with this: "So, based on your answers, this little girl will end up dead. She is going to commit suicide because none of you have an answer and it's over." **You could hear a pin drop and feel the discomfort within the room.**

I gave them a moment to reflect before speaking again. "Let me tell you how we were able to help her. Morgan, her parents, and I were in a meeting and I asked Morgan, 'What if you believed that you and your parents would all go to heaven when you die? According to the Bible, there's no marriage in Heaven. Everybody is your brother and sister. You live for eternity and you can spend time as a family for as long as you want. There's no more pain and no more tears in heaven. What do you think about that? Do you think you could just hold out for that day?'"

At that moment, Morgan's eyes sparked, showing a ray of hope. Her beautiful answer to the question was, "Yes. I believe." That day, hope was all she needed. Faith is just one of many concepts that Heart Transformation® uses in its approach. *This nugget of hope that had been presented to her that day was perceived by her as love.* **Hope and love are not restricted to time and distance. What was once an impossibility had suddenly become a possibility.** *Real enough to save her life.* From that moment forward, this little girl not only excelled in the treatment program, but she went on to live a successful life.

I concluded this interaction with these mental health specialists by sharing, *"In all of your studying and in all of your learning, you failed to study one thing: the principles of faith, hope, and love applied directly toward the heart as a viable form of medicine."*

A love like we've never known

This is not only a story of faith and hope but one of love. Morgan did not have to change anything to receive the gift of love and acceptance without condition. It comes natural to humans to love on the conditions of their expectations and standards. A spiritual renewal of mind and perspective is required to love someone unselfishly. We call this Heart Transformation®.

In performance-based love, emotional approval or withdrawal become the reward or punishment for performance and behavior. Soon children start thinking that their self-worth is in the things that they do instead of who they are in their identity.

It sets up expectations and timeframes that a child may or may not be able to live up to in that moment. *Think back to when you were a child.* Did you always meet your parent's expectations? When you didn't, how did you react? Depending on your personality whether passive or aggressive, compliant or stubborn, or something in between, it still hurt the relationship and it caused you to internalize those feelings or act out and rebel.

Disappointment is a toxic emotion that breeds false identity

It's not just parents, either. The same expectations are put into play with teachers, coaches, family, and friends. One of the worst forms of not feeling loved is when in our own perception we feel as though we have become a disappointment in the eyes of those we care about. An even worse scenario is to be governed by what others think of you. Especially when those expectations are of people who really don't care about you, or don't have your best interests at heart.

Expressed disapproval from those whose opinions we value can make us feel like a failure or we self-destruct and justify ourselves as being bad people. It isn't uncommon for the girl next door to call herself a bitch these days. These learning moments can devastate the psyche, which shapes their future. They may end up:

- Deciding to no longer care—they're going to do what they "gotta do," regardless of what anyone else thinks.

- Subscribing to the fact that they are a failure so why bother trying—they cannot succeed. It's not worth the effort because they can never please their parents no matter what they do.

Children suddenly agree with the conclusion of someone else's unfulfilled expectations and succumb to the idea that they were born this way, it's who they are and there's nothing they can do about it.

Perceived Love

As adults, these confused children pass on these values as truths to their peers and on to the next generation. The human psychology (soul and mind), regardless of religion, race or gender, responds profoundly to the thought that God, the universe, a higher power or whatever deity they call him, is now upset with them. Suddenly God is viewed as an angry judge ready to punish, instead of being a friendly and loving Creator. Before we know it, bitter perceptions are formed against God. Other times it's a lot easier and even less painful to not believe in a God that is difficult to please. More times than not, religion, along with its own set of conditions, further aids this false mindset. Fear of God's rejection and efforts to acquire blessings or "get right" with him causes people to live a life of repetitive, religious calisthenics that they mistakenly call "spiritual." Religion teaches us to pray with remorse and regret, be faithful to certain activities, give money, do this and don't do that—all to please God. Yet the only thing that pleases God is our happiness and our acceptance of his unmerited forgiveness, love and favor which was established long ago before we were born. It's no different than a child trying to please their parents for approval instead of relying on the security that comes from the relationship. Changing someone's ideas and behavior is so much easier to accomplish when one perceives they're loved.

Toddlers and children are constantly pressured to perform for fear of losing mommy and daddy's hugs and smiles. By around 11 to 13 years old, they become rebellious towards parents. Soon the tables turn and children administer emotional rewards and punishments on their parents in order to get what they want. Professionals call this manipulation, but it is learned behavior that parents teach. Most of our frustrations with another person are rooted in our own unfulfilled expectations. *If our expectations haven't been fulfilled, how can we fulfill another person's?* We get stuck—giving up on love. We make canned statements such as, "I am worried about you because I love you," or "I'm upset with you because I care about you." My favorite one is, "God hates the sin but loves the sinner." Try telling that to someone who has their identity wrapped up in their behavior along with all the self-fulfilling prophesies that have been spoken over them, "If you keep behaving in this or that fashion, you will end up a loser," Before you know it we have forged a false identity based on behavior instead of our true identity; God's beloved child.

The answer to feeling loved and valued is found in five sequential steps which starts with God's love.

FIVE STEPS OF DISCOVERING LOVE THROUGH HEART TRANSFORMATION®

How do we really find love so we can experience it and understand it?

1. **Believe who God is** - At some point in time every person will have a need to seek a greater love beyond themselves, the ones they care for, and the ones they are cared by. God is that father to all of his creation and has reconciled his relationship with fallen mankind by forgetting all their wrongs committed. He is committed to the relationship and promises to never leave you or forsake you. You don't have to fear being judged and you can't disappoint him. He has peaceful thoughts toward you—nothing else.

2. **Believe who you are** - If you're a Peterson and on occasion you wear a mustache and a sombrero, it doesn't make you a Gomez. You're still a Peterson regardless of the costume you decide to wear. You are a child of God. You are more than a conqueror. You can do all things and nothing will be impossible for you to accomplish. That is your identity regardless of how you behave—nothing can change that.

3. **Believe you are loved** - There has to be someone, somewhere in the universe who can truly accept and love you just the way you are. That person is God and he is love and he wants to live in each and every person. Wherever there is true love, God is indiscriminately present regardless of anyone's religious views or lack thereof. You can't love God, yourself or anyone if you don't understand that he loved you first. It is far more important to know that God loves you.

4. **Learn to love yourself** - It's impossible to truly love, forgive and accept yourself with all of your imperfections until someone has role-modeled this love to you. Only God is capable of such love. It takes

experiencing genuine love in action for you to realize that you too, can accept yourself just the way you are. Not until then, will you will be able to honestly tell yourself, "I love me, just as I am."

5. **Learn to love others** - Freely you have received and now you can freely become that vessel of joy to the depressed; peace to the fearful and anxious; good to the undeserving and love to the broken-hearted. You will give to others what you have longed for yourself. It's like discovering the cure to cancer and wanting to share it with the whole world.

Follow these five steps and over time, the law of love will exceed the requirements of rules and morals. In time the fruit of change will blossom in your life; All in God's time and nobody else's.

THE SCIENCE OF HEART TRANSFORMATION®

The energy of love is the last frontier of scientific discovery. It can create the change we've envisioned! It can give us wholeness of mind and healing of emotions. Imagine, a force so powerful that it could guarantee to keep the flame alive in couples. Parent-child relationships can become more intimate and honest over time. Families will be able to trust in happiness. Mankind has made huge advancement in technology, information, medicine and economics. **But now we have the greatest scientific discovery which solves the human condition:**

IT IS HEART TRANSFORMATION®.

About Robert

Robert Torres, a straight "A" student during his elementary school years, was recruited into the Mentally Gifted Minds program. As Robert approached his adolescent years, he got trapped into a culture of promiscuity, partying and substance abuse. It eventually led to a life of crime and gang violence. By age 18, Robert had come to the end of his rope and ended up behind bars.

While in jail Robert, out of boredom, picked up a Bible and read about a man who loved and accepted sinners. He was intrigued by the fact that Jesus was merciful to the rejects of society but harsh towards religion, it's leaders and the self-righteous. The idea that all his crimes were all forgiven over 2000 years ago and that he could receive the free gift of righteous standing and be totally acquitted undeservedly boggled his mind, but sparked a tiny ray of hope in his heart.

The course of Robert's life had changed which led him to help others like him to turn their lives around. By the time he was 28, he had raised a family and became an accomplished business entrepreneur. Robert founded several non-profit organizations to help families in crisis with troubled teens. Unbeknownst to Robert, religion would become his new gang and self-righteousness would become his new crime. Even though Robert had helped families around the world, his initial relationship with God eventually degenerated into religion-ship.

His performance-based religion had crumbled and ended in moral infidelity and financial bankruptcy. Through his loving wife, Ceci, he would come to rediscover God's mercy and goodness. It was there, in the dark shadows of the valley of failure, that Robert discovered God's acceptance and love towards him had not changed one bit from the time he was just a lost teenager.

It was in that valley of his life that Heart Transformation® was birthed. Heart Transformation® was created by Robert which now certifies accredited residential inpatient and intensive outpatient programs that provide mental health treatment services anywhere in the world. Heart Transformation® is the first biblically-based treatment modality in the history of mental and behavioral health.

It is a therapeutic approach based on how God treats the heart and the relationship, in spite of behavior. When administered correctly, it has the impact to change hearts, heal emotions and restore mental health resulting in a transformed life.

C.A.R.E.S. Treatment™ is the first CARF internationally-accredited residential treatment facility to offer Heart Transformation Treatment ™.

To schedule a speaking engagement with Robert Torres or if you just want more information to learn how Heart Transformation® can heal your loved-ones' emotions and restore soundness of mind, visit: http://hearttransformation.com and http://hope4teens.org for residential inpatient treatment or intensive outpatient tele-therapy from anywhere in the world on any device.

You can also post questions and comments for Robert on Facebook at: http://facebook.com/hearttransformation.

CHAPTER 31

CHAMPIONS NEVER QUIT!

BY THELMA SAMPLE

Dear mind... "Creativity flows, captured thoughts, endless hope, determination penned to reality, dreams caught, limitless possibilities, stretch for the moon, be bold, you are strong, and achieve your goals..."
~ *Champion* by Thelma Sample

"Ladies and Gentlemen, I have the privilege and distinct honor of introducing you to a true champion who 'never quit' even though for many years, he was in bondage by the choices he made in his life. He was sick and tired of being sick and tired, and he made a bold decision to take his stumbling blocks and turn them into stepping stones. His story is heartfelt, and full of compassion; it was written to inspire and to encourage you to push yourself, beyond the distractions and detours of life." It's a story that defines hope in its rarest form, and it's a reminder to us all that "we are our choices."

Dominic knew his strength lay buried, hidden in his struggles, he had abused drugs and alcohol for over 30 years and had been to prison seven times. One particular day, he was depressed and thinking about all of his past mistakes. His cellmate Keith was reading a book called *Rich Dad Poor Dad*, by Robert Kiyosaki, and he told Dominic if he wanted to change his life, the first thing he needed to do was to change what he believed about himself, and change his thoughts, and to stop filling his empty voids in his life with drugs and alcohol. Furthermore, in the words of Robert Kiyosaki, "It's not what you say out of your mouth that determines your life, it's what you whisper to yourself that has the most power." Dominic had a defining moment, and he began to realize he could not have a negative mind and expect a positive life. He took 100% ownership for the things that happened in his life thus far; he did not like the man he saw in the mirror. At that very moment, Dominic made a powerful decision: this is not how his story will end. Intentionally, he started to believe that he could change, and with that powerful thought the path to freedom began. He internally created a new belief system that started with his mindset. His life had a God-given purpose.

In the words of Mark Twain, "The two most important days in your life are the day you are born and the day you find out why." Dominic realized he had been living his entire life wrong and with the help of God, and through the guidance of Keith, strongholds were broken that day and the old Dominic died. His new adventure in this funny thing called life was birth, and he was now the author.

Keith was able to help Dominic turn his dreams into a well-written plan of action that became his daily routine. His plan consisted of the following habit-forming activities which included: studying his Bible daily, time-stamped goal setting (daily, weekly, monthly, and yearly), accountability partner, reading one personal development/self-help book a month, and using his remaining time wisely. Upon release, he found a job as a Sales Consultant at a major firm, and he quickly climbed to the top of the company in six months!

For the first time in his life, Dominic had a clear vision of his future, and he was determined; he was disciplined; and a hard worker. The good news is that he did it without the use of drugs and alcohol. Dominic had made his mind up. Quitting was not an option anymore and no more excuses, just continual self-improvement. There were over 100 sales consultants at his job, and he was the #1 guy in the company! The person he thought he was, was no match for the person he was becoming, and his best was ahead of him. Dominic stayed the course and after three years he left the company and started his own firm. He was ready to create his own opportunities – his persistence and ambition were in overdrive.

It was in those quiet times that Dominic remembered the powerful words of Keith, and prayed and meditated daily for clarity. Dominic then stepped out in faith and started his own business. Dominic was well prepared for the risk factor of being a business owner and the challenges that lay ahead, and he pressed on in pursuit of his dreams. He had a slow start financially, but each morning, he studied his written blueprint.

After 18 months in business, he had made over a million dollars! Moment by moment, he was tenaciously building himself to become a millionaire. He was very grateful for his massive success, and wondered who he could help? How many more untold, unwritten, history changing, 'Dominic stories' were out there? Dominic never gave up and he continued to challenge himself to grow mentally and to develop intellectually. Walt Disney said, "If you can dream it, you can do it."

Dominic had beaten the odds! He had never met his biological father, he was GED educated and not qualified in the eyes of society. However, he had overcome unimaginable odds and reached milestones many thought were impossible. Dominic was a truly a champion whose journey began at the end of his comfort zone!

Let's explore the **7-Step Road Map** that revolutionized Dominic's life. I challenge you to search inside your life and explore how these steps can help you take action **TODAY!**

1. **Mindset:** The mind is the greatest asset you have; the question is, are you feeding it or starving it? As human beings our minds are more powerful than we can imagine. Our thoughts are either serving a purpose in our daily lives or taking up space in our finite mind. Brian Tracy said it best, "You can accomplish virtually anything if you want it badly enough and if you are willing to work long enough and hard enough."

   Beyond our DNA, our power to grow and develop, to be innovative and creative, our key to change is deeply embedded in our minds. It all starts with our mindset and our belief system is the only thing that sets us apart. Ask yourself, "What do I believe about myself?" "Are my thoughts toxic or healthy?"

Tip: On 3 x 5 notecards, write down positive affirmations, words, and/or phrases to repeat to yourself daily such as: "I am enough, God loves me, I am powerful, I am a champion, I have a great attitude, I am fearless, I am a winner, good things will happen to me today, I live in abundance, I am a visionary!"

2. **Plan of Action:** *Without a plan, the people perished.* Proverbs 29:18. Your goals must be well written and time-stamped with deadlines. Life happens to all of us, there will be roadblocks, distractions, and emergencies, and losses sometimes, beyond our control.

> ***Commitment is the sacrifice you make regardless of the storms of life.***

Be on purpose – (destination highway): Don't get buried in the day-to-day and lose sight of your goals. A useful way of making goals and objectives more powerful and measurable is to use the **SMART Mnemonic**—which stands for Smart, Measurable, Attainable, Relevant, and Time Bound.

Write down your goals in complete detail and check them off as you achieve them. Make sure you include short and long term goals you want to accomplish and go for it! Champions, this is your life, enjoy it, design it, and create experiences so amazing that you WOW yourself!

Every day for 5 minutes study your goals and envision them coming true.

The Bible says, "Now faith is the substance of things hoped for, the evidence of things not seen." (Hebrews 11:1). Put the **Law of Attraction** to work by putting your goals on a vision board. A vision board is a fun and creative visualization tool that represents your goals and a glimpse into the future you want to live. They say, "A picture is worth a thousand words," make sure you choose words and images that represent the vision for your future. A Vision Board is a daily, visual reminder that keeps you focused on your goals and dreams. See it, believe it, and receive it! ***Boldly tell yourself, "I can do this!"***

Tip: Wake up every day with a plan and say "Today will better than yesterday." Review your goals daily and stay committed to achieving them. You are the author of your life, write a bestseller *TODAY!*

3. **Implementation: Getting Started – Someday is not a day,** it is an excuse. Wake up every day and write out how you will spend your day. Remember, there is no easier, softer way, nor

is there a magic formula, and no one is coming to rescue you. ***You are 100% responsible for your life.***

The simple fact is that everyone has the same number of hours in a week – 168 to be exact. The key is to be consistent and stay committed to your vision that motivates you. God has given each one of us a purpose in life. We all have a set of talents and gifts that makes us unique and extraordinary. Time does not stand still for anyone. Successful people have excellent time management skills. Evaluate how you are spending your time and minimize unnecessary activities (time wasters).

Ask yourself:

- What am I doing with the life God gave me?
- What is my daily routine?
- How do I spend the majority of my time?
- Why am I not where I want to be in life?
- What changes can I make to live the best life possible?

Tip: A great acronym to use throughout your day is **P.O.P. = Priorities over Pleasures**, remember there is never going to be a perfect time to get started, you just have to do it! Don't give up, the beginning is always the hardest. Envision the finish, that's the most rewarding.

4. **Measure the results: Self-Evaluation** – Time to take actions toward your written goals and form new life-changing habits. Research shows it takes 21 days to fully break/form a new habit. Interestingly, 21 days is the time required for new neuropathways to be fully formed in your brain! Building better habits is an effective self-improvement tool because it is simply an investment in yourself. You are an eyewitness (just like the cocoon to a caterpillar to a butterfly), to the transformational process in your own life. Wow, that is something to get excited about! You must embrace the process and commit to the 21-day system, and take steps toward the best life you desire.

Let's talk about the negative people, the dream killers – they are EVERYWHERE!

They sound like this:

- You can't do that.

- You'd better stop dreaming and get to work.

- You don't have the money.

- You don't have the experience.

- You are going to fail. …etc., etc., so on, and so on…

Mark Twain said it best, "Keep away from people who try to belittle your ambitions. Small people always do that, but the really great make you feel that you, too, can become great."

Literally, guard your ears from negative, unmotivated people who will steal, kill, or rob you of your dreams. Furthermore, give yourself permission to make mistakes or fail, it is ok, get over it. Many successful people failed their way to success. One of the hardest things in life is working on yourself, and evaluating the people in your life. Be brave enough to surround yourself with assets not liabilities.

Tip: Take small steps every day toward your victory and do more than you did yesterday. Make a conscience effort to track your progress, and measure your results. After you have accomplished one of your 21 day goals, check it off the list. Accept the next goal challenge. Keep going!

5. **Accountability Partner:** Accountability partners are great encouragers and the true definition of a champion. They pick you up and dust you off when all hell is breaking loose in your life. They are a second pair of eyes and ears on your goals and vision board to help you achieve them and live the kind of life you desire.

Tip: An accountability partner is a great asset in your life and for the future life you want to create. Be open, and honest about what you want to accomplish, and lean on them for support, and encouragement. Life is full of unknowns. The good news is you don't have to face it alone!

6. **Wake Up Motivated:** Zig Ziglar said, "Motivation is like bathing, you have to do it daily." In order for your life to change, you have to change. Change is constant and inevitable. Each morning, wake up armored and ready to conquer the day. You must be focused and on purpose with your day-to-day routine.

Remember, Dominic's entire world changed when he began to practice the daily habits such as prayer time, meditation time, visualizing the day ahead, studying his written goals, and speaking positive words of affirmation into the universe (Law of Attraction). Listening to motivational material daily is a powerful tool as well.

Tip: "Don't be upset by the results you didn't get with the work you didn't do." ~ Author Unknown.

Nothing is more of a waste of time, than to be motivated and not take action.

7. **The Power of YOU:** *If life does not challenge you, it won't change you.* Look in the mirror that's your competition. In order for real, long term change to be effective, you have to evaluate all the areas of your life. Give attention to the areas that need personal growth and development. The only thing standing in the way of your success is YOU! Wake up each morning believing you are strong, powerful, and capable. Don't let anything stop you! Always dream big!

Tip: Michael Jordan said "the best thing I ever did was believe in myself." There is always room for improvement, it's the biggest room in the house. Your life can be what you want it to be when you believe in the power of you.

Dominic could not erase the mistakes of his past, but he started with a blank canvas, and created a one-of-a-kind, priceless masterpiece. The champion within him found light in the cracks of his life where darkness had lived for so long, **and he made his mind up to not give up!**

Dear mind: "You were determined, a mission deemed impossible, fear cheated me, the unknown robbed me, addictions were hostile, I died to me, thought about quitting, that's EASY, looked back for a minute, long paused... was I interested? Or fully committed?"

~ Champion by Thelma Sample

About Thelma

Thelma Sample is a humble servant of God, devoted wife, proud mother, a professional speaker and business owner. She is a graduate of the University of Phoenix – Houston Campus, where she pursued a B.S. in Business Management with a minor in Marketing.

Thelma is passionate about helping people reach and aim high for their God-given purpose in life.

Matter of fact, while working for one of the largest tax resolution firms in the country, she generated over $4 million in gross revenues personally in less than three years. Upon being promoted to management, she coached, trained, motivated and developed teams on mastering the art of the one call, along with giving them the necessary tools to enhance their personal and professional growth.

Along with her husband, she currently owns a tax firm, **Success Tax Relief,** which they started with $1,200 of their own money, and it has grown to over a million dollars each year they have been in business!

She has over 20 years of experience in the rewarding field of sales in the following industries: automotive, restaurant marketing and promotions, commercial collections, insurance benefits, and tax resolution, respectively. She is a "sought after" trainer in the arena of sales. Some of the companies she has previously worked with are: Sonic Automotive Group, Brinker International, Ambit Energy, Tax Cite, NKS Debt Recovery, and Coast to Coast Tax Relief. She is a member of International Association of Coaching, Expert Rating Business Coaching, La-Porte-Bayshore Chambers of Commerce, Better Business Bureau, American Society of Tax Problem Solvers, and BOD-Millionaire Mastermind Alliance Group, to name a few.

In her free time, she loves riding her bike while listening to her favorite artist Beyoncé, she enjoys various women church events, spending time with her family, writing poetry, and attending classic car shows. Her ultimate goal is to leave an impact on the lives she touches.

CHAPTER 32

CRISIS AND CHANGE

BY STEVE WOOD

There is nothing special or different about Daniel. In fact, he is the epitome of an ordinary guy and always has been. He was an average student. He got a steady job after college, and dated a few girls before he met the love of his life, Jeanie. They were married young, he was under 20, and started out on the adventure of life. He and his wife would sit for hours and talk and dream and make plans for their future. Of course not everything went according to plan, there were hiccups and trials and tests along the way, but with support from each other they were able to overcome the obstacles and move forward together.

They scrimped and saved to get the deposit for a house – a small, modest house, but their house. Then, according to plan, it was time to start a family, and according to plan, the babies arrived. First a happy, bubbly, baby boy. Two years later another baby boy, not so bubbly, and three years later a beautiful baby girl.

Daniel and Jeanie had a good life. Sure they had the usual inconvenient debts; mortgage, car payments and household bills, but they managed to have a holiday most years and still put money away for the future. But something else was going on.

Slowly but surely Daniel's life changed from being free and easy, to the regimented life of providing for a family, raising children and working around the children's schedules. Daniel's life became less and less about his and Jeanie's plans and more and more about the plans for their children.

It all began innocently enough. "Can you drop the kids off at play school? I will pick them up later." "You take Joey to Chris's birthday party and I'll take Mike and Jane to Billy's party." Then it was "Joey's got practice at 6 in the morning, can you take him? I've promised Jane I will take her to swimming class." Both Daniel and Jeanie kept up with the "obligations" and in fact enjoyed doing it. As time went on they all developed routines and habits to accomplish things with the minimum amount of effort and in the shortest possible time.

One day, not long before his fiftieth birthday, Daniel realised that the first half of his life had already passed by, but he had been too busy being a husband and a father to notice, and now what did he have to show for it? A mortgage, debts and of course three children that had grown into decent people, and left home, married and began their own life adventures. What more could he ask for, he thought. "Nothing" was his reply and he sat for a moment thinking about his past life and feeling proud of how he and Jeanie had raised their children. Then he said to himself "so why do I feel so down, so empty, so lost, so fed up with my life, as if I've been a failure, as if I have no future? Geez! I'm not even fifty, yet."

As I said at the beginning of the story, there is nothing special or different about Daniel. He had just reached a crisis in his life and although this story was about Daniel, it could just as easily have been about Jeanie, or you or me. Crisis doesn't distinguish between the sexes or individuals. Anyone and everyone can be a target for crisis and at any time in their life. Some of us meet crisis more than once.

If we look up the meaning of crisis in any dictionary we find there are many definitions, but if we focus on the definitions related to people we will find they are mostly to do with change, transition, turning points, making decisions and emotional upheaval due to change or loss, especially of a loved one.

We need to understand that a crisis is a point in time, where circumstances change. Circumstances will always be different from this point forward, for better or worse, and there is no going back to the state before this point.

Once we have reached a crisis and we understand there is no going back, the best way to view the situation is as a challenge because that is, in fact, what a crisis is. The challenge is to make a decision as to which way we want to proceed. It's like driving down a one-way street in a strange city and coming to a stop sign at a fork in the road. We stop the car and think, "now, what do I do? I can't go back, it's a one-way street. If I take the left fork I'll be going west, if I take the right fork I'll be going east, if I stay here I am not going anywhere. What is it I want to do?"

Let's go back and analyse Daniel's story and see what got him to his turning point where all those emotions, feelings and thoughts were playing with his mind.

He had spent the last 20 to 25 years taking care of his family. Everything he had done was based on what he felt was best for the family. He scheduled his vacations around school vacations and the children's commitments. He purchased cars, even down to the sound system, based on what was practical or desired for the whole family. They chose a house based on what he and Jeanie felt was best for the children. A relatively safe neighborhood, well-lit streets at night, good public transportation and plenty of amenities for children to socialize, and of course, good schools.

Now none of this mattered. His last child had left the nest and taken his place in the world along with his other children. Of course he still loved his children and they still loved him. He and Jeanie, their children and their spouses all met regularly and had a great time. But things were different. Daniel was no longer the number one go to guy. His daughter no longer went to him for advice and help with minor problems, she went to her husband instead. His sons were eager to be the best husbands they could and were developing their independence by showing their wives that they could handle problems and were quite capable of performing repairs around the house. His children had other loved ones in their lives and responsibilities to those people.

Daniel was experiencing a lot of emotional upheaval, most of it to do with issues related to change. He will continue to go through mental turmoil until these issues are resolved. So let us talk about change, what it is, how it affects us, how we typically respond to it and how we can use it for our benefit.

CHANGE

Change can mean many things. The change I am referring to here is the introduction of something that takes people out of their comfort zone. Depending on the individual's point of view, change can be good or bad. The physical acting out or performance of the change is relatively quick and simple, but the mental transition to change is not so quick or simple. People need time and often instruction to mentally adjust (transition) to change; the amount of time depends on the individual and the circumstances. People who are more "easy going" toward life, generally take less time to transition to the change than people who are more fixed in their approach to life. Change can be awkward at first for everyone, but some people thrive on the challenge while others continue to resist and never feel comfortable with the change. We need change, especially if we are unhappy with where we are, or when the old ways of doing things no longer work.

Some things to understand about change:

1. It is about doing something we are not used to doing

2. There is always a reaction to change

3. Change often leads us to think about what we have lost, instead of what we could gain

4. Although some of us might be happy to greet change, for many it can be worrisome and overwhelming

5. If the pressure or desire to change is removed, we will return to our previous behaviors

Some Myths about change:

1. Change always comes with resistance or conflict
   • This is totally false. It is true that many people resist change but it is also true that many people seek out change and purposely introduce change into their lives as a way of reigniting a passion for life.

2. We must plan ahead for every aspect of change
   • Again this is not true. Sometimes, we are totally unaware that change is about to happen so how can we plan for it?

3. No one will embrace it
   • As I said in #1 above, some people seek out change.

DEALING WITH CHANGE

Adapting to change is about dealing with the transition to change; this can be a stressful process, the earlier we can identify our goals, the better. (Habit #2 from Steven Covey: Begin with the end in mind.) We may need some guidance to understand the new direction our life has taken, and our place in it. Talking to others can be a double-edged sword, so seek out people who have a positive outlook and who can see the positive side of change.

Positive stress (aka *eustress*) can be a very helpful tool in dealing with change. Positive stress motivates, it increases energy levels, and can drive people forward to embrace the change, this decreases the transition period

What about having no stress at all? An absence of stress can lead to boredom and/or frustration, which in turn can lead to fatigue. A balance of positive stress is ideal, although what is good stress for one person can be negative for another.

STRESS MANAGEMENT TECHNIQUES

There are a number of methods to help manage stress. Don't try them all at once, but a combination of several techniques can help us to approach change in a healthy and resilient way.

1. Humor:
Laughter truly is great medicine. In this day and age, however, we have to ensure that jokes and humor respect the people around us. Avoid jokes that may hurt other people's feelings, for instance but not limited to, racial, political, or religious sentiments. Jokes are only a small part of humor. For the past 20 years, one of my goals has been to make everyone I meet smile, not by telling jokes, but by simply engaging in light conversation. It has done wonders for my outlook on life.

2. Music:
Music is another stress reducer for many people. People may select music that helps them to relax, almost meditate, or they may prefer music that helps to provoke intensified feelings of energy.

3. Exercise:
Exercise, because of the hormones released, is an excellent way to reduce stress and put us in a good frame of mind.

4. Deep Relaxation Techniques:
Achieving a state of deep relaxation takes practice. However, once you

have learned a particular technique, you will be able to become deeply relaxed within a few minutes. If you decide to try deep relaxation, choose the method that appeals to you most. Don't expect dramatic, overnight results. Relaxation does not eliminate tension entirely if you are extremely upset, but it will reduce the tension.

5. Momentary Relaxation Techniques:
You can use Momentary relaxation whenever and wherever you like so it is more practical than deep relaxation. Developing a habit of taking short breaks throughout the day can counteract stress build-up.

6. Deep Breathing:
The rhythm and regularity of deep breathing can have a calming effect on your nervous system. Sit quietly, close your eyes, and let your attention focus on your breathing. Breathe through your nose and let your shoulder and neck muscles relax.

7. Visualization:
Imagine yourself in a restful place (e.g., on a beach). Try to imagine all the sensations you would feel: sun on your face, wind in your hair, and the sound of waves lapping against the shore and the sound of seagulls. The more detail you add, the more quickly you will relax.

Now, let's go back to Daniel's story. . .

If you remember, he said he was feeling down, empty, lost, and fed up with his life. He felt as if he was a failure and had no future, yet he wasn't even fifty. After carrying these feelings around for awhile he did something that most men don't like to do. He confided in a friend, and then another friend. He soon realized he was normal, and that these feelings he was experiencing were also normal. His friends told him he needed to do something about these feelings or they would pull him right down. "What can I do?" he asked, and they reeled off the following list of options as Daniel made notes:

1. Stop looking at everything from the negative side and start looking from the positive side. There are always two sides.

2. Make a list of things you would like to do. Then make plans to do them with specific time lines. For example, take dancing classes with Jeanie, or make a list of different restaurants you

and Jeanie would like to try over the next year and put it into a schedule so it happens.

3. Join an organization like Rotary that meets on a regular basis. Their schedule will be your schedule.

"The list is endless." they said, "but whatever it is, it needs to have a schedule, because schedules create deadlines and deadlines make us do things."

Fast forward ten years. Daniel has a very happy demeanor. He took the advice his friends gave him which led him to attend some council meetings. He became so interested in the council meetings that he ended up running for council and has been a councilor now for the past five years. He often thinks back to the time when he felt so down, and then says to himself, "What a kick in the pants that was!"

About Steve

Steve Wood, C.Aed, DTM, lives in Ontario, Canada.

Steve was born in Liverpool, England where he attended college and obtained his mechanical engineering degree. A couple of years later, he and his wife decided to emigrate to Canada. He loved his new life in Canada but soon realized there would be more opportunities for him if he had an electronic background. So while working fulltime, he went back to college parttime (four hours per night, four nights a week, for two years) to obtain his electro-mechanical engineering certificate. This enabled Steve to get his dream job in robotics. While working in this field, Steve's position morphed into training others in this area and topics like health and safety.

Steve wanted to be a better trainer / presenter, so he joined the Toastmasters organization to improve his communication skills. Steve soon realized he loved seeing folks improve their skills and develop confidence in themselves. Helping others improve their lives became his passion, and Steve once again went back to college to obtain an Adult Education Certificate.

Steve is an award winning, high energy speaker and trainer. Clients applaud his effectiveness as a trainer and motivator. Steve's natural and easy humor style, engages and motivates his audiences and they leave with a newfound belief in their abilities.

Having gone through crises himself, Steve draws from his own experiences and has led thousands of folks to pivotal change in their business and personal objectives. Steve has helped folks overcome their fears and has paved the way for many of his students to learn to embrace change and ignite their lives by making change work for them.

To learn more about Steve, visit his web site at: www.stephenkwood.com.

CHAPTER 33

THE GIFT OF INDEPENDENCE
—Finding resiliency after a traumatic event

BY CHRISTINE M. BOORAS

The 4th of July was always one of my favorite holidays of the year and the one in 1990 was to be no exception. The day was to be focused on celebrating our country's independence and witnessing spectacular fireworks, but my highlights were to indulge in more than my share of Bar-B-Q chicken and banana pudding. With visions of sugar-laden desserts swirling in my brain, I set out for a long bicycle ride at two-o-clock in the afternoon in an effort to burn off some pre-buffet calories. The outdoor temperatures exceeded ninety-eight degrees, so my prediction of caloric expenditure was to be accurate. But what I did not anticipate was having an encounter with a stranger that could have ended my life.

While riding my bike on a public road in an affluent subdivision about two miles from my house, my pleasurable outdoor experience was abruptly interrupted when a guy on a motorcycle sped up from behind and kicked me on my low back as he zoomed by. Propelling forward at high speed, I crashed and skidded on the newly paved asphalt road, tumbling violently. The left side of my body took most of the impact and it felt as though fire had erupted on my skin, which ended up being freshly poured asphalt embedding into my arm, head, shoulder and leg.

315

Lying face-up in a semi-conscious state in the middle of the road, I heard the motorcycle engine stop and footsteps thudding heavily and quickly in my direction. The motorcyclist had parked and was running back to help me - or so I assumed. I hadn't opened my eyes yet but felt him kneel down at my side. Putting his hand on my abdomen, he whispered, "Are you okay?"

With my eyes still closed, I exhaled with relief. But my relaxed state was short-lived. To my disbelief, the stranger took advantage of my downed state and launched himself on top of me. Aggressively groping and pulling at my biking shorts and tank top, I desperately struggled under him, kicking, squirming and cussing with all my five-foot two-inch body could muster. Pinning my hips with his lower body he was pulling at my clothing but I kept writhing, making it difficult to latch on. Eventually I was able to roll over on my side into a fetal position, trying to protect as much as of my body as possible as he sat on top of me fighting to make progress.

His intentions were now very clear: he was trying to rape me - in the middle of the road - in broad daylight.

In twisting under his body my head wound up being directly under his, which was to my advantage. He was still wearing his motorcycle helmet, pressing it against my head, and it gave me something to grab on to. Fumbling frantically, I was able to insert my right hand under the helmet by his face and tugged as hard as I could on the mouthpiece. Surprisingly, my quick jerking motion was enough to forcefully flip him off of me. He landed with a thud about six feet away. Instantly reacting to my freedom, I scrambled to my knees and sprung up like a jack-in-the-box.

I was in a total state of shock and felt numb everywhere, having just been violently knocked off of my bike and then pounced upon like prey while lying in the road. But I was also furious and felt anger spiraling up my spine. Standing as tall as I could and putting hands on both of my hips, I felt my eyes shrink to slits and steam exited both eardrums. I shot dagger-like looks at the punk, now standing directly across from me, and yelled "What is your problem?!"

He paused momentarily, then lunged forward and punched me in the face - twice. It happened so fast I didn't have time to block or deflect his strikes. Again, shock and disbelief. My legs wobbled like rubber bands and I felt woozy, but I didn't go down. The "flight or fight" response finally kicked in and my body sensed the need to prepare for battle. Throwing both of my hands up like a boxer, we squared off - me and this stranger in the middle of the road. I had no idea what to do but going down like a pansy was not an option.

The attacker just smiled - a sickening little smile from a coward that hid behind his helmet and sunglasses. I started seething and could feel my whole body tightening and blood pressure rising. I wanted to pulverize this guy, but I knew I couldn't. Plus, he had the advantage - I was wounded.

"Keep standing up! Damn it! Stay up! Stand up!" I was now talking to myself aloud, trying to grasp what was happening.

The attacker started hopping around like he was performing in a boxing ring for a cheering crowd, throwing jabs at me that I miraculously redirected or blocked. He had gotten in his first two punches, but I wasn't going to let any more touch me if I could help it. He didn't seem to be trying very hard; just toying with me. But that gave me time to settle my breath and gather my wits. I was trembling violently, and felt exceptionally weak, but a feeling of calmness unexpectedly cascaded over me and I started smiling. The whole situation was bizarre and just plain weird.

Shaking my head back and forth I said aloud, "I can't believe this is happening." He must have thought my comment was amusing too because he started smiling and hopping around, jabbing even more energetically like a tiger playing with its victim.

That *really* pissed me off.

"You're sick!" spewed venomously from my mouth. The stranger paused briefly from his antics and his smile grew wider, showing the space between his two very white front teeth. To my surprise, I reflexively provided a quick kick to his groin while my trembling knees barely held my weight. It felt like I had only brushed a butterfly from my shoe, but the blow was apparently enough to be effective, or he was shocked that I had made contact. Dropping his boxing stance, he just stood there looking at me.

"You're just sick!" I shouted ferociously. Deliberately pausing, he suddenly lunged towards me and I instinctively jumped back. But it wasn't me he wanted; it was my stereo headphones that had fallen to the asphalt, knocked off of my head during the scuffle. From five feet away I watched the attacker casually retrieve his consolation prize. Wrapping them around his neck and smiling smugly behind dark glasses, he spun around on his heels and slowly strutted off like a peacock down the street towards his motorcycle. I began fuming at his cockiness and felt flames rising from the hot asphalt under the soles of my feet rushing directly to my head.

"YOU SON OF A BITCH!" I screamed hysterically and started sprinting after him like a crazed cheetah, adrenaline in hyper-drive. I think my aggressiveness and deranged behavior startled him because he started running too, quickly arriving at his motorcycle. I had already slowed my pace after only about twenty yards, knowing that I could never catch him. And I also knew he could come back and finish me off. The attacker had strategically parked his motorcycle far enough away, around a curve and hidden from my view, so obtaining a good description would be impossible. I heard him start his motorcycle and speed off. Remaining still for a few moments, I listened for the high whine of his engine just in case he decided to circle back and give me a little more abuse. For what had seemed like an eternity, not a single car or person came to my aid and it was one of the longest ten minutes of my life.

Pausing for a moment in silence, I stumbled back to my bike which was crumpled and bent in several places from crashing on the asphalt. Lifting it up I began walking towards the main road which was only about fifty yards away. Then it sunk in about what had just happened. Shaking and sobbing, it felt as though my feet weren't touching the ground and that it was all a dream. I kept saying aloud repeatedly, "This can't be happening."

But it was. And it had.

Upon reaching the main road, a car with an elderly couple inside pulled up beside me, rolled down their window and asked if I was okay. Limping along the road with torn and bloodied clothing, it was obvious that I wasn't and they directed me to a guard gate of the community. It was surreal to see just how close this incident had occurred to where others could have been a witness or heard what was going on. Timing is everything. And you can be in the wrong place at the wrong time - and I certainly was that day.

From the guard gate the police were called and the staff provided me with ice for my swollen face. After about thirty minutes an officer arrived and I began detailing the event to him, which even he had a hard time believing had happened without any provocation on my part. Because it was a physical assault, a detective had to be called in to assist in writing up the report. For the next two hours I provided as many specifics as I could about the attacker, completed the necessary paperwork and then asked for a ride home since my bike was totaled. A police report was filed and the incident was documented as "Attempted Sexual Battery" and I was provided with a copy as a memoir.

After showering, I drove myself to the hospital emergency department where I spent the rest of the evening having the staff perform x-rays and scrape asphalt out of my shoulder, arm and knee where it had been deeply embedded while sliding on the road during my crash. I was given a tetanus shot in one arm and another shot in the other arm and sent on my way. Surrounded by exploding celebratory fireworks that night, I felt thankful to be alive but my nervous system was jacked up to Level Red, wanting just to go somewhere and hide.

The days, weeks, and months to follow were a challenge on not only a physical level but emotionally as well. Especially how I was treated by others. To my surprise, when I would describe what had happened, the most common response I received was, "Well, what do you expect? Riding by yourself? And wearing shorts?"

What? I was shocked by how insensitive people were being, judging me as though I deserved it. Apparently, I should have known better than to venture out alone at two o'clock in the afternoon; to ride my bike by myself on a neighborhood street; to wear shorts and a tank top when it's only ninety-eight degrees outside. Shame on me!

These reactions were disappointing and frustrating, tainting my attitude towards people - how unfair and judgmental some can be. According to the detective contacting me afterwards from the Sexual Crimes division of our Sheriff's Office, this type of reaction is common when people hear about something bizarre or cruel being done to another person. As human beings we search for a coping mechanism in efforts to rationalize why someone would purposely harm another without being provoked. We have the need to blame someone - and often times it ends up being the victim.

Being an overly-sensitive introvert with extremely low self-esteem most of my life, receiving this criticism and blame for what had happened could have plummeted me down into an emotional abyss. But fortunately, in the early 1980's a friend had introduced me to a self-help program by Brian Tracy entitled "The Psychology of Achievement." The cassette tape program truly changed my life. I had absorbed, practiced and instilled the principles contained within them and they would serve as powerful tools for not only my survival but success. After the attack, I went through ups and downs but listened to his tapes daily for assurance and motivation, finding these five principles to be the most empowering:

1. **Take 100% responsibility for your life and the choices you make.** I could have said, "Why did this happen to me?" and kept a victim mentality, but realized it would only weaken me. Things happen, and they may not be your fault, but you need to move on with your life. Acceptance of responsibility is not optional: it is mandatory.

2. **Avoid catching the crippling disease of "excusitis"—it's fatal to success.** We can always come up with reasons why we can't do something, but if you want it bad enough, you will find a way to overcome obstacles.

3. **Establish personal goals to provide a sense of meaning and purpose.** I set goals for my physical body which gave me self-confidence and strength, pursuing certifications as a Personal Trainer and Group Fitness Instructor. And I started taking Kung Fu, ultimately holding a U.S. Open title and national ranking in the top five of my division during my first year of martial arts competition. All humans have a success instinct but we must set it free to do the work.

4. **Say "I like myself" several times a day.** It's not being conceited. It's about being the person you want to be. Don't let judgments by others determine who you are.

5. **Stop blaming others for where you are in your life right now and do not accept being blamed by others for their situation.** Responsibility looks to the future and blame looks to the past. The key to ridding yourself of negative emotions is to eliminate blaming others for where you are in your life. Replace blame with "I am responsible".

July 4th, Independence Day, is the day the United States of America was declared a free nation and is one of celebration. As a human being, I feel we all have the right to be free, no matter what area of the world we live in. We strive for it and too many have died for it. Once we become of legal age, we have the right to do as we choose, and must pay the price and consequences if we make poor choices. Blaming others for our predicaments is futile.

Our current situation is always a result of the choices we have made in our life or have allowed others to make for us. Peace of mind means freedom from fear. We can change our situation, but it takes courage and tenacity. Realizing that we can obtain that peace of mind by taking responsibility for our lives is truly empowering.

About Christine

Christine Booras began her professional career working as a Manager of Human Resources in a corporate environment for Southeast Toyota Distributors, Inc. after graduating from the University of Florida with a Bachelor's degree in Psychology. Throughout her long-term employment with Toyota she gained valuable experience in conducting training programs, communicating with both salaried and hourly employees, and organizational management. During her tenure with Toyota she also pursued licensing as a Massage Therapist and certifications in personal training and group fitness.

In 1995, she said goodbye to the corporate world and opened her own business offering therapeutic massage and group fitness classes in yoga, Zumba and Tai Chi. In 2005, she added another skill to her professional toolbox and obtained her Florida Real Estate license. She continues to be an agent today, working with Continental Realty of Jax, Inc.

In addition to wellness and real estate, Christine is a published author of various publications and a memoir focusing on personal growth entitled: *Me, My Ferals & I: How a colony of cats freed me to discover the feral within.* Having pets as a child, she has always had a strong bond with animals, wildlife and nature and has volunteered with various animal groups and sanctuaries, including the Jacksonville Zoological Gardens and Marineland in St. Augustine, Florida. She is currently a professional member of the Cat Writer's Association and Dog Writer's Association of America.

Christine's interest in pursuing unique hobbies and physical activities gives her the ability of pulling from a colorful array of past experiences. Staying with the more conservative sports and group activities in her younger days, such as basketball and marching band, she gradually expanded her horizons, venturing into competitive bodybuilding, fencing, K9 Frisbee competitions, Kung Fu, Tai Chi and Iaido (Samurai Sword). She will often include performing Qi Gong movements for stress reduction in her presentations, encouraging audience participation.

After two knee surgeries, Christine is now involved in less physically demanding yet mentally challenging activities – which include shooting traditional archery and playing the Highland bagpipes. Currently a member of both Jacksonville Pipes and Drums and Jacksonville Fire Rescue Department Pipes and Drums, she performs at special events for individuals, corporations and official city and state celebrations. Christine's business has evolved into Dragonfly Warriors, LLC, offering a variety of health and wellness services. With an emphasis on self-empowerment, her eclectic personal experiences and knowledge makes her a well-rounded presenter and guide for individuals pursuing optimum physical, mental and emotional health.

Christine is a native of Jacksonville, Florida where she currently lives with her husband and menagerie of animal companions.

You can connect with Christine at:

Email: DragonflyWarriors@gmail.com
Website: www.christinebooras.com
Facebook: www.Facebook.com/ChristineBooras

CHAPTER 34

PERFECT PRACTICE MAKES PERFECT

BY CHRISTINE ROMANI-RUBY, PT, D.Ed., MPT, ATC, PMA®CPT

Ignite your life. When I was invited to write a chapter in this book, I found the title intriguing. As I began to make a list of the important points that I wanted to share with you, I centered my thoughts on success in business, in personal life, and in health. However when I read over my list, I realized that igniting your life isn't about being successful, it is about enjoying life. It is about optimizing your human experience.

So what does it mean to optimize the human experience? It means having the ability to embrace all that life makes available to you. In my work as a physical therapist, I spend a great deal of my time working with clients who are unable to fully embrace their lives, due to disabilities, illness, or impaired movement. Their life experience has become difficult because they are unable to move to enjoy their life. There are times when I come out of an initial meeting with a client thinking, "How does one let it get this bad?" Sure, there are accidents and diseases that can limit the ability to move, but often it is just simple neglect of the human frame that has lead clients down this path to immobility.

In the race to success, some clients lose their way. They forget to care for themselves. I have had clients so engrossed in their workday that they sit for hours on end without moving. Or, they are so engrossed in thought about their children or their household, that it becomes a cage for them. Clients repeat the same activities day after day in the race to success and their bodies adapt and conform, building a posture to complete only those tasks efficiently. This then leads to either no movement at all or poor movement at best.

For years we have thought of disability as a result of an accident or an illness. There is an event that leads to poor movement. But in more recent years we are exploring the idea that this process can happen in reverse. Poor movement can exist for years before wear and tear creates pathology. My response to this is, why do we wait? Why do we wait until there is pain or pathology to evaluate our movement and our posture?

With my clients, I often use the example of the 6-month dental appointment. Most of us visit the dentist for a biannual check up to avoid tooth decay. Why is there never a checkup on movement or posture to avoid pathology and dysfunction? I remember even before I became a physical therapist, I wondered why one had to wait until they were injured to seek the expertise of a physical therapist. If physical therapists were the experts in movement, then why wouldn't I seek a regular check up?

There is a great deal of information available on the importance of regular exercise and its ability to decrease the risks of diabetes, heart disease, and cancer. Many people have recognized this and have incorporated regular exercise into their lives. Unfortunately so many people have no idea what to choose for their exercise program or even how to perform that program effectively. For example, I have middle-aged clients that choose running for exercise and even decide to take on the challenge of a marathon. Six months into their training they find themselves stricken with plantar fasciitis or Achilles tendonitis and unable to continue. They started into their program with no attention to the detail of the movement and without experience with this activity. That, combined with weakness and deconditioning, caused them to fail. Possibly, it is time to think of exercise as more than just meaningless movement for burning calories or building muscle. Could it be more precise, and could its practice actually build healthy movement patterns?

In my practice, I incorporate the Pilates method for exercise that was developed in 1920 by Joseph Pilates. Joseph Pilates professed that we cannot separate the mind, body and spirit. Exercise should incorporate the mind as our mind controls our movement. In recent years, the Pilates method has gained a reputation for strengthening the core musculature, but its true benefit is in bringing the mind into exercise and requiring precision and breath in movement. "Perfect practice makes perfect" was what Joseph Pilates professed and this is the only way to regain and maintain healthy movement. If you want to ignite your life, practice perfectly!

One of the biggest obstacles to regular exercise is time. Everyone will tell you that in the hustle and bustle of life that they just can't make the time. My advice, start with something small. For example, something that won't take more time, like getting in and out of your chair properly or standing in good posture. These small daily life activities can be a start to building healthy movement patterns through muscle balance and you can perform them in your normal day. No extra time needed.

There are many misconceptions about posture. For most people, the only ideas that they have about their posture are "stand up straight" or "pull back your shoulders" that were probably preached to them by their mother or teacher. Or, maybe they just focus on having the proper chair, desk, or shoes because they saw an advertisement. Posture is much more than being in a position; it is a working balance, a mental state, and it is poise for movement. If a movement starts from poor posture, the person fails before they begin, as they will certainly have poor movement patterns and over time, pain.

Good posture is a state where muscles are balanced and powerful, where the body can move freely without tenseness, where breathing is effortless, and where gravity is used as an opposition. Posture needs to be visualized. It cannot be dictated. It needs to be felt and practiced so that it becomes natural and even automatic. Good posture should be a habit that can be produced without deep thought or effort. When standing in good posture, our muscles balance one another, which creates both flexibility and strength that will keep us healthy and ready to move efficiently. So, think of standing in good posture as part of your daily exercise. One problem expressed by my clients is that they feel they must make extra time to exercise. It is a wonderful thing if you can take an hour each day to exercise, but if that is too overwhelming, incorporate your exercise into your daily activities.

With one look at standing posture we can identify age, athleticism, personality or pain in another person. We can sense a mood or power without even knowing. Our posture can work for us or against us and we create it with movements and feelings.

Because posture is so interconnected it can be used to create better impressions, improve mood, decrease pain, boost confidence and improve performance. But what defines good posture? Here are some visual cues to help you find good standing posture:

1.   Stand with your feet hip-width apart and stack your hip joints directly over your ankle joints. Feel your weight slightly in your heels. Avoid shifting your weight to just one leg.

2.   Bend at your hip joints to bring your torso slightly forward. Your hips are actually where your leg bends from; I call it your swimsuit line. Then pull your pubic bone toward your nose with your deep abdomen and the back of your legs. Avoid tightening your buttocks to perform this.

3.   Lift your kneecaps and push the ground away with your feet. The front of the thighs will feel engaged.

4.   Reach out of the top back of your head as if your head were the top of a coat hanger on a bar.

5.   Use the hanger of your head to hold your shoulders and imagine your arms hanging like the sleeves of a shirt on the hanger. Notice that the spine holds the arms, not the shoulder blades.

6.   Position your arms at the sides of your body, never behind your body, on your hips, or across your chest. Lengthen your arms by reaching from the elbow and keep the palms facing the sides of the body. Think about holding your arms with your spine rather than your shoulder blades.

7.   Lift your sternum as if to show off a necklace and stack your ribcage over your pelvis. If your ribcage were a large flashlight pointing down toward the floor, the light would shine directly through your pelvis.

8.   Breathe in fully through your nose while expanding the ribs to the sides and the back. Then exhale completely through your mouth without force or strain. I tell my clients that if they were

blowing on a candle, it would flicker, but it would not blow out.

Posture is something that we move in and out of. Do not expect to hold this posture indefinitely, instead strive to pass through it often from memory and habit. It will become home, a place of comfort and strength that your body naturally returns to.

Remember that practice is key. At first, you will need to think hard and produce the posture on purpose but with practice it will become natural and effortless.

My expertise is in the treatment of clients with back problems and this keeps my office full. Eighty percent of adults will experience back pain at some point of their lives and, for most of them, the back pain will never completely go away. Spine problems such as degenerative disc disease and spinal stenosis are not curable. Most back pain is ultimately caused by poor movement patterns and weakness. Aging can be the root cause of both of these and this can begin as early as age thirty years old. Beginning at the age of thirty, adults lose ten percent of their strength every decade and they begin to move less in their hip joints. Both of these changes cause a great deal of stress to the spine. The good news is that research demonstrates that both of these changes can be significantly diminished and even completely avoided with a regular exercise program using proper movement patterns.

The best exercise is one that offers the opportunity to learn better movement patterns. One of the programs that we offer in our clinic is the YUR BACK program. This program is designed to assist those recovering from back pain in re-learning healthy movement patterns through exercise. The program uses the Pilates reformer or Pilates mat exercises to guide clients in new movement patterns and regain strength. The goal is to provide an exercise program that will not cause pain, but will teach healthy movement patterns and good posture. That learning takes patience and practice. A constant rehearsal of good movement is the only way to make good movement a habit and that is the ultimate goal. Clients come to our clinic to study their movement and learn how to improve their movement in daily activities. With good movement patterns as a habit, they are able to fully embrace all of the activity that life has to offer!

About Christine

At PHI Pilates, Dr. Christine Romani-Ruby engages her clients and students in the study of movement. Chrissy enjoys sharing her expertise with clients that may be recovering from an injury and with teachers learning to teach movement. Her studio in Pittsburgh's motto is "The Study of Movement." For over 10 years, clients have been going to Phi Pilates Studio to study their movement and improve their life experience through movement. Teachers in training have been coming to hone their skills in screening and instruction so that they can improve movement in their clients.

An internationally-renowned presenter, Chrissy has a strong background in both teaching and movement with a Doctoral degree in Education from Indiana University of Pennsylvania, a Masters degree in Physical Therapy from Slippery Rock University, a Certificate of Athletic Training from West Chester University, and Bachelors degrees in both Natural and Exercise Science from Indiana University of Pennsylvania. She is also certified as a Pilates instructor by the Pilates Method Alliance. She has authored 6 books and 18 DVD's and founded PHI Pilates that is both a studio and a Pilates teacher training school for fitness and rehabilitation professionals. The school has branches in the United States, Japan, and South Korea.

Chrissy has published in journals and magazines and presents internationally on the subject of Pilates for wellness and rehabilitation. Her clinical experience spans 25 years as a physical therapist and she has worked with clients ranging from young children to professional athletes.

With 25 years of clinical experience as a physical therapist, Chrissy is an expert in movement and she specializes in movement issues of the spine. She has created the YUR BACK program, a unique program of exercise for those recovering from back pain that can be done at home or with a licensed YUR BACK instructor. The program is matched to the client's condition and offers an exercise program that can be performed without risking further injury or pain. Many clients never return to an active lifestyle after back pain because of fear of re-injury. The YUR BACK program takes the fear out of returning to movement and teaches more effective movement patterns.

In addition to running her own studio and school, Dr. Romani-Ruby is an Associate Professor in the Exercise Science and Sport Studies Department at California University of Pennsylvania.

You can connect with Dr. Romani-Ruby at:
- cruby@phipilates.com
- www.phipilates.com

CHAPTER 35

WHAT KIND OF S.M.I.L.E. IS IT THAT CAN MAKE YOUR LIFE CHANGE?

BY FRANKY RONALDY

Man. Because he sacrifices his health in order to make money.
Then he sacrifices money to recuperate his health. And then he is
so anxious about the future that he does not enjoy the present;
the result being that he does not live in the present or the future;
he lives as if he is never going to die, and then dies having
never really lived.

~ Dalai Lama

This might be the first book about self-motivation or inspiration you've read in a long time, or maybe ever. What is your dearest wish? What dreams do you have for the future? What do you want to be or do? Imagine your dream coming true. How wonderful it would be. How fulfilling. What is holding you back from realizing your wish? What is it in you that stops you from really going for it?

It all started from a smile. Would you feel better when people smile at you compared to a frown? It takes fewer muscles to smile than frown. Some claim it takes 43 muscles to frown and 17 to smile. In light of this, you should smile more often and you will look better as a bonus point. The smile, transmitted either consciously or subconsciously, is viewed across cultures as a sign of friendliness, especially when greeting someone. As part co-founder of a powerful system that can be integrated into our daily life to achieve our goals in life, we named it **The Triple-S™** framework. It stands for **The Super S.M.I.L.E. System**.

It comprises five components in this framework to ignite your life and will shine like a flashlight to brighten your path while you walk along your life journey.

S stands for *Self-Motivation*

M stands for *Managing Expectations*

I stands for *Inspiring Others*

L stands for *Learn*

E stands for *Endurance*

I want to take you one step further by giving three "**charms**" for each of them. It is the quality of delighting our daily life which makes it as easy to remember as ABC.

1. SELF-MOTIVATION

*The only conquests which are permanent and leave
no regrets are our conquests over ourselves.*

~ Napoleon Bonaparte

CHARMS: DESIRE | COMMITMENT | DETERMINATION

DESIRE is a fundamental motivator of all our actions. We have a desire to eat because of hunger. What is your most compelling desire? Do you hunger for success? Do you hunger for love? Do you hunger for money or happiness? Extreme starvation incites us to take action to find food. Suppose we have a desire to achieve our dream, the push-factor is how great our desire or how hungry we are to have our dream come true? Allow the hunger desire to become great self-motivation to push you to take action to achieve your dreams.

Most of us love to decide not to decide. It causes us to get stuck and we cannot move on. **COMMITMENT** sometimes intimidates us. Why? Because when we commit to something, this means no excuse is acceptable. One easy way out is by saying "I'll try." If I asked you to attend the meeting, would you say, "I'll try."? Are you suggesting that you will lean towards attending the meeting? NO! No such "try," either you will go or you won't. Are you worried? Be true to yourself. Even though in the end you were not able to go and attend, but at least you proudly say "I did it anyway." It's better than never. Will it be easy? NO! Will it be hurt? YES. Will it be difficult? YES. Even though it is not easy and will hurt and pain, so what? NO PAIN NO GAIN!!!

Focus and gain clarity in your thinking on what you want to achieve. To be a great athlete, you must go through continuous training and exercise. To go through it requires **DETERMINATION**. Be stubborn to your dream. Developing a simple routine for your action which you can implement immediately is a key

2. MANAGING EXPECTATIONS

The three great essentials to achieve anything worthwhile are, first, hard work; second, stick-to-itiveness; third, common sense.

~ Thomas A. Edison

CHARMS: FREEDOM | APPRECIATION | GIVING

Everyone needs **FREEDOM** to do anything without boundaries and be mindful of others. The key problem of human in this century is emptiness. Not only that many people do not know what they want; they often do not have any clear idea of what they feel. We generally can talk fluently about what we should want and expect more, rather than what we ourselves want. Where can we find freedom in life? We get the freedom through playing. It is the excitement that we experienced which makes us feel the happiness and freedom.

All our responsibilities have indirectly created expectations in us. We can't remove our responsibilities, but we can give them secondary importance by putting **APPRECIATION** first. Appreciation begins with the inner self, in the place that is closest to us: Home. Thus, appreciation should start from housework. Start telling the person who did the housework how much you appreciate them.

Some people say there's no such thing as a selfless act. Any time we do something to help another person, we get something in return, even if it's just a warm fuzzy feeling. What is my expectation before I do something for another person? A bit cheesy, but honestly speaking, I want to feel good and show care and love to others. Strangely, when I release the need to control what I get for giving, somehow my expectation starts to get enough. **GIVING** and expecting from others cannot co-exist – perhaps by holding someone's hand when they feel vulnerable can let them know you haven't judged them. Releasing expectations doesn't mean you give other people permission to treat you thoughtlessly. It just means you check in with your motivations and give because you want to. People who care about you will be there for you in return. It is about how do you give just to show you care.

3. INSPIRING OTHERS

When one door closes another door opens; but we often look so long and so regretfully upon the closed door that we do not see the ones which open for us.

~ Alexander Graham Bell

CHARMS: INFLUENCE | GENIUS | DEDICATION

No source of **INFLUENCE** is more powerful and accessible than the persuasive power of the people who make up our social networks. Savvy people know how to tap into the source of influence in hundreds of different ways, and they do so by following one rather simple principle. Be confident. We have to be a role model that it's safe to share bad news and failures, without any artificial words. We dress ourselves well at all times, regardless of the good, the bad and the ugly.

Everybody born with a **GENIUS** within. A toddler doesn't stop learning to walk when they fall. However, we, as adults, stop learning when we fall down (commonly known as *"failure"*) either in business or other areas of our lives. How can we reveal the genius in ourselves and put it to good use? We don't spend enough time thinking because we are often looking for answers. People don't like to think and find solutions, and instead, they complain or wait for someone else to find the answers. Unfortunately, nobody has all the answers. Stop waiting around for someone else to come up with a solution for our difficulties and obstacles. When you think, you will start to reflect and seek ways to achieve your dreams. This is when the genius in you is revealed.

In life, we would rather inspire people than discourage them. To inspire others, we need **DEDICATION**, but it takes a lot of effort to be dedicated. Perseverance is an important part of dedication. Just as with prayer, we have to give all of our dedication. Hence, we should inspire others by dedicating ourselves through praying. Regardless of our beliefs, everyone prays in certain situations. We pray for good, for our family or for safety. This is because everyone has hope, and prayer gives us hope. We inspire others because we hope for good. By inspiring others we also inspire ourselves.

4. LEARN

Well done is better than well said.

~ Benjamin Franklin

CHARMS: CURIOSITY | GROWTH | EXPLORATION

To continuously and actively learn, we need to be curious. We need to ask questions to know more. Through **CURIOSITY**, we explore and have fun. Every failure is part of the learning and growing processes. However, many people do not appreciate learning once their formal education is complete. Always encourage yourself to keep learning and to have a curious mind by asking questions. Use a fun and relaxing method when asking questions to avoid feeling silly. Do not stress and pressure yourself during the process of learning, and making learning fun can be stimulating.

What is the purpose of learning? It is for **GROWTH**. There are many ways to learn. Learning is a life-long process. Every day we must eat, whether you like it or not. If you don't eat there are warning signs triggered from your gastrointestinal tract. To grow, we cannot stop learning. Whenever you feel too drained to learn, think about eating. You must eat to grow and stay healthy.

Humans are born explorers who like to seek new things. Every day, we encounter unexpected events, and like driving a car, anything can happen. We need to keep ourselves focused in our driving and in our **EXPLORATION**. Being an explorer, you tend to always be aware of your surroundings. When everything is interesting to you, you tend to enjoy the journey more. This is why new ideas are easily generated during the process of exploration, because you are driven to reach your destination. Life is like an adventure for you to experience, and having the mindset of an adventurer will make it easier for you to accomplish any undertaking.

5. ENDURANCE

Fate gave to man the courage of endurance.

~ Ludwig van Beethoven

CHARMS: PASSION | REINFORCEMENT | SUSTAINABILITY

Live your life with zeal, because without energy, life is dull. Everyone has energy when they are shopping for their wants and needs because of **PASSION**. Endurance requires energy and, at times, it will drain us more than help us. To overcome this, you must recall your passions while you are out shopping. There are times you might need to shop around to search for the product that you want. This is similar to the process of achieving your dreams, because the first stop may not be the right one. Don't stop if can't find what you are looking for.

To keep our focus, we need **REINFORCEMENT**. Small achievements are reinforcements, which assure us that we are on the right track. Feedback from others is also reassuring, so make sure you are listening to the universe. Listen to your surroundings because the universe sends us signs through our environment. See beyond the surface of things and also try to listen beyond what you usually hear. Your inner self will encourage and strengthen you.

If you can't find sustainable ways to keep your energy, determination and passion at a high level before you reach your goal or dream, chances are you will stop. It is important to constantly revitalise ourselves. **SUSTAINABILITY** and endurance are friends. Watching motivational videos and reading books to continuously rejuvenate our minds is a good idea, but no one-time effort will last long enough for you to reach your goals.

THE TURNING POINT

Yet dreamers are not often doers. Life is not a fairy tale which is predictable; most of times it did not turn out as we expected. Should we feel desperate and disappointed? We should be able to discern between all the options facing us and accurately compute their value – not just in the short term but also in the long term; and we should choose the option that maximizes our best value. If we're faced with a dilemma of any sort, we should take a step back to give ourselves space to see the situation clearly and without prejudice, and we should assess the pros and cons.

We know that action is the first step to success, yet we procrastinate. We live our life assuming we have plenty of time. Keep focus on what you really want. Do not be afraid of making mistakes. Mistakes are the mother of learning. *Done is better than perfect.* Embrace it and let go of unattainable standards. Life is an asset not a liability. Action seems to follow feeling. How about when action and feeling are aligned? It will be like:

The Sun can melt ice, but a SMILE can ignite your life.

Finally, I came across this quotation and would like to share it with you:

> *The dream in your mind is Possible.*
> *Attitude controls it.*
> *Momentum maintains it.*
> *Passion protects it.*
> *Leadership guides it!*
>
> ~ Author Unknown

About Franky

Franky Ronaldy was born in Bandung, Indonesia, in 1977. In 1995, he enrolled at the Bina Nusantara University, receiving his Bachelor's Degree in Computer Science from the school three and half years later.

As a young child, Franky proved to be a bright and conscientious student. He showed a sharp intelligence, and enjoyed delighting his fellow classmates. Over the course of his long career, he built a goal to share the knowledge of the purpose of life, and the drive to push the limits of understanding and life's meaning seemed to point his life in a very specific direction.

Franky has read dozens of books, watched countless videos and conducted extensive research on the details of human behavior in addition to the business topics he covers. Striving to be able to help people around the world, and with dogged determination and in relentless pursuit of excellence, he developed a strong will and he made a successful breakthrough to pursue his dream. He has a strong belief in self-happiness and laid the foundation for his life experiences. He has written and published his first book. As a co-writer together with his wife, and both known as Best Selling Authors of Life Sucks! A book which focused on living a happy life. His book has struck a chord with a population hungry for self-improvement. These experiences have guided him to take ownership of everything that happens in life, and Franky believes happiness must come from the bottom of each person's heart. But the most important obligation is his determination to help others overcome obstacles and regain happiness.

Franky made another breakthrough and became co-founder of the *Triple-S Framework™*, which is the powerful system to regain true happiness in life. The system, as easy as ABC, which translated from extraordinary term into ordinary term for most people who are hungry for self-improvement. Franky has given a glimpse as to how to be a happy person.

Franky perceived that the most successful people in any given industry were not those with the most technical know-how, but rather those with the best people skills. He envisioned limitless potential, and through his background he fought to cultivate understanding, and he became aware of everyone's unique essence. Despite hardship, immense suffering, and unspeakable circumstances, Franky has faced his own fears and strongly believes it has evaded his fears. This has spurred Franky onto his life-changing success.

Franky's life-time vision is to uncover the true meaning in life so as to choose his moment and live it. With this vision, it helps him to choose his purpose in all life's challenging and rewarding situations, and to shape his life around the right decisions and direction for him.

You can connect with Franky at:
frankyronaldy@magtim.com
www.frankyronaldy.com
www.lifesucksbooks.com
www.twitter.com/lifesucksbook
www.facebook.com/lifesuckbook

CHAPTER 36

IGNITE YOUR LIFE WITH NLP
—From 911 depressed guy into Successful NLP Master Trainer and Executive Coach

BY JIMMY SUSANTO, MH, ACC

911 — WORLD TRADE CENTER

I watched a movie a few nights ago starring Nicholas Cage in World Trade Center, a true story based on two Port Authority New York Police Departments survival under the ruins of the 9-11 Attacks at the World Trade Center back on September 11th, 2001 suddenly brought back my own memories regarding the event. From the spring of 2000, I was pursuing an Associate Degree at Columbus State Community College, Ohio, USA. At the time, I had some issues with the weather. The weather where I grew up in Jakarta, Indonesia has only two seasons, which are the summer season and the rainy season, while the U.S. has four seasons in Columbus, Ohio, like most other states in the U.S. During the winter season, my skin would have skin rashes, while in summer, my skin would be exfoliated. So, my parents and I decided to go back home to Indonesia to cure or find a solution for my skin issues in August 2001.

My skin issues were assessed and were being treated for several weeks until one night I was informed by the news of the plane that hit one of the Twin Towers of the World Trade Center. During the night, I kept on watching CNN or Fox News for the updates, and somehow it caused me a greater damage in my life for years ahead. I wasn't aware that watching over and over again, with negative comments, would affect my mind consciously and unconsciously, especially during the nights before I went to sleep watching the twin towers collapse. So that affected my brain somehow, that and my own projection of what would happen to me, because I couldn't return to the US due to security reasons, and also with the news from friends who were still in the U.S. who stated that the country was not safe; it was a place where you could not even drink water from a tap, nor open any letter due to the anthrax threat.

With the worries and thoughts in my head that my future was gone, and that I couldn't continue my studies in US, I couldn't carry on. This kept running through my head and started to give me a blank stare -- with more worries for my own future. What could I do without any education? What would my friends say about my lack of education? . . . and what would other families say about me behind my back. The more I saw the Twin Towers falling in my mind, the more I believed that my future was falling along with it.

I couldn't even sleep at nights; it was like a horror movie that kept on rolling through my mind; there was the thought of what would my future look like, and sometimes I even thought of suicidal jumps from the third floor of my house. With the sleepless days and nights, I finally collapsed and was taken to the hospital. I was treated for few days, then released so my family could get me medical treatment and help from professionals to take medication, and of course, sessions with the doctor. After a few months of sessions and medical treatments, I was healing and recovering in my body, mind and soul.

MOTIVATIONAL WITH NEURO LINGUISTIC PROGRAMMING.

My recovery took about six months of my life. I didn't continue my college or my education – neither in Jakarta nor the US. Instead, I went into the family business of property development for the next few years. During those years, I started to develop an interests in books— especially motivational books. Two interesting books to me were *Law of Attraction* and *The Secret*, and then I started to think differently, change my mindset, my values and my beliefs. During the years since then, I attended lots of seminars to update and upgrade my knowledge and my education. In 2008, I had a desire to obtain new knowledge, either Hypnosis or Neuro-Linguistic Programming (NLP). However, it was not until 2009 that I managed to take an intensive seven-day NLP certification program.

The NLP program really changed my mindset on the things that happened to me, especially those from 2001. The depression that engulfed me was merely a visual or picture in my mind, and future expectations projected by my mind were not necessarily true in reality. If NLP was introduced to me earlier, I think I might be much further ahead, and a different person overall. What I learned from NLP is that the human is equipped with excellent capabilities and knowledge to make his or her life better or worse by simply using their mind. Later on, I was persuaded to learn from the creator of NLP himself, Richard Bandler, in 2012 for twenty-five days in Orlando, Florida, so I could improve myself to a higher level, and also expand the business opportunities as an NLP Trainer. Later on, I developed my own training company.

NLP has become one of the best approaches to maximize human potential and its performance. It is also the secret behind lots of successful corporate and famous speakers, such as Anthony Robbins. Therefore, as a motivational speaker with an NLP background, I continued to gain further knowledge on Coaching and Hypnosis. I also proceeded to work with executive clients, helping them with their varying conditions and mindsets using my coaching services.

HOW I USE NLP IN MY EXECUTIVE COACHING CASES

Since then, I have helped numerous coaching clients, with both executive and corporate backgrounds, with hundreds of coaching hours – handling issues in business, sales, and management, and even personal and family issues. One of the more effective tools is *Time Line* that I often use in my coaching sessions – the idea of the Timeline is to take learning from the past, bring the same learning to the present, and thus prepare for the future. The timeline normally has three different positions with past, present and future.

One of my clients was having a hard time forgetting her past and hating her own current life. She felt stressed with her current work because her parents told her to take a Pharmacy major which she wasn't fond of. My client was also not comfortable with her work and life balance due to too much stress at work, while also coping with not enjoying her work at the same time. So she came to me for a session and after getting a brief description of her condition and her outcome, I decided to use this NLP tool, *Timeline,* to help her. In the coaching session, I asked her to "fly" back to her past where and when she got the first memory of her parent asking her to study Pharmacy instead of her favorite major – which was Accounting.

During the past timeline of her own projection in her mind, I asked her to rate her own feelings at that time; she rated herself at three out of ten. Still in her past, I asked her to think of at least three ideas in learning at that moment which she can bring to her present life. I told her that she could keep the ideas to herself or repeat them out loud. As she kept her silence, I assumed that she wanted to keep the ideas to herself, then I asked her to let me know whenever she got at least three ideas for her current life. After a few minutes, she nodded her head and said that she got five instead of three for her present situation. She moved forward in her mind into the future, which is the present timeline, where I asked her to implement the five ideas that she got back in her past timeline. Soon, she nodded her head and she looked at me which I assumed was her signal that she was ready, and I asked her to rate her feelings and condition where she was formerly three out of ten in her past timeline, and she responded quickly, saying she was six out of ten – which is double her previous rate. With her present timeline, I also asked her to give me three additional lessons that she got from her current life projected into her future, so she could have a greater and brighter future. She said she was ready for her future, then I asked her to move forward in projecting her future timeline, and implement the five thoughts from the past and three thoughts from the present into her future. Afterwards, I asked her for her rating for her future and was surprised when she said eight out of ten, which showed great progress – showing that she was confident about her future and of course, was experiencing great relief in her present lifestyle.

The other effective and favorite tool from NLP is *Swish Pattern.* It's the best and fastest tool to help clients overcome whatever that might occur in their heads, especially regarding expectations in life. It is normally based on projections of visual images or pictures in their mind. The modifications in their own mind are simply made by changing the pictures that they don't want, to something totally different – which is something that they want to happen (normally between good or bad, right or wrong, positive or negative, something to compare), in contrast to making it reality.

Recently, I had a client that was referred to me by a high school friend who believed I could help his brother in a way that he was unable to. As usual, I took information before I agreed to take the case, using pre-coaching analysis in one short meeting with the client. I found out that this guy was at the productive age of twenty-eight. He was having what he called anxiety issues when meeting new friends, even when chatting or meeting his current friends, including ones in the office sharing the same room. In my opinion, his condition was not healthy for a young adult male who wished to have a family, or if he had to meet a new girl that his mother might introduce to him as a prospective future wife, if he needed to meet with a new client to work on new task, or even for communicating well with team members.

When I took his case as a client, I set up a coaching agreement for a six-month period with a three-month evaluation period for his progress. If he was able to keep up with his work and home-fun after three months, then we would proceed for the three additional months. This method was to ensure the accountability of the client. If he was unable to deliver his own work for his own progress, how can a coach help this client. Directly in the first session, I introduced him to a very effective NLP tool, *Swish Pattern*. As I sat beside him, I asked him whether in the future, he wanted to chat with any female in the office with whom he wanted to talk. He said, "Yes, I have this one female colleague that I wish to talk with over lunch, yet what comes into my head are the objections from her and laughter of other colleagues." I decided to not only apply this NLP tool to him, but also to teach him how to use it whenever he wants. At the end of that session, I gave him a mission to ask her or someone else out as long as it was a female colleague. Now, the session has passed the three-month evaluation period, he is now much more confident and thinking of the next step as an entrepreneur, and finding the right girl for a wife. I, as a coach, will support him during the upcoming three-month coaching sessions.

These coaching sessions with clients are one of the main reasons why I am still doing what I do best with NLP, because it is from my own experiences that keep me going to help more people who might experience the same or worse than I had. I know a lot of people out there who are suicidal because of simple issues that they cannot solve at that moment. It's a permanent solution for a temporary problem. Besides coaching executive and corporate clients, I actively do NLP training, Trainer's Training and coaching training to create more people in this helping industry.

Recently I expanded my business into a publishing company for international best-selling authors and books to be translated into the Indonesian language, including Co-Creator NLP Richard Bandler and executive coach Marshall Goldsmith as some of the first. I am just the proud father of two children with a beautiful wife who is a medical doctor; a therapist who would consider myself as a family-comes-first guy. I am looking forward to collaborating with you all in the near future.

About Jimmy

Jimmy Susanto, MH, ACC is an NLP Master Trainer and Executive Corporate Coach with more than twelve years experience in business – in management, sales and marketing – in various industries from advertising to property development companies. Since 2012, Jimmy established a training and coaching company based on Neuro-Linguistic Programming (NLP) to help companies ranging from Small-to-Medium Enterprises (SME) to Public Listed Companies in Indonesia.

With his expertise, he has given training and coaching across Asia especially in Malaysia, Thailand and Singapore. His focus is in helping his clients build their systems, developing human performance within the organizations of the companies using an NLP Coaching System. The coaching sessions with clients is one of the main reasons why he is still doing what he does best with NLP, because from his own experiences, that keeps him helping more people who might experience the same or worse than he did. He also has the passion to train more people in this industry, so they can help even more people in this world.

Indonesia Coaching Alliance is one of the organizations that he co-founded with the NLP Coaching System and which focuses on client-centered coaching to improve the client's potential through NLP and Coaching. He also co-founded NFNLP Asean, an official affiliate with NFNLP USA for NLP training and certification in Asia. Along with NFNLP Asean, they are focusing on providing NLP training and services using highly standardized NLP training for executives and corporations. NFNLP Asean also trains NLP Trainers and NLP Coaches in the Asian region, especially in South-East Asian countries.

Beside training and coaching, Jimmy also established PLP Book, which is an international publishing company in Indonesia that provides best-selling books and authors around the world to be translated into the Indonesian language, with emphasis on NLP, motivational, coaching and self-help books – including books from the co-creator of NLP Richard Bandler, and executive coach Marshall Goldsmith.

Jimmy Susanto was born and raised in Jakarta, Indonesia and was educated in Malaysia and the United States. He is also the proud father of a daughter and a son, with his beautiful wife (a medical doctor). He considers himself as a family-comes-first guy. For social work and charity, he is active in Rotary International, and in the Buddhisme Organization, he is active in both charity and fundraising.

You can connect with Jimmy at:
info@jimmysusanto.asia
https://www.linkedin.com/in/jimmysusanto

CHAPTER 37

RE-IGNITE YOUR ENTREPRENEURIAL SPIRIT

BY PRERAK PATEL

Business owners face many challenges- there's no doubt about it. What matters is how one accepts those challenges as part of the quest to achieve success, while living their best life. As a successful, serial entrepreneur, I work with both small and large businesses. I have learned that leading any size entrepreneurial business can put you on a direct path to your best life, for professional and personal success, for wealth generation, and for good health. Just as you would nourish your garden with the right nutrients for it to grow to its fullest potential, it is important to **"nourish" your business with the right marketing tools** and systems so it may grow to its maximum potential and bear maximum fruits, or riches in this case.

Nourishing your own business to grow successful financially is one of the main goals of entrepreneurship. Wealth is certainly one of the most desired outcomes one has when hoping to create not only a successful business but also a successful personal life. Success in our world is directly correlated to the amount of wealth one obtains. This is because with wealth, you can exponentially multiply your own success, achieve desired material possessions and experiences, and create beneficial partnerships with other successful people. Wealth can also provide the opportunity for things you cannot control when working for someone else or in a dead end situation- time with loved ones, time to create unique experiences including travel experiences, resources to help you expand as a global entity, and the means to give back to the community. Wealth ultimately encompasses the factors which allow you to become a key person of influence in today's world, instead of just another business entity.

All that said about wealth, we know it is worth nothing without health. What good is achieving financial wealth and successful entrepreneurial relationships if you are sick and unhealthy? Stress is one of the biggest toxins in our lives today. We all know stress can make you very sick and ultimately kill you, one way or the other. Numerous studies have found one of the major causes of stress in people's lives is work. By being in charge of your own life, by being an entrepreneur, you can control the factors and time needed to embark upon a healthy lifestyle, a lifestyle corporate America does not often afford. In reality, *true success must be measured by the amount of both wealth and health* one obtains. For *optimal* success, one cannot exist without the other.

If you think about it, we are all born with an entrepreneurial spirit. Once able to, babies cherish the process of exploration—with their eyes, their hands, all their movements. Once able to walk, a baby is quick to take off and suddenly parents are childproofing everything! Of course childproofing is meant for safety, but a baby will still possess the urge to explore and embark into unknown territory. Innately, a baby knows this is all part of growing and maturing. Being an entrepreneur is much the same. I believe we are all born with some level of an entrepreneurial spirit, but most people get stuck in that **"childproof"** **mindset** and become accustomed to a mundane everyday life, scared to venture out of what they think provides safety and stability, scared to leave their comfort zone. I'm here to tell you that it's never too late to ignite, or in some cases, **RE-ignite,** your entrepreneurial spirit.

As a third generation entrepreneur, I am very familiar with the benefits of entrepreneurship and how it can completely turn around one's life for the better. One of my most important clients is testament to this fact. My wife is a dentist who successfully completed years of challenging schooling. Upon graduation, she earned a job working in her field as a dentist. She had achieved her goal and was well on the path to success… or so we thought. Despite working in a field she was thoroughly trained for and enjoyed being part of, she was unhappy. She was earning less money than she deserved, therefore unable to maximize her wealth. She was working long hours and unable to provide her patients the level of service she wanted to provide them. This caused her great stress and limited her time and resources with our family, negatively impacting her health. Overall, her level of wealth and health were at much lower level than she desired and was easily capable of, negatively affecting her personal and professional success.

We knew this was unacceptable and decided to take action. The first decision we made for the better was to live our success in the moment, to embrace a positive mindset and take massive action. *We knew moving away from the 'doing it' mindset and transitioning to the 'getting it done' mindset was essential.* Instead of waiting for something to happen, we decided what needed to happen. We knew the best course of action was for her to begin her own practice, instead of working as an associate in someone else's practice. The catch was, how could she run a successful practice while also having the healthy work-life balance that would lead to the greatest personal and professional success?

Luckily, I realized I could use my expertise as a serial entrepreneur, with a specialty in Internet and digital marketing, to help her practice become a successful venture. I knew one of the toughest challenges entrepreneurs face is how to market themselves and determine key elements in today's digital world that will ensure their business is visible and attracting clients. It is my experience that utilizing strategic digital marketing to create a sales funnel of clients is vital to ensure success for any business, large or small, including my wife's dental practice. In combination with a solid brand, thoughtful digital marketing strategy is key to achieving success in today's online business environment.

BRANDING AND POSITIONING

Developing your brand and positioning is vital to the success of every business. Building a strong brand is about building confidence and trust with your clients. An optimized, solid brand will help clients see you as a trustworthy business and authority. This can be an important deciding factor, or quite often *the* factor, in a customer's decision to choose your business. Building a brand and positioning your business as trustworthy can be especially crucial if you're a new business determined to get off to the best start possible.

Your quality of interaction with your clients is where you will have the most personal flexibility with your brand. It is also where you have the greatest opportunity to build your brand. Businesses that are deeply committed to providing clients with top quality service or products, and advice, are naturally at an advantage. As a business, your brand will be built on your quality interactions with clients, in their reviews, word-of-mouth references, and, of course in the results from your product or service. This makes having a comprehensive online presence all the more important, vital even to success as an entrepreneur.

It is well known that a good relationship with a client can lead to a client relationship that lasts a lifetime. It is important to realize that in today's digital world you must not only keep each individual happy to retain their individual business, but also to retain the good image of your brand. A word of mouth referral or positive review has more power in today's world as it can be quickly shared with a large audience using a variety of digital mediums. A bad review can travel across the web and social media even faster. For that reason, building a robust brand and protecting it is more important now than ever.

DIGITAL MARKETING: INTERNET STRATEGIES AND SOCIAL MEDIA

Businesses must recognize consumers are becoming incredibly reliant on online and mobile sources for information about services and products. To be successful, entrepreneurs must utilize advanced digital marketing strategies to meet consumer demands for online and mobile information. Whether it's through social media, or search engines like Google, Yahoo, or Bing, there are more vast numbers of people looking for business providers online than there are phone books in American homes. You owe it to yourself to grow your business the smart way, by becoming an online authority presence. To do this, you must pay special attention to social media and Internet marketing strategies.

DIGITAL MARKETING
THROUGH SOCIAL MEDIA

If you aren't already involved with social networking platforms, get involved now! Social networks have become the preferred method of communication between professionals, businesses, their demographics, and the everyday public. Networks such as Facebook, Google+, Instagram, Twitter, LinkedIn, Pinterest, and more have all become part of the digital marketing sphere. The call and response nature of social media means your prospective clients can not only learn about you, but have the potential for direct interaction.

An active social media presence shows you have faith in your reputation and good work. As an entrepreneur, word of mouth can net a lot of business through referrals. When customers leave positive reviews on your social media page, or when the public sees you patiently answering questions and giving advice, it "warms" your image considerably and projects an image of you as an authority in your industry. This adds value to your business and your overall brand.

As an added bonus, an active social media presence improves your search engine optimization, or SEO. This includes any video content you may upload to YouTube, pictures you share on your business' Instagram account, and more. Get creative, and you could be the "before and after" reference video or infographic that people share when they talk about specific products or services your business offers.

DIGITAL MARKETING THROUGH
INTERNET STRATEGIES

The first Internet strategy you must embrace is to *stay active and dominate the Internet.* Constantly update your website with meaningful content and consider adding a how-to or advice section, which can boost your online reputation. Work to build a local presence so that you are the go-to provider whenever consumers are in need of the product or services you provide.

Optimize your online visibility by ensuring your site has organic content. Search engines favor top-notch, organic content over paid advertising, banner ads, and other forms of online marketing. Organic content includes positive reviews consumers write for your business on sites like Yelp, and also relates to the amount of content your site has, its relevance, and metrics that determine its quality.

Act now to join online directories for services or products your business provides. Google+ and Angie's List are just two examples of incredibly popular online directories that can send potential customers to your business. Even better, these directories can help to boost your local SEO rankings. When users search for your service or product in your area they are more likely to find your business with that advantage.

Finally, avoid marketing shortcuts and the temptation of "DIY" marketing or taking a cheaper route. Investing in marketing doesn't need to be a huge burden on your budget, but it's also not a task you should delegate to a staff member's cousin who happens to know a bit about SEO, word Pay Per Click or online media buys, social media, or WordPress. Much like your business works, digital branding and Internet marketing is its own entity. The most successful campaigns and predictable results will be created by people with the know-how and have expertise in the field.

If you focus on building a strong brand and utilizing thoughtful digital marketing, you can achieve professional success and live your best life. You can be in control of your own business and have the ultimate responsibility for your professional and personal success. The work-life balance you have always dreamed of can become a reality. Simply re-ignite your entrepreneurial spirit, create a positive mindset, and take action! Set yourself on the path to personal and professional health, wealth, and success.

About Prerak

Prerak Patel is a successful entrepreneur, a business professional, and a visionary. After graduating from the University of Houston with a concentration in Computer Engineering Technology, Prerak set himself on an entrepreneurial path immediately. He foresaw that Internet and technology would have an extreme impact on any business model at any stage, whether it be a start-up, mid-level or an established large company. In order to brand themselves effectively and progressively, businesses would need advanced digital marketing strategies and automated systems. As a result, he founded Mightus Media.

Since starting Mightus Media, Prerak has expanded his services to provide Internet and Direct Response marketing to all businesses. His clientele enjoys the expert problem-solving practices that Mightus Media offers in developing profitable and sustainable campaigns.

Due to his expertise, Prerak has been featured in *Forbes.com, Inc.com, Entrepreneur. com* and many other publications. His team consists of experienced marketers that have assisted many businesses and brands to grow and exponentially increase their revenue. Contact Mr. Patel at: info@mightusmedia.com

CHAPTER 38

THE SELF-COACHING SYSTEM TO SUCCESS

BY MIKE STONE, MBA, RFC

"How to get what you want."

It was a rainy morning in Boston. Springtime was slow to arrive as winter refused to leave. I walked up to an impressive brown stone office building just around the corner from the Boston Public Gardens. Even on this gray day, I was inspired by the beauty and the history of the entire area. I wondered who had walked these roads in the years before me. Ben Franklin? Paul Revere? What about just an average colonial citizen? No doubt many different people, all with hopes, aspirations and goals just like us today. Entering the building I walked over ageless marble flooring and past impressive granite pillars. My meeting was with a veteran stockbroker at a large well-known exclusive bank. We met several weeks before at an investment management conference in New York. Kevin, I had come to understand, had plateaued, not only in his business, but in many areas of his life as well. He felt frustrated, stressed, and often angry. Over dinner, he shared that his business results were disappointing. He was not accomplishing his goals and he was seriously considering quitting. As I got to know him better, I offered to share with him something that I had recently discovered. Something so revolutionary, yet so simple. Something that anyone could implement and immediately use to breakout to new heights – in their business goals, their personal life, or in anything at all.

~~~

I began my career in business – in banking and finance – multiple decades ago. My MBA classes taught me the latest and greatest strategies from academia. My large Fortune 100 employers sent me to the finest sales and management training courses around. As a young and eager banker I devoured all the self-development courses I could find. Anthony Robbins, Zig Ziglar, Brian Tracy and the like became my preferred reading. I learned about positive affirmations, which sounded so simple. Just think it, recite it, and you get it. How easy is that? I set about my goals and my affirmations. "I earn six figures," the penniless rookie recited. "I weigh 180 lbs.," said the 225 lbs. version of myself. Indeed, my business thrived quickly. I climbed the corporate ladder to Vice President and Sales Management levels. My income kept pace. Evidently positive thinking and affirmations were all that was needed, I naively thought. However, strangely my weight loss goal didn't follow so easy. Nor did a multitude of other goals and affirmations of mine follow the successful course. As time went by, even my business success proved to not be responsive to affirmations, typical positive thinking and goal setting. Business cycles, economic cycles and the reality of life events seemed to always throw a curve ball. As time passed, I paid less attention to affirmations and self-development material. I continued with the endless process of designing grand goals, implementing big plans, striving to push the rock up the hill, only to have repeated fallbacks, over and over again. I have distinct memories of one such planning session in the Orlando Marriott Airport hotel with my business partners, where we diligently planned out our ambitious goals and plan of action, so sharply and detailed that surely success would be ours. I can remember the table we sat at and the suit and tie I was wearing. They were grand plans. They were big. I also distinctly remember that although I felt hopeful, I didn't really believe it and I certainly didn't feel it. What I don't remember at all, is when and how fast it all went off track. We never got to the end goal. I am sure there were good reasons. The economy? Regulators? Personal stress? A multitude of other circumstances no doubt. There would be a multitude of other goal sessions on a myriad of objectives, business and otherwise. Some reached, some half accomplished, and some... well, crash-and-burn comes to mind.

~~~

Why do we sometimes succeed at accomplishing our goals and at other times fail? Is it just up to luck? Or are there special "chosen" people who are destined for success? Could the key to accomplishing any goal be identified and explained? Was there a way to develop a useful and repeatable procedure to help accomplish goals? In an effort to answer these questions, I went back and thoroughly examined my 30 years of experience in business, sales and marketing. I re-studied the key concepts of behavioral psychology and personal development. I reflected upon what I learned as an endurance athlete. I analyzed all the training, coaching, reading, classes, seminars and education I experienced throughout my life. Was there a secret method to success? Suddenly, almost out of the blue it hit me! The key missing ingredient that ties it all together was not a new concept or strategy. Rather, it is in fact how you use these universal key concepts. It is:

- *how you work yourself through it.*
- *how you apply it.*

The key I discovered, is to *coach yourself* through it. With this in mind, I set about designing a self-coaching system. A process to move back and forth between critical causes and effects. A *cause* is WHY something happens. An *effect* is WHAT happens. This simple system can allow anyone to self-identify what is secretly preventing them from reaching any goal or to getting anything they want, and then *shift* these causes and effects to their advantage. I have taught this simple process to many different types of people, business people, sales people, executives, athletes and parents. The results I have seen have been life changing

The principles of the system are deeply grounded in the roots of personal development and advanced business training. It draws heavily upon the study of psychology, but is also cross-referenced with the latest advances in neuroscience and the study of how the brain functions. The system incorporates lessons from the Bible and lessons from the great first century philosophers. None of this material was invented by me, however, I have assembled it together into a system that is laser-focused to direct us to a specific and improved course of action. Importantly, it clearly explains my lifelong experience of goal setting and planning, and why some goals seem easy to reach and others seem unobtainable.

Accomplishing any goal or getting anything you want requires two very simple sounding, yet immensely complex, steps: *You know what to do and you are doing it.* The inverse is also true. If you don't have what you want it is because you *either don't know what to do, or you're not doing it.* This is one of those simple, but not easy concepts. Both of these points take thoughtful work and reflection that only you can do for yourself.

This is why self coaching is the key. We will call these two points **Self-Coaching Zones**. One is how you *think* and one is how you *act*. This self-coaching system incorporates both of these zones as equally critical elements. This chapter focuses on the most elusive part of this work that holds back many successful people from breaking out to higher performance. "You know what to do but you're not doing it."

THE SELF COACH SYSTEM

Life Events/Circumstances==>create==>Thoughts/ Beliefs==>drive==>Feelings/Emotions ==>influence==> Actions/ Plans/Habits==>create==>Results

What we think affects how we feel. How we feel affects how we act. How we act creates our results. If you don't have what you want, it is because of one of these two reasons I call *self coaching zones*:

Self Coaching Zone I - Thinking:

You know what to do, but you're not doing it. Change your thoughts and self coach yourself with this system. Your thoughts create your emotions. When your beliefs and emotions align with your goal, you'll find yourself automatically "doing it." Are your thoughts serving you? Do you feel it?

Self Coaching Zone II - Actions:

You don't know what to do. Learn what to do and get a good plan. Study, ask, get a mentor, seek out those who are doing it and do the same. Take MASSIVE Action. Implement a plan using S.M.A.R.T. goals. Defined as Specific, Measurable, Achievable, Results-focused, and Time bound.

~~~

I approached the reception desk at Kevin's office, an impeccably-dressed receptionist seated at a thick mahogany oak desk greeted me immediately. My arrival was announced with a thick Bostonian accent that seemed to match the environment just right. Shortly thereafter, my new acquaintance Kevin strolled down the hallway. We went to a large, but surprisingly understated office. Pictures of his family were on prominent display, as were numerous awards and certificates. There was no doubt Kevin had reached an enviable level of success. Yet, why so unhappy? Why frustrated and angry? And why were his business results suffering?

It was there, over a cup of coffee, that I shared the system that I had finally discovered. Kevin was indeed frustrated with many aspects of his life. He felt trapped. Pressures from his employer, the regulators, the economy, his family, seemed to be everywhere. These were his subconscious thoughts that surfaced automatically. He believed he *ought* to be more successful and that it *should* be easier after ten years in business and all his hard work. These beliefs were causing him to *feel* depressed at times, confused and angry at other times. Kevin had developed a belief system. These were deep-seeded thoughts at the subconscious level, meaning he automatically thought these thoughts.

We began to examine these thoughts and the various circumstances that were triggering his thoughts. We began to dispute Kevin's automatic conclusions. We challenged his thinking. In a matter of days, Kevin learned that he could indeed manage his thoughts at the conscious level and thereby train his subconscious thinking. In doing so, he could instantly change his feelings. He shifted his thoughts from those that did not serve him to those that did serve him. As he shifted his thoughts his feelings changed. Instead of feeling angry, depressed and afraid, Kevin's feelings switched to feelings that empowered him. This was not simply positive thinking. This was a *change of thinking* from automatic and invalid thoughts that did not serve him, to those that did.

When his feelings changed, Kevin suddenly started to execute on his business plan with enthusiasm. New ideas developed seemingly out of nowhere. These new actions he took led to the results that he had been looking for. Kevin had been stuck thinking he had misfortune and should have had more success; he had become resentful of numerous life events and circumstances from a volatile stock market to the economy and more.

But then, he decided to dispute these thoughts. Was the market out to get him? Did the economy only affect him? Hardly. He began to understand these were invalid thoughts. He changed his thinking. He thought how lucky he was to work in a dynamic and exciting environment, and how the volatility made him much more helpful to his nervous clients. He worked and reworked his thinking until he felt positive and relaxed. He coached himself. His actions then aligned with this new thinking. He changed his client mix and products to eliminate much of the volatile, uncontrollable situations that caused conflicts. And with his thoughts and actions aligned, he achieved the results he wanted.

~~~

Shakespeare wrote, "There's nothing either good or bad, but thinking makes it so." The scientific evidence is clear that it is possible to change our thoughts. It starts with recognizing what is actually occurring, and following a definitive process. Realize, the outside world is what it is and you have no control over it and you cannot change it. These are life events, circumstances, people, your past, etc. These are facts. You can "want", you can "wish", but you cannot change them. They are neutral, neither good nor bad. Don't waste energy wishing they were different. Be alert for your automatic thoughts about events and circumstances that your subconscious mind will automatically make. Look for thoughts with these judgmental words: *should, ought, must, always, prefer, wish otherwise. "Traffic shouldn't be this bad."* No. Traffic is what it is. *"People should treat me fair all the time."* Sound rational?... hardly. *"I ought to make more sales; if I don't I'm a failure."* No, that's not true. *"This person must love me, appreciate me, etc."* No. We don't control anyone. Pay particular attention to *limiting thoughts*. "I can't lose weight". "I'm too young, old, poor, etc."; "I'm not smart, pretty, wealthy enough." Not relevant and not true. Challenge those self imposed limits.

Use your conscious mind to override your automatic subconscious thoughts. You begin by disputing and challenging these thoughts. Is there another viewpoint? Are your thoughts absolutely true beyond a shadow of a doubt? Are there alternative reasons or explanations for your difficulties? You will soon see that your thoughts aren't in line with reality. And with a little work, those thoughts will start to change. Many of your deep irrational beliefs are not immediately obvious. Sometimes you'll have to dig to find them. And you'll need to dispute them a fair amount before new reasonable beliefs kick in. With work you can make progress, and in time these thoughts will seep into your subconscious and become your new automatic thoughts.

You can bridge the gap from where you are to where you want to be. Examine your thoughts. Take them one at a time. Your job or business, your marriage or family, your health and fitness, people. Anything and everything that is outside of you and your control. Start with the area of your life that you want to improve the most. The area where you don't like the results you are getting. What outside events, people, and circumstances impact this area of your life. How are you responding to them? What are you thinking about them? How do you feel when you think about it? Does it bring optimism, excitement, happiness, or enthusiasm? Conversely, does it bring confusion, frustration, anger, or stress? Are there exterior triggers that unleash the thought?

Repeatedly work this out and come to understand this. Some beliefs are blocking you from reaching your goal before you even get started. Some beliefs are causing you to quit on your goals midway through. This is why we start a diet and quit it, or start a business plan and give up. Our thoughts and beliefs do not align with our actions and we are at risk of feeling like giving up. Every thought we have is our own opinion and therefore it can be changed, challenged, manipulated and managed to serve ourselves. I encourage you to begin to self-coach yourself. You will be amazed at the results.

About Mike

Michael J. Stone, MBA, RFC, Ironman is a proven business leader who runs a very successful Financial Advisory Business, Income Tax business and a Consulting and Coaching Business, specializing in Sales and Marketing and overall goal achievement. Mike is a man who has experienced success in many areas, including as an author, keynote speaker, business and executive Success Coach, sales and marketing trainer, mentor, high performance motivator, Ironman, triathlete/endurance athlete, financial advisor (26 yrs.), entrepreneur/business owner x3, blogger and real estate investor. He is a self made man.

Mike's interest in high performance training and personal development began in the early eighties. Mike brings a successful background of over 30 years of Sales, Marketing and Management experience in the Banking and Financial Services industry. Mike achieved Vice President and Management levels with some of the world's largest banks and investment firms. As a proven and successful business owner, he has succeeded in some of the most competitive business environments. Mike also has experienced ample setbacks, failures and challenges in life, both personally and in business. He understands the required mindset necessary to persevere through the tough times, valuing the lessons of humility, gratitude and compassion he learned while rebounding back to even higher levels of success.

Mike brings to the table a background of thirty plus years as a Triathlete and all around Endurance Athlete, including the ultimate physical and mental test of the Ironman. He has competed in hundreds of swimming, running, and biking endurance events. Mike strongly believes in health, fitness and nutrition to fuel the mind and body to maximum performance. Further, Mike has extensively studied and exhaustively researched the areas of behavioral psychology, motivation, personal development and achievement. Mike has completed coach training and certification from a well-known national coach training school, and is a practicing Success Coach and Consultant for business executives, professionals and athletes. Putting all of this together, Mike has perfected a system of High Performance self-coaching that can guide you to a path to accomplish and maintain any goal.

Last but not least, Mike has been married for 27 years and is the father of four terrific and successful children. The life lessons learned from all of these endeavors have prepared Mike to literally deal with anything – to handle any situation and any chaos with calm assurance. They have also strengthened and deepened his understanding of what it takes to support personal growth, behavior modification, goal-setting, and achievement. Mike is the one you need on your side.

Mike has combined personal development, behavioral psychology, business planning and sales management with sports training, coaching and motivation into a unique and highly efficient and effective approach to help guide you to achieve the very highest levels of success in your chosen field, sport, or endeavor. Mike is a proven expert in high performance. Inspiring, motivating and supporting others as they discover their true potential is something that Mike is not just passionate about, but one at which he excels.

For more on how to self-coach yourself to success, you need to read his book: *Get it Faster & Keep it Longer.* You can reach him at: www.imhighperformance.com

CHAPTER 39

THE EIGHT ARTS TO EMPOWERMENT

BY MISS JO

Hello, as you read, please focus on how the information relates to you:

At four I made a decision, by the age of twelve I had a clear vision of how I was going to change the world. I have successfully used these skills in secret for over thirty years remaining virtually ANONOMOUS. So what could possibly be so life changing? A simple skill I have personally researched and honed for over three decades. So time for a few ancient secrets:

1.) ...

I am saving number one for last. It is a two-part powerhouse you use at will to create real, lasting empowerment.

2.) Start where you are. If you wait for ideal conditions, you wind up with excuses instead of results. This is the procrastination graveyard many of us have made. Where you are is your starting point and key to your success.

3.) Make a MAP (Master Action Plan). Before GPS, everyone had maps to plan where they are going and what is required. This step helps clearly outline your progress as well as what you require in undertakings.

4.) Expert advice comes from experts. If expertise is required, get your information from an expert in the field. Too often people seek advice from friends and/or family who have none. This creates stress and negative undercurrents in relationships and is self-sabotaging.

5.) Change is your friend. Change is inevitable and as you make changes you may find some goals change. Keep what is important and embrace the changes, as they will often create long-term goals faster.

6) TAKE ACTION DAILY! Success is not a goal it is the accumulation of little everyday habits that allow a person to live unconditionally, leading an empowered life. Daily action is essential to personal development and achievement.

7.) Be grateful! Gratitude does more than convey appreciation. It is one of the great reciprocators that brings back many times what we put out. Smiles, saying thank you, handwritten notes, you have a variety, . . . use them!

8.) Receive, Conceive, Believe, Achieve. Many think receive belongs last. The reality is by being open to receiving accelerates the process. It is about what you give AND receive with a grateful heart that empowers your process exponentially.

These **Eight Arts to Empowerment** are a strong foundation you can build a legacy on.

My research and stories are from my vast experiences. I draw from this resource teaching my classes and with my clients to create a personalized experience that is relevant to the individual(s) I am working with. If you have no basis for comparison it can prove more difficult. Questions and an objective listening skill can help create this for you.

Before the age of sixteen I was a retail owner, manager, and was earning over $10.00 per hour when I was hired by other business owners to work for them. I negotiated my price with no help and no experience. I could do this because I knew what advantages and disadvantages were in play. I held my head up, looked adults in the eye, had a firm handshake, and made certain I knew their business before I went in. I was young, and to some that means inexperienced, so I knew that showcasing my skills was essential. I would ask questions directed at their expertise and how they viewed their business, and what their goals were. I had experience and would use personal details that aligned with their ideas to show how having me was an asset to them.

I was in a small tourist town where highly skilled workers were needed, but there were few. Almost everyone owned a business, and there was a shortage of reliable staff. I owned a business in town too, and was looking to make extra money by helping others after the main hours were over. This is when shop owners wanted time to relax and spend time with their families. I was able to do simple tasks, keep their stores open longer, and earn them more profits. I worked five jobs that summer, including my own. After taking one night per week off to go out to dinner and daily expenses I made enough to go on three out of town shopping trips for school clothes, music, and jewelry and still had enough left over to spend on things until the next summer. I did my shopping in couture boutiques, custom stores and the like.

I did well because I expected to be exceptional. I made a plan based on relevant information, set my goals, and kept going until I succeeded. I started with my own shop, and got to know others. I observed behavior, and listened to what people wanted and found a way to present it in a way they felt filled their needs. This brings us to the ever-important #1 on the list. These are the two inseparables at the center of a person that show whether they truly live or simply exist:

1-A) I am the most important person in my life.

Your life is absolutely and uniquely yours. Your life is shared with the world around you since you live in it. Being the most important person in your life ensures that you are the best version of yourself. It allows you to embrace and utilize anything empowering to achieve your goals. It makes you better in all your endeavors. It makes you the best kind of friend, spouse, parent, boss, or any role you choose in life.

1-B) Make a decision.

Just as everything in existence was first a thought, what made it reality was a decision. We are our decisions and how we have used them. When you make the decision to be the most important person in your life, will you commit? Decisions are commitments and they create powerful changes when followed through. A thought is simply an idea or fleeting moment. A decision to use that idea and create from it is a commitment.

What is important is how this works for you. So let's do that, this is how you make it work:

- Repeat aloud: "I am the most important person in my life!" Pause. "I am grateful for everything this brings me." (Be grateful!)

- Decide where you are and focus your mind on a goal you want to achieve. This can be simple, and something you can do alone. This part of the process identifies the learning process you use daily to achieve. (Be grateful!)

- Be open to receiving what it is you decided on. You conceived it, now believe in it. Then you take what steps are necessary to achieve it. (Be grateful!)

- What are the things you need to do to achieve your goal? (Make your MAP. Be grateful!)

- Do you need to consult an expert? (If so do it! Be grateful!)

- Take daily action on your goals! Obviously this will vary according to what those goals are. (Be grateful!)

- As you achieve, change, reset, recharge, grow, empower, whatever you do and however you do it, be grateful!

Gratitude is essential to the empowerment and success of anyone doing anything. People gravitate to specific things because of what they feel. When you feel gratitude and practice feeling grateful, it becomes a power source.

I have always had successes because I expected to be successful yes, but I was always focusing energy and time on gratitude. I have also failed more by the time I turned sixteen than some people do in twenty years. Even in the present I fail more often every day than some people do in a month. I don't enjoy it, but the alternative is not even worth considering.

In conversation, I frequently remind people to invest in themselves. Many try to make small of it, and my response is always the same. "You will always be the most important investment you will ever make."

If you are reading this you have already accomplished numbers 2, 4, 5, 6, and part of 8. Quite possibly you also have begun or achieved all or part of 1, 3, and 7 as well.

The natural state of any being is one of being empowered. This has become set-aside in much of society almost as if people have become afraid of it. I mentioned my failures. Not even trying is worse than failure. When I was younger I gave up something most people never even get a chance to do.

I was twelve and loved horses, so I received English riding lessons for my birthday. Inexplicably, I was riding during the first lesson. (I've ridden since I was two.) I knew everything they were showing me to do, so I was able to ride. There were always people coming and going, and one day my instructor asked my mother to introduce me to someone. He was the authority on sending people to compete in the equestrian events at the Olympics. My instructor wanted to see if he would take me on, she thought I could make it. Both my instructor and my mother were so excited that my answer never occurred to them. I said no, I never met him, and I never found out if I could have made it.

Could I have been an equestrian in the Olympics? Could I have been a medalist in one of the most prestigious competitions in the world? Maybe. No one will ever know. For the record this was not a failure, you can only fail if you attempt. To not even make the attempt... Well, you get the point I'm sure. Never knowing what would have happened is far worse than any failure could have ever been!

Lesson learned, so please remember you will always be the most important investment you will ever make. Take the Eight and use them as a solid foundation to ignite an empowered life.

To your great success, Jo.

About Jo

Given the opportunity to study a wide variety of techniques with healers from around the world by age eleven, by the age of seventeen Jo owned multiple businesses which included her practicing and teaching Psi-Quanta healing. From the people she taught in her time this has split into many other names, techniques, and disciplines. She has been a business owner for over thirty years, a Social Entrepreneur for more than 20 years, an author, a Martial Artist, a full time parent, and the list goes on.

Jo continues to practice life in the NOW. She avidly keep's herself updated on the most important industry and life knowledge. This includes investing in people who are ready to invest in themselves.

When she is working with people her focus is on their goals, lives, and process of creating their dreams. Jo uses over thirty years of personal experience, and expertise from owning multiple businesses which have provided the tools of success.

If you require access to all the tools you need, an effective and proven format to apply them and you are ready to make it happen, make an appointment; ask for Jo at:

infiniteempowerment@icloud.com

CHAPTER 40

THE SPARKS THAT IGNITED MY LIFE

BY WANDA GOZDZ, CAPS, ALLIED ASID

It often takes more than one spark to ignite a flame, and I have been very fortunate to have had many sparks to kindle and fuel the flame that has ignited my life.

The first spark happened when I was much too young to realize its force. The desire for a better life was ignited in 1951 when my parents, Antoni and Maria, my brother George and I emigrated from Germany and boarded the USS General ML Hersey, a military cargo ship that carried supplies to Germany and filled the void on the return trip with immigrants to the U.S. The voyage was long and the seas were rough. My mother sat against the bed and clung to her two-year-old daughter and one-year-old son as desperately as she clung to the hope of a better life for her family. With the symbolic flame from the Statue of Liberty beckoning us, we arrived in NY harbor on December 25 and celebrated Christmas Day on the ship because Ellis Island was closed. We were processed on December 26, 1951 under the "Displaced Persons Act", given a train ticket and a brown bag lunch and sent to our sponsor family in Ramsey, NJ. We lived in a chicken coop on a farm for one year as indentured servants. But in a mere three years my parents purchased a house where we grew up, and my parents lived till they died.

Our sense of family was strong, and my father was responsible for the series of sparks that nurtured me throughout my childhood and continue to sustain me today: a strong sense of faith, fortitude, and the knowledge that I am a limitless person. From him, I learned that all things were possible if I believe in myself, work hard, respect others, save money, got a good education, and love and support my family. All seven Gozdz children worked to put themselves through college, and now hold Master's and Ph.D. degrees.

My parents nurtured our strong Polish culture, which provided another early spark for my growing flame. We spoke only Polish at home, so on my first day of kindergarten, my teacher spoke in a foreign language – English. As a five-year-old eager to be accepted into her new country and eager for education, I learned my new language in just three months.

My childhood seemed to vanish at a very early age, when I had to care for my six siblings while my parents both worked. I believe this early responsibility for the welfare of my family sparked the care and concern for the elderly and their families that eventually led me to my current vocation.

When I was ten, my parents took my brother, George, and myself to a Polish summer camp in Canada. Returning home, the U.S. Border Patrol guard asked to see my green card, which had been burned in a fire. Fearing that the agent would detain me, I started to cry. I was allowed to return home under the condition that I reported to immigration within a week. It was the scariest week of my life because I remained terrified that I would be separated from my family. When I finally received my duplicate green card, I vowed that when I turned 18, I would immediately apply for U.S. citizenship so that no one could ever tell me that I couldn't go home. In 1968, I became a naturalized U.S. Citizen and was given the greatest gift that all U.S. citizens enjoy – the right to vote. I can assure you, I have exercised that privilege with pride throughout my adult life.

Wanting to create my own family, I got married at 21 and taught school for a short time. My first boss taught me the fundamentals of business ethics. Eventually, the company merged with another distributor and I became a purchasing agent, where I expanded my work knowledge for 7½ years. However, my longing to be my own boss drove me to start my own business.

After a short marriage, I became a single mother and worked at my sister's company, Library Update, Inc., where I learned to manage library resource centers. In an effort to start a new life with my two children, I filled a

U-Haul truck with all our worldly possessions, and left with $1,000 in my purse. My brother, Henry, drove us to Florida, where I would live with my brother, George, while I started my new business.

Just two months later with a mere $250 in the bank, W. Gozdz Enterprises was incorporated. Within 30 days, my library management consulting company had its first client, Deloitte & Deloitte. I joined the local accounting association, advertised in their professional journal to brand my company, and continued marketing to the Big Six accounting firms and law firms.

A key move for me was joining the National Association of Women Business Owners (NAWBO) to network and get support from others like myself. As a board member of NAWBO, I was elected a delegate to the 1984 and 1995 White House Conferences on Small Business, which made 100 recommendations to Congress on issues that impacted the growth and prosperity of small companies, including Equal Access to Credit for women. I also served on NAWBO's National Public Policy Council, helping write and pass legislation that impacted women business owners. For the next 25 years, I held many offices on a local, state and national level and was mentored by great NAWBO leaders like Terry Neese, Barbara Kasoff and Jimmie Rogers Gregory.

In its early stages, W. Gozdz Enterprises wasn't yet able to fully support my small family. To supplement my income, I made and sold vacuum-formed and magnetic display signs to local gas stations, dry cleaners and retail stores. During this time, my brother, George, and my parents assisted me in purchasing a townhouse to raise my two sons and grow my businesses.

My brother, Kazmierz, provided the spark I needed to automate and expand the company's consulting practice. Together, we created a strategic plan, but growth was slow because of my initial resistance to change. When I finally saw the light, the company began to grow and prosper. By the time Kaz left three years later to pursue his PhD, we both acknowledged that we learned a lot from each other.

By the late 90's and early 2000's, we were faced with challenges on a variety of fronts:

- Information technology was gaining momentum, with the World Wide Web providing access for both consumers and professionals to a huge variety of information and data.

- Publishers were starting to offer legal resources in electronic format.
- We lost a large client of 25 years, along with its six-figure revenue stream.
- In 2004, Florida got slammed with Hurricanes Francis and Jeanne, destroying homes, businesses, and much of the State's economy.

To counter these events, we downsized, reorganized, and reduced my salary to a minimum. On the plus side, we still had clients, my employees had jobs, and my family had a roof over its head. We added technology management to our services, but it couldn't fully replace the revenue we lost as firms began to downsize their print resources.

It was at this time that I realized the importance the role that independence has played in my life. Is not independence the promise Lady Liberty holds out to all new citizens coming to America? Is not her flame a constant reminder of that hope? I decided to look into a way to assist the elderly to maintain their independence. First, I began looking ahead for other opportunities in related markets. From the U.S. Census Bureau, I learned that the "Aging in Place" market was going to explode over the next 25 years. The first Baby Boomers would turn 65 in 2014, and by 2025, there would be 78 million Boomer retirees. (Of course, I would be right there with them.) I knew that if I could design and organize library resource centers, I could do the same for Baby Boomers.

So, at the age of 60, rather than retire, I began to reinvent myself. I went to college nights and weekends and earned a degree in Interior Design Technology, focusing on residential design and the "Aging in Place" market. My undergraduate degree in education reignited my passion for teaching. I relished the challenge of educating, inspiring and motivating students to make a difference in the lives of seniors.

I have said that not all my life sparks came from positive sources. Around this same time, my mom came down with cancer and needed modifications to remain in her home. She was adamant that she would only leave "feet first." On top of that, I broke my right hand, which took six months to heal. So here I was experiencing the difficulties of a physical handicap, even if only temporary.

In 2009, I created a business plan for a new venture, Golden Age Living. I became a "Certified Aging in Place Specialist" (CAPS), which gave me additional credibility and expertise in assessing and remodeling homes for seniors. I networked, joined boards and made a lot of free presentations to get my name out into the community.

I looked "outside the box" for my target audience, creating an electronic marketing campaign. I also created an exit strategy for retirement by becoming an instructor for the National Association of Home Builders (NAHB), and developing a tailored teaching schedule that allowed me both flexibility and a reliable revenue stream.

Today's retirees, in addition to looking for beauty, ease of use, safety and security, strongly desire to remain in their home forever, just like my mother. To paraphrase a TV commercial, an educated consumer is the best customer. So I organized free seminars to educate the aging population and their families on the opportunities and challenges of "Aging in Place".

But the professionals that serve the senior market – interior designers, builders, remodelers, architects, realtors, equipment specialists, occupational therapists and others that serve – also need to be educated on how to best serve their aging clients. We set out to educate and empower these professionals to identify and understand the characteristics of the Aging in Place Market and how to design for and sell to that market. In summary, it is all about education, education, education.

Looking back, the success of my company has been driven largely by a commitment to both customers and employees, treating employees as family and clients as customers for life. But just as important have been all the events – large and small – that have sparked my zest for my family and my business and ignited my life.

Someone once asked me if I ever thought I would fail. My response was, "As a single mother of two, failure was never an option." I had to provide a secure home, put food on the table, and clothe and put two sons through college.

The greatest sparks came from raising my sons to become self-sufficient, self-reliant and independent adults, and to watch the next generation of my family grow. James Wortman, Jr. is the Director of Enterprise Imaging

& Cardiovascular IT&S at St. Barnabus Health, and Ryan Wortman is Squadron Superintendent, 50th Operations Support Squadron, Schriever AFB. They have given me eight beautiful grandchildren that I cherish and love.

In conclusion, the sparks that ignited my life started with my parents, who laid a foundation of values and beliefs, and my brothers and sisters, who have supported and loved me through both my challenges and my triumphs. Sparks included teachers who inspired me; friends who supported me and professionals who helped and mentored me. I have been blessed with good health, a great support system and opportunities and experiences that opened doors to growing my businesses and moved me up the ladder of success. It took commitment, dedication and hard work to reach this pinnacle of my life, but it also involved being open to change and knowing when to seek and accept help from others. And most of all, it involved persistence in the face of adversity.

I asked an acquaintance who was blinded by a roadside bomb in while serving in Vietnam, what "ignited your life" when it changed? He responded, "Regardless of your circumstances, live a life of gratitude rather than attitude." He focused on his *abilities* rather than his (dis) ability, and used them to lead him to greatness. He went on to become the National Salesperson of the Year in his industry and is a motivational speaker today.

He expressed exactly what I would state as *the* top recommendations for taking advantage of the "sparks" that can ignite your life:

- When you go to bed at night, review the things you have to be thankful for from your day.

- When you wake up in the morning, be grateful for the wonderful day you have been given.

- List at least three positive outcomes you want to experience each day.

- Create your circle of influence by surrounding yourself with people who will be a truthful sounding board, are supportive of your dreams and wishes, hold you accountable for your actions and challenge you to be the best each day.

- Respect everyone, regardless of their station in life.
- Identify the people you want to emulate.
- Learn something new each day.
- Give back to your community.
- Tell those you love how much you love them each day.
- Say "thank you" often.

I am so grateful to my wonderful family, including my youngest brother Edward and my sisters Lucy Rieger and Sofie Empel. I dedicate this story to them and to my grandchildren, Mason, Max, Sophia, Lucia, Charles, Jake, Jordan and especially, James E. Wortman III, who at nine years old declared that his goal is to be President of the United States! I hope I can be one small spark in achieving his goal and an inspiration to all. And, wouldn't it be great if I could get to sleep in the White House!

I sincerely want to thank my co-editors, Denny Floden, Penny Callas and Marty Buckley and those that sparked my business life, Tom Smith, Mike Burgio, Maria Kondracki, Phil Guerra (now deceased), Dr. Nancy Bredemeyer, Karen Kane, Deborah Hamilton, Joe Carpenter and Allen Furrer.

About Wanda

Wanda Gozdz is Founder and President of Golden Age Living, LLC, a consulting and interior design company whose mission is to empower the aging to live independent quality lives in their home and work environments, with an emphasis on sustainable design. Her goal is to inform consumers on the changes they need to make to adapt their homes to their changing lifestyle and to educate professionals that serve the senior market on how to help their clients and their families "Age in Place."

Wanda began her career as a teacher and moved into the business world to become a purchasing agent. She left after seven years and learned to manage library resources which provided the foundation for starting W. Gozdz Enterprises, Inc. in Florida.

Wanda Gozdz joined the National Association of Women Business Owners (NAWBO), while continuing to market to Big Six accounting firms, law firms and law libraries. She served on NAWBO's National Public Policy Council, which helped pass legislation supporting women business owners. Gozdz was award the 1995 Public Policy Advocate of the Year award from NAWBO and that same year she was also named Small Business Woman of the Year.

Because of her determination to stay in her own home "forever," her mother inspired Gozdz to move into the Aging in Place arena. Gozdz pursued a degree in Interior Design and became a Certified Aging in Place Specialist (CAPS). Today, she is an instructor for the National Association of Home Builders (NAHB), which named her the 2014 CAPS Educator of the Year. She teaches nationwide and frequently presents at national and international conferences on the topic of "Aging in Place".

Wanda Gozdz authored *Sensible Smart Tips for Living in Your ForeverHome™*. Karen Kane of Karen Kane Interiors and Gozdz received the 2013 Laurel Award for Residential Construction less than 10,000 feet from the Green Building & Remodelers Council of The Treasure Coast Builders Association (TCBA) for their design work for the Lobby Project at Hibiscus by the Sea. She also received the Golden Mouse Award for Digital Devices from Women in Ecommerce for creating an encrypted flash drive for storage of confidential information.

Wanda has served on the Florida Board of Architecture and Interior Design and on the Advisory Committee of Indian River State College, Interior Design & Technology Department. She is a member of the American Society of Interior Design (ASID), Interior Design Society (IDS), International Furnishings & Design Association (IFDA),

National Kitchen and Bath (NKBA), Association of Aging in America (AIA), and Builders Association of South Florida (BASF). She is an avid runner, finishing first in her age group in the 2015 Fort Lauderdale Marathon.